# THE EARLY COLOMBIAN
# LABOR MOVEMENT

COLOMBIA

PANAMÁ

VENEZUELA

COLOMBIA

ECUADOR

Barranquilla
Cartagena

Sinú R.
Cauca R.
Magdalena R.

Cúcuta
Bucaramanga
Socorro
Medellín
Vélez
Rionegro
Tunja
Honda
Zipaquirá
Ambalema
BOGOTÁ
Ibaqué
Meta R.

Cali

Popayán

Pasto

Elevation 1000 Meters
or greater

0  50 100 150
Kilometers

Tunja

Honda
Magdalena R.
Zipaquirá
Ambalema
BOGOTÁ
Ibaqué

N

0  1000  2000  3000  4500
Elevation in Meters

0                    50
Kilometers

12° N
8° N
4° N
0°
4° S

12° N
8° N
4° N

76° W          68° W

76° W

# THE EARLY COLOMBIAN LABOR MOVEMENT

## Artisans and Politics in Bogotá, 1832–1919

# DAVID SOWELL

Temple University Press : PHILADELPHIA

Temple University Press, Philadelphia 19122
Copyright © 1992 by Temple University. All rights reserved
Published 1992
Printed in the United States of America

The paper used in this publication meets the minimum requirements of
American National Standard for Information Sciences—Permanence of
Paper for Printed Library Materials, ANSI Z39.48-1984

Library of Congress Cataloging-in-Publication Data
Sowell, David, 1952–
The early Colombian labor movement : artisans and politics in
Bogotá, 1832–1919 / David Sowell.
p.  cm.
Includes bibliographical references and index.
ISBN 0-87722-965-1
1. Artisans—Colombia—Bogotá—Political activity—History—19th century.
2. Labor movement—Colombia—Bogotá—History—19th century.  I. Title.
HD2346.C72B657   1992
322'.2'0986148—dc20                                    91-45958

# CONTENTS

# PREFACE

I N MAY 1846, 230 ARTISANS PETITIONED THE COLOMBIAN CONGRESS
to maintain existing levels of tariff protection against foreign
merchandise competitive with their own products. Rumors that
the congress would soon lower tariff rates sparked fears among
craftsmen that the availability of greater quantities of competitive
products would make their already precarious economic situation
untenable. Speaking in the name of some 2,000 artisans and their
families living in Bogotá (*bogotanos*) and for tradesmen in other
areas of the country, the petitioners argued that they constituted a
crucial productive sector of the domestic economy and that reper-
cussions from the damage they would suffer would be felt by other
social sectors—as the artisan class became less productive and the
economy in general deteriorated. Besides, they complained, lowered rates were unjust to artisans with years of service in the national guard.[1] In spite of these arguments, congress lowered tariff
rates by about 33 percent the following year. The same tradesmen
thereupon formed La Sociedad de Artesanos de Bogotá in order to
undertake political action to raise tariff rates to previous levels.

Bogotano craftsmen first entered the formal political process because they felt threatened by increased amounts of foreign manufactured goods in the local market. War and financial crises had
already hurt their accustomed lifeways; further competition might
cause them to lose the independence that their work brought
them. In expressing their concerns, tradesmen thought it impor-

tant to stress both their socioeconomic importance as producers and their civic services in support of the legal constitutional order. Artisans feared that the new legislation would jeopardize not only their own fortunes but also that of their families, other social sectors, and even the country as a whole. The artisans who presented this petition to the congress clearly did not view themselves in isolation, but as important components of a social environment that in its largest manifestation included the entire nation.

This study traces artisan political activity in Bogotá, Colombia, during the "long nineteenth century," from the 1830s through the 1910s.[2] It reveals the social, economic, and political goals sought by artisans through active participation in a political system normally described as oligarchic. The long nineteenth century serves as a useful conceptualization of the transition from the colonial period to the establishment of national political, economic, and social norms—a process not completed in Colombia until at least the 1910s. Bogotá and Colombia experienced marked economic and social change during this period. Bogotá had a largely self-sufficient economy in the 1820s, which was supported by traditional industries and linked by mule and human carriers to a limited regional market. By the 1910s the Colombian capital was in the throes of industrialization and had been integrated by steam and rail transportation and commercial networks into both national and international markets.

The transformation of Bogotá's and Colombia's economies had a fundamental impact upon bogotano artisans. As the local, regional, and national economies evolved, a variety of forces threatened artisans. Many craftsmen suffered economic dislocation or proletarianization through the loss of their once isolated and protected economic niche. A few artisans emerged as small "industrials" who operated shops employing up to thirty people, but most suffered deterioration of their social and economic positions while they continued their craft activities. Artisan social relations were affected by changes in their productive function and in the larger economic environment. Relationships with other members of their class were redefined, as were those with individuals of other classes. The host of socioeconomic changes created special problems, which in turn called into being new class interests that evoked individual and collective responses by craftsmen.

In order to understand the context in which artisans pursued their specific concerns, much attention will be directed toward Colombia's political system. The struggle for power between elite-dominated Conservative and Liberal parties constituted the catalyst of nineteenth-century Colombian politics. Elites strove to implement their own ideological programs and competed for limited governmental positions. They drew non-elite social groups into the political process in the effort to enhance their partisan chances for domination of the state apparatus. The competitiveness of the political system first enabled artisans to gain a political voice and in time offered them the opportunity to express their class objectives. Artisans were not wholly dependent upon elites for political mobilization however; at times they organized for satisfaction of their own ambitions. Yet tradesmen could not isolate themselves from established parties, and thus the narrative of their political activity is closely intertwined with that of the larger process.

Both changing socioeconomic conditions and the general political environment affected the tempo of artisan political activity. It is possible to speak of a more or less homogeneous artisan class in the beginning of the national period. Internal stratifications were present, but these did not override its essential homogeneity. The most cohesive artisan organizations existed during the generation before a profound crisis in the 1860s transformed earlier social and economic norms. As Bogotá's economy evolved during the last third of the nineteenth century, differences in the artisan sector became more pronounced. Fragmentation of the artisan class resulted in the demise of broad mobilizations. By the beginning of this century, skilled independent craftsmen, journeymen associated with the emerging industrial concerns, proletarianized laborers, and various other types of workers made up the city's working population. This division of the labor force, clearly visible by the 1910s, coincided with the gradual replacement of artisans as leaders of the Colombian labor movement by workers associated with industrial production, transportation systems, and the production of coffee.

Nuanced attention to the artisans and labor movement of the nineteenth century is absent in standard Colombian labor histories.[3] Aside from the multitude of studies on the mid-century Sociedad Democrática de Artesanos de Bogotá, very little is known of other workers or of organizations in which they were influential.[4] Miguel Urrutia, for example, in *The Development of the Colombian Labor Movement*, examines only the Democratic Society in discussing labor in the nineteenth century. Urrutia briefly mentions the formation of mutual aid societies in various cities (though he does not include those of Bogotá), but allows them no political role.[5] Edgar Caicedo, the longtime editor of the Marxist newspaper *Voz Proletaria*, notes that "the activities of mutualist organizations, from the middle of the nineteenth century, constitute only the prehistory of the syndicalist movement. . . . Those organizations were heterogeneous groups of artisans, principally, with confused trade ideologies and limited objectives. To say this is not to lessen recognition of the important social and political struggles undertaken by artisans of the Democratic Societies in the dawn of Colombian capitalism."[6] Urrutia and Caicedo represent common tendencies in Colombian labor historiography, the focus upon twentieth century industrial and/or organized laborers, often from a traditional Marxist perspective. Few words have been dedicated to the social, cultural, or economic experiences of workers. Historical examinations of workers in cities other than Bogotá have been even sketchier. In short, little is known of organized labor activities by artisans or of the role of craftsmen in the transition to the modern labor movement.

The institutional focus and predominantly Marxist methodological analysis that dominates the study of Colombian labor history is equally apparent in the historiography of other nations of Latin America.[7] Students of Latin American labor history have, for the most part, bypassed the nineteenth century in the rush to examine the twentieth century. Labor and syndicalist activists long dominated the discussion of the labor movement, adding a sense of urgency to their interpretations seldom found in the works of non–Latin American scholars.[8] Representative of the traditional Marxist approach are the works of Argentine sociologist Julio Godio, who places a great emphasis upon "ideological influences" and the development of labor unions. Godio, in referring to the nineteenth century, analyzes the 1850–80 period as one of a "workers' movement without a working class" and the 1880–1918 period as the years in which both the class and the movement itself came into being. While Godio recognizes the importance of mutual aid associations as precursors of latter-day syndicates, he fails to appreciate the conservative nature of these artisan-dominated bodies. For Godio, their importance was as a "brewing pot" for revolutionary ideologies.[9]

More recent attempts by U.S. academicians to pen histories of the Latin American labor movement have contributed to the rapid expansion of Latin American labor history. The works of Hobart Spalding, Jr., and Charles W. Bergquist stand out as stimulating interpretations of Latin American laborers within the context of national economies defined by their dependence upon the dominant North Atlantic economic structure. Spalding posits three general periods of organized labor in Latin America, each corresponding to a stage of integration into dependent economic relations. He concludes that governments have successfully restrained radical demands of laborers, thereby co-opting their movement and keeping Latin America "safe" for foreign capitalists.[10] By contrast, Bergquist suggests that pressures by laborers in the export sector challenged the historic social indifference of many Latin American governments to the needs of the people and, in doing so, have ameliorated socioeconomic conditions in many countries. He allows that workers have been powerful agents in shaping nations in twentieth-century Latin America, with largely positive results.[11]

Both of these works require the establishment of dominant export industries and dependent economic relations as catalysts to the Latin American labor movement. This approach seems partially appropriate for the comprehension of the twentieth century, especially in the analysis of Bergquist. It fails to address, however, the struggles of laborers in most industries, domestic service, non-export rural activities, and other types of work to provide for their own basic needs. Nor does it illuminate organized activity by laborers in the nineteenth century, before a dependent export economy was fully operative. Moreover, political activity undertaken by nineteenth-century laborers is often ignored, despite Bergquist's observation that developing political systems in the nineteenth century strongly color the character of this century's labor movements.[12]

Although "Latin American labor history has come of age," the study of nineteenth-century artisans has not kept pace with examinations of twentieth-century wage laborers.[13] This stands in marked contrast to historiographical trends in European or United States labor history, fields that have often favored the nineteenth-over the twentieth-century laborer.[14] Especially in England and France the reactive mobilizations and violent political movements of craftsmen against threats to their labor and lives have attracted a host of scholarly studies. The same is not true of the Latin American artisan. These different trajectories are shaped in part by the perceived utility of labor studies. Imbedded in the scholarship of Europe and the United States are criticisms of industrial society and the effort to examine the characteristics of preindustrial Europe. Similarly, much of the thrust of Latin American labor history is provided by condemnations of twentieth-century social, economic, and political norms, which are frequently related to the emergence of dependent economies and exploitive relations between polities and organized labor—both of which are seen more typically as phenomena of the current century. The resolutions of these problems are not, however, for many Latin Americanists, to be found in an "idyllic" preindustrial culture such as E. P. Thompson describes for England, but in the rectification of contemporary structures of injustice. Only recently have historians begun to study nineteenth-century labor movements on their own terms. The best of these studies trace the transition from the colonial to the national periods or assist in the understanding of the transition from the early (artisan-based) to modern (wage-based) labor movement.[15]

The failure to investigate craftsmen and their organizational efforts clouds our understanding of the transition from colonial to "modern," twentieth-century Latin American societies. The years after independence established social, economic, and political patterns that helped to mold contemporary Latin America. The study of artisan-based labor activity illuminates the foundations of contemporary societies. Such a project necessarily considers the socioeconomic and political contexts in which artisans labored. This simple axiom is frightfully complex. It requires the consideration of economic structures, social relations, and political machinations—unique variables for each country. Each of these themes relates to earlier patterns and to those that followed, in addition to the topic under immediate investigation. Not disregarding the peculiarities of national histories, the investigation of artisans—a social sector defined by a mode of production found in many societies—lends itself to comparative analysis. Further, nineteenth-century Latin American governments imposed essentially the same political economy, and most nations followed a similar economic trajectory. Considering the nature of artisan production, common economic policies, and similar routes of economic development—qualifications that can serve as guideposts—the study of Latin American craftsmen offers promising findings.

This effort represents one step toward that end. A detailed investigation of the artisan class of nineteenth-century Bogotá in the tradition of the once "new social history" is hampered by the availability of sources. The *alcaldía,* home of information on local taxes, juridical procedures, and city government, burned in 1903. Departmental archives and part of the archives of the diocese were destroyed in the 9 de abril riot, which followed the assassination of Jorge Eliécer Gaitán, a popular political leader, in 1948. Notarial archives are extant, but disorganized to a point of limited utility. Consequently, the nature of available sources dictates the political emphasis of this study. Fortunately, abundant data on artisan political history of the period is available in the Archivo del Congreso, the archives of the Academia Colombiana de Historia, several outstanding newspaper collections, and, perhaps most important, fine collections of political handouts and broadsides. Yet, while good data are available, their limitations define the scope of this work. Information on the artisan elite is more common than on the "rank-and-file" artisan. One can locate data on artisan political societies, but not have access to their internal functions. Informal associations are particularly difficult to document. Information on trade activities, including apprenticeship systems, are almost nonexistent, although complaints about tariff policy abound. Social information must be carefully gleaned from sources and employed with more generalization than would be desired; the data that remain dictate a political emphasis, balanced by an orientation toward social history. This includes a constant attention to economic conditions, changing modes of production, attendant cultural norms, and precisely analyzed attention to the intercourse between artisans and the polity.

# ACKNOWLEDGMENTS

I T IS A PLEASURE TO ACKNOWLEDGE THE PERSONAL, SCHOLARLY, AND financial support that helped to sustain this project. My deepest gratitude is to my wife, Chris. Little did she (or I) suspect what "walking in the Andes" meant or how much "artisans of Bogotá" would become a part of our lives. Chris has been an astute critic (to whom I have not always paid sufficient attention), a willing workmate, and a steadfast friend. She has nurtured our child, Emily, in settings as varied as Bogotá, western Kansas, and south-central Pennsylvania as the research and preparation of this book took place. For her love, companionship, and help I am thankful.

I owe countless debts to David Bushnell, a gentleman and scholar of the highest caliber. Bushnell's editorial help and keen knowledge of Colombian history have improved this project since it began, though I often wished for more direct guidance on the latter and less of the former. Charles Bergquist has been an inspired critic, first at the 1988 meeting of the American Historical Association and, more significantly, during the final stages of manuscript preparation. His observations have greatly improved the presentation and conceptualization of this work. J. León Helguera read the manuscript closely and alerted me to many of its shortcomings. From him I have learned the meaning of patronage and friendship that have defined so much of Colombian history.

Long hours in the Sala Colombiana of Colombia's national library were enlivened by the friendship and wit of Oscar de J. Saldarriaga

Vélez. Our many discussions over *tinto* and *aguardiente* helped to define the orientation of the project. Conversations with Mauricio Archila and Gary Long further stimulated my thought. James Amelang offered me crucial guidance for the study of labor and social history, as well as helpful criticism. Hermes Tovar Pinzón helped to locate the elusive 1851 census. The encouragement and assistance of Jane Landers over the past decade is gratefully acknowledged. Glen Ames, John French, Frank Safford, Hobart Spalding, and Consuelo Valdivieso helped in many different ways. The staffs of the Archivo Histórico Nacional, Archivo del Congreso, Archivo Central del Cauca, Academia Colombiana de Historia, Biblioteca Nacional, and Biblioteca Luis Angel Arango were courteous and helpful.

The author extends his appreciation to the laborers at Temple University Press who helped in the preparation of this manuscript, especially to Doris Braendel and Jennifer French, as well as to freelancer Caterina Mercone. My sincere appreciation is extended to all these people and to others unnamed for their friendship, instruction, and assistance. They have substantially improved this work through their advice and suggestions; the errors and shortcomings that remain are the sole responsibility of the author.

Financial support from a Fulbright Grant and a Tinker Field Research Grant sustained field research in 1984 and 1985. A Fort Hays State University summer stipend underwrote the coding and analysis of the quantitative materials.

David Sowell
Huntingdon, PA

# THE EARLY COLOMBIAN
# LABOR MOVEMENT

# ONE

# ARTISAN SOCIOECONOMIC EXPERIENCES

N INETEENTH-CENTURY BOGOTÁ, IN THE WORDS OF GABRIEL García Márquez, was "a gloomy city where on ghostly nights the coaches of the viceroys still rattled through the cobbled streets. Thirty-two belfries tolled a dirge at six in the afternoon."[1] Santa Fé de Bogotá had served as the viceregal capital and, although its name had been shortened to appease republican sentiments, the city retained much of its colonial character through the nineteenth century. The prominence of the cathedral in the city's center reflected a highly religious society, one whose daily patterns were deeply influenced by the Roman Catholic church. Essential social divisions changed only slowly over this period. And, although García Márquez does not say so, neither did economic patterns depart severely from the time of Santa Fé. Bogotá and the province of Cundinamarca remained physically remote and economically isolated, not only from neighboring provinces, but from the outside world.

The Colombian capital is located on the vast *sabana de Bogotá*, a fertile highland plain that had yielded grain, vegetables, and meat for the city and region since prehistory. The 8,500-foot altitude of the sabana frequently spawns cold, drizzly conditions, though summer days are glorious in their clarity and splendor.[2] The sabana descends to the west and northwest to the lowlands of the Magdalena River valley and is interrupted to the northeast by a series

1

of peaks and ridges that separate Cundinamarca from the province of Boyacá. Travelers approaching the city 160 years ago noticed first the massive crests of Guadalupe and Monserrate that determine the city's eastern boundary and direct its urban development along a general north/south contour.[3] From the mountain peaks flowed the San Francisco and San Agustín rivers, now covered by thoroughfares such as the Avenida Jiménez.

Rugged mountains and dismal transportation conditions kept Bogotá isolated from most of the country and the world through the nineteenth century. Passage from the northern coast to the capital required weeks of boat travel up the unpredictable Magdalena River. After arrival at the river towns of La Vuelta or Honda, the arduous ascension to Bogotá over treacherous mule paths required several days before the sabana opened to the traveler or merchant. The governments of the 1820s sponsored efforts to develop steam navigation on the Magdalena River, but, despite their best intentions, pole-propelled skiffs dominated the nation's primary transportation artery until the 1860s. Permanent steam service was in place by 1847, which reduced upriver transportation costs by up to one-half by the 1860s.[4] Even with steamboats on the Magdalena, mule teams carried most imports up the rugged mountains from the river to the capital until early in this century, when rail lines finally connected the capital to the river.

Bogotá was, until late in the century, divided into four wards (barrios) that surrounded the Plaza de Bolívar, the symbolic and physical heart of the city. Las Nieves is situated to the north, San Victorino to the west, Catedral in the more central location, and Santa Barbara to the south. Most of the streets were cobblestone, although those further from the center were dirt. Many of the streets had gutters cut in their middle to drain the refuse, wastes, and runoff from rain into the rivers. Only those streets in the business section had appreciable sidewalks. Their two-foot width seldom allowed persons walking in opposite directions to pass. When two persons met, the person with a lower social station stepped aside.[5]

The spatial distribution of socioeconomic groups became increasingly distinct over the course of the nineteenth century. Social elites traditionally clustered around the central plaza, often in two-storied houses, while Las Nieves, the "artisan barrio," and the other wards were dominated by one-story adobe houses. Shops or stores commonly occupied either the first floor or front of a house. Artisans and small shopkeepers lived in the house with their shops more frequently than did the city's elite, many of whom rented the first floor of their houses for craft or commercial use. Lower-class individuals and new migrants resided on the city's periphery, often in mud and thatch dwellings.[6] This spatial distribution changed toward the end of the century, as the middle and upper classes moved northward, settling around the suburb of Chapinero.[7]

In its demographic expansion during the nineteenth century, Bogotá parallels that of those Latin American cities that did not experience marked levels of foreign migration. (See Table 1.) There is little evidence that changes in birthrates or mortality rates dramatically affected the city's size until the twentieth century. Instead, civil unrest, migration from the countryside, and the pace of economic expansion determined the rate of urban growth. Economic stagnation and widespread civil disorder during the post-independence period helps to account for the slow rate of expansion in the 1820s to 1860s, while the improved economic situation of the city and region accounts for the growth after the 1870s.[8] These same variables determined the tempo of expansion in Lima, Peru. Buenos Aires, by contrast, displayed a markedly distinct growth pattern due to high levels of foreign immigrants and its sustained economic development.[9]

A description of the city's social structure is complicated by the failure of social scientists to agree upon a common set of criteria by which to stratify the society of the nineteenth-century city. The two-class model that dominated analyses of the region through the 1950s has given way to various analytical constructs with at least three layers that contain major substrata variously defined as subcultures, classes, occupations, or social classes.[10] R. S. Neale's five-class model, though elaborated for England, is particularly instructive for this study. Neale isolates the upper class, middle class, middling class, working class A, and working class B within the context of political and social conflict of nineteenth-century England. His image of class divisions revolves around access to the polity and socioeconomic status, both of which are revealed by social tensions. For Neale, these considerations combine to make the middling sector a critical barometer of change in representative politics and economic growth. During periods of growth, the upward mobility of working class A into the middling class is more

TABLE 1: Latin American Urban Expansion

| Bogotá | | Lima | | Buenos Aires | |
|---|---|---|---|---|---|
| Population | Date | Population | Date | Population | Date |
| 21,394 | 1801 | 52,627 | 1791 | 40,000 | 1801 |
| 40,000 | 1843 | 54,628 | 1836 | 55,416 | 1822 |
| 40,883 | 1870 | 89,434 | 1862 | 177,787 | 1869 |
| 95,813 | 1895 | 100,194 | 1895 | 663,854 | 1895 |
| 121,257 | 1912 | 143,000 | 1908 | 1,575,814 | 1914 |

Sources: Amato, Elite Residential Patterns, 138; Boyer and Davies, Urbanization in Nineteenth Century Latin America, 7–11, 37–39, 59–61; Anderson, "Race and Social Stratification," 215.

possible, as is the shift of the latter into the middle class, which contributes to increased pressures for an expanded voice in the polity. Periods of decline restrict upward mobility, forcing many in the middling class downward, producing tensions of a different nature.[11]

The distinct levels of industrialization in early nineteenth-century England and Bogotá give different weights to the compositions of these five classes, especially in the middle, middling, and A working classes. The Colombian capital had smaller numbers of professionals, relatively few members of the industrial proletariat, but significantly larger numbers of artisans. Consequently, artisans had a proportionately more important role in Bogotá than in the English urban setting. Moreover, the impact of economic change upon that sector, in combination with the crucial role of the urban middling class in the formation of Colombian political culture, suggests that, in the Colombian setting, artisans served as a critical indicator of urban economic and political change.[12]

The full weight of Neale's image of class contention becomes apparent only when variables of social stratification, social class, class consciousness, and relations to authority are considered in combination.[13] José Escorcia's studies of nineteenth-century Cali argue that property ownership (or the lack of it), ethnic stratifications, and political power combine to define the social structure of the Cauca valley. In the city, merchant and mining interests, "second step" creole elites, an intermediate strata of small property owners, artisans, and controlled-wage laborers served as nubs of social identification. Social conflict revolved around how these multiple sectors were affected by property interests, ethnic rivalries, and access to political power.[14] Together, these factors, which parallel those in Neale's five-class model, contributed to a period of intense social conflict in western Colombia.

The lack of anything resembling the archival data that supports Escorcia's analysis complicates the construction of a comparable profile of Bogotá. (See Tables 2 and 3.[15]) The analysis of extant data on various occupational categories, assigned essentially according to levels of skill, reveals that the relative composition of each category remained rather constant during the course of the nineteenth century. This is especially true of the skilled-labor sector, which was by and large composed of artisanal workers. According to the 1851 census of Las Nieves, just over 36 percent of all adult males with stated occupations called themselves artisans. Only 1 percent of the women referred to themselves as artisans. Clearly crafts*men* is an appropriate label. Demographic information from the 1880s suggests the same 36 percent, a figure that coincides well with the 31 percent artisan share reported in an 1893 directory. The 1912 census enumerated 28,027 workers in the city, 32 percent of whom were classified as practicing *artes y oficios* along with their apprentices. (See Table 4.) These data fit within the range of artisan compositions reported in other nineteenth-century Latin American cities.[16] If we interpret these data with healthy portions of salt, the argument that artisan workers persisted as important components of the productive structure seems plausible.

Qualitative descriptions of Bogotá's social stratifications reinforce the quantitative data's suggestion of less radical social transformation during the nineteenth century. The Scottish-born John Steuart, writing in the late 1830s, noted three strata: the poorest, made up of peons and "lower" house servants; the second class, which consisted of artisans, small shopkeepers, and the "best" servants; and the *gente decente*, the highest level of society, which included *hacendados*, larger merchants, and holders of important political posts. Dress habits accentuated the class distinctions: artisans and their peers wore *ruanas* (a Colombian poncho); the up-

TABLE 2: Male Occupational Structure

|  | 1851 | | 1888 | | 1893 | |
| Category | N | % | N | % | N | % |
|---|---|---|---|---|---|---|
| Unskilled | 69 | 12.7 | 89 | 20.1 | 21 | 1.1 |
| Semiskilled | 13 | 2.4 | 11 | 2.5 | 34 | 1.8 |
| Skilled | 196 | 36.3 | 163 | 36.9 | 582 | 31.4 |
| Commercial | 57 | 10.5 | 52 | 11.8 | 610 | 33.0 |
| Religious | 21 | 3.9 | 5 | 1.1 | 13 | .7 |
| Professional | 26 | 4.8 | 17 | 3.8 | 208 | 11.2 |
| Other[a] | 158 | 29.3 | 105 | 23.7 | 383 | 20.7 |
| Total | 540 | | 442 | | 1,851 | |

[a]Includes police and military.

Sources: Manuscript Returns, 1851 Census, AHN: República, Miscelánea, Tomo 17, ff. 65–165; El Telegrama, data extracted from October 1887 through December 1888; Cupertino Salgado, Directorio general de Bogotá. Año IV, 1893 (Bogotá: n.p., 1893).

TABLE 3: Female Occupational Structure

|  | 1851 | | 1888 | | 1893 | |
| Category | N | % | N | % | N | % |
|---|---|---|---|---|---|---|
| Unskilled | 574 | 78.2 | 316 | 79.0 | 334 | 50.3 |
| Semiskilled | 55 | 7.5 | 22 | 5.5 | 34 | 5.1 |
| Skilled | 7 | .9 | 11 | 2.7 | 12 | 1.8 |
| Commercial | 89 | 12.1 | 38 | 9.5 | 261 | 39.3 |
| Religious | 1 | .1 | 4 | 1.0 | 0 | .0 |
| Professional | 6 | .8 | 5 | 1.3 | 16 | 2.4 |
| Other | 2 | .3 | 4 | 1.0 | 7 | 1.1 |
| Total | 734 | | 400 | | 664 | |

Sources: Manuscript Returns, 1851 Census, AHN: República, Miscelánea, Tomo 17, ff. 65–165; El Telegrama, data extracted from October 1887 through December 1888; Cupertino Salgado, Directorio general de Bogotá. Año IV, 1893 (Bogotá: n.p., 1893).

TABLE 4:   1912 Occupational Categories

| Category | N | % |
| --- | --- | --- |
| Domestic servants | 1,695 | 6.0 |
| Day Laborers | 2,895 | 10.3 |
| Industrial | 6,553 | 23.4 |
| Manual Arts | 8,968 | 32.0 |
| Empleados | 3,564 | 12.7 |
| Fine Arts | 450 | 1.6 |
| Liberal Professionals | 1,455 | 5.2 |
| Other[a] | 2,447 | 8.7 |
| Total | 28,027 | |

[a]Includes police, military, and clergy.
Source: *Censo general de la República de Colombia levantado el 5 de Marzo de 1912* (Bogotá: Imprenta Nacional, 1912), 181.

per-class men wore coats; and the *pueblo* (lower classes) walked barefoot.[17]

Two travelers in the 1880s commented upon similar divisions, albeit with somewhat less distinct boundaries and more complex strata. According to the Swiss Ernst Röthlisberger, the "people" (*gente del pueblo*) occupied the lowest rung on the social ladder. They toiled as agricultural workers, day laborers, water carriers, and servants. Moneyed aristocrats and a "nobility" (*nobleza*) consisting of liberal professionals such as doctors or lawyers occupied the upper class. Alfred Hettner agreed on the composition of the upper classes, which included both the upper-class and nobleza groups, but added the middle classes, which consisted of artisans, *empleados*, shopkeepers, and the like. For both travelers, the use of the ruana generally divided the middle from the upper sectors, just as the non-use of shoes divided the pueblo from the middle classes. Both Röthlisberger and Hettner noted, however, that by the 1880s many artisans dressed like members of the upper class and exhibited similar material characteristics, suggesting a weakening of these social distinctions.[18]

Casta considerations inevitably enter the discussion of Latin American social stratification schemes. The correlation between racial labels and occupational practice becomes very difficult to establish when examining the republican period, when racial labels were removed from most public documents. At best it is safe to say that Bogotá was largely a white/mestizo town in the later colonial period and probably remained so through the nineteenth century. A 1789 parochial census labeled 91 percent of the population as white or mestizo. Blacks made up 5.7 percent of the population and Indians 3 percent.[19] However imprecise this count, it seems that most of Bogotá's late-colonial residents were either white or mestizo, an assessment with which travelers throughout the nineteenth century concurred.[20] The 1917 national census estimated that whites or mestizos constituted 93 percent of the population, blacks 1 percent, Indians 2.7 percent, and the remainder was unknown.[21] While one cannot extend the argument into occupational analysis with great confidence, nineteenth-century observers noted the lightest skin at the upper levels of society and the darker tones at the lower, suggesting that *casta* and class were positively correlated, a pattern common to much of Latin America.

## Artisans

Defining *artisan* is an arduous task. From the point of view of production, distinguishing the skilled craftsman from the unskilled laborer is relatively simple. However, the label *artisan* had a social meaning that overshadows its productive function. An early eighteenth-century definition introduces the problem. It describes artisans as those "who earn their daily bread with their hands; and it especially means that they have a public shop and are involved in mechanical trades. Also called . . . oficiales, . . . obreros [or] menestrales."[22] The *Oxford English Dictionary* seconds the importance of the manual, industrial arts in defining the term.[23]

In the Hispanic context, ascribed social position and the social stigma of manual labor complicates the matter. According to Spanish law in the Americas, only pure-blooded Spaniards could gain membership in guilds, denying mixed bloods, at least in theory, access to the organized trades. In fact, mestizos and mulattos regularly joined guilds, although they were less frequently represented among the masters. Moreover, manual labor was thought by many to be a less than honorable way to earn one's living. One artisan noted in 1858 that the colonial belief that "the arts are dishonorable" handicapped the efforts of manual laborers to earn public recognition of their social value.[24] Manual labor brought with it a social stigma, one that forged among craftsmen a shared identity in opposition to those who thought themselves above such toil.

Scholars who define the artisan in the non-Iberian context tend to stress different variables. Karl Marx characterized artisans as members of the petit bourgeoisie who lived off their own labor but also the labor of others, especially journeymen and apprentices who toiled in the shops of master craftsmen.[25] Eric Hobsbawm, following the analytical insights of Frederick Engels, identifies the artisan as the "labor aristocrat" of late nineteenth-century England.[26] The skilled manual labor required for work, in combination with control over that skill, is a frequently cited mechanism for defining the artisan. Many classify artisans as skilled manual workers and make little effort to isolate other characteristics of labor activity.[27] Howard B. Rock defines the artisan as "a skilled handicraftsman, owning his own tools, who worked either for himself or as a foreman for a contractor or merchant, in which case he was master craftsman, or else for a daily or weekly wage in which case he was a journeyman."[28] E. P. Thompson's masterpiece (itself an artisan word), *The Making of the English Working Class*, extends the conceptualization of artisans, suggesting that class is an experience that "happens when some men [people], as a result of common experiences (inherited or shared), feel and articulate the identity of their interests as between themselves, and as against other men [people] whose interests are different from (and usually opposed to) theirs."[29] Artisans worked as skilled craftsmen who shared not only patterns of labor but also experiences of life, including trade or guild membership, social standing, cultural practices, and, often, economic fortunes. Artisans became members of a class when their experiences produced a consciousness and set of activities that distinguished them from other social sectors.

Bogotano artisans were defined first by their status as skilled manual laborers. Those skills, acquired through a lengthy apprenticeship, afforded craftsmen a middling social status and a degree of economic and social independence, especially for master craftsmen. As independent producers, artisans were less beholden to others, which set them apart from the majority of urban dwellers. At the same time, manual labor in the Hispanic context carried a social blemish that separated artisans from higher social strata.

Second, insofar as most artisans were apprenticed in the shop (*taller*) of a master, they acquired not only the skills of a trade but also the social traditions of the shop. Apprenticeship initiated the artisan into both the "society" of artisans and the world of the skilled laborer. Artisans learned social values in the shop, which, in combination with the independence that came with their labor, sustained the pride "de ser artesano" (to be an artisan). Craftsmen not only did skilled manual labor, they *were* skilled manual laborers. Thus, *de ser artesano* implies not only a collective identity emanating from a shared productive function, but also common social values, and position vis-à-vis other social sectors. Changing economic conditions over the course of the nineteenth century threatened many artisans, heightening this sense of shared identity. So, too, did their recruitment into the political arena by partisan elites. Economic threats and political recruitment forged an artisan class during the middle decades of the century, a class that (as will be seen) articulated its ideology most forcefully in the Union Society of Artisans (1866–68).

*Artisan* nevertheless served as a variable label according to the context in Bogotá. For example, an "artisan" newspaper in the 1860s argued that craftsmen constituted two-thirds of the nation's populace, if one included seamstresses and displaced craftsmen in that portion. The same paper frequently complained of the indiscriminate use of the term *artisan* and attested that only 10 percent of the city's population deserved the title.[30] The obviously contradictory usage stems from the fact that in one instance an appeal was being made to the broader population and in the other instance artisans were seeking to set themselves apart from the "mass" for purposes of identification. Artisans saw themselves as both a part of and distinct from the pueblo as it fit their purposes. This indicates a middling social position that linked artisans to two social worlds, both of which might be used to certain advantages in the political context.

Only general insights about craft stratification are available. The absence of formal guilds stimulated viceregal officials during the Bourbon reform era (1777) to establish such a system, but with little success.[31] Guilds did not become firmly established, however, and their abolition in 1824 evoked little opposition.[32] Nevertheless, an 1858 account, "The Artisan of Bogotá," claimed that during the colonial period, masters (*jefes* or *dueños del taller*) and journeymen (*oficiales* or *jornaleros*) were clearly distinguishable, both socially and economically. Masters exerted some control over prices and successfully kept journeymen from establishing their own shops. Masters' control over journeymen was shaken by the disruption of the Independence period, but not eliminated.[33] In keeping with republican notions of equality, masters who tried to maintain their traditional powers were attacked in the press during the 1820s.[34] By the 1830s, journeymen reportedly could establish their own shops and many were undermining masters through lower prices. Masters complained that while the journeymen's labor was cheap, the quality of their goods was poor.[35] Despite these changes, masters and journeymen remained linked by collateral relations, by wages, and by more informal, traditional bonds. Masters still tended to dominate the relationship within the shop, but they lacked sufficient power to control all journeymen activities.[36] By the end of the century, internal trade distinctions appear to have given way to the economic reality that the pinnacle of the craftsmen's profession was shop ownership.

Many artisans continued to operate their own shops with a few journeymen, thus maintaining their economic and social independence throughout the nineteenth century, even though their production undoubtedly represented a decreasing percentage of the city's output. Others, such as the shoemaker Martín Silva, labeled themselves "industrials" by the beginning of the twentieth century. Industrials were generally craftsmen who had successfully used the division of labor to change their shop to a small manufacture. Silva, for example, practiced his craft as the owner of a shop that became increasingly larger until, in 1908, he employed thirty workers, produced a wide range of shoe styles, and had two sales rooms.[37] The "industry" of Silva did not compare to the fully mechanized Bavaria beer factory, which by the same year had almost four-hundred wage laborers, but it was probably typical of shops whose owners had taken advantage of the division of labor to expand their productive capacity. Of the workers who toiled for Silva and other industrials, most probably faced a life of wage labor. Some realistically might hope to achieve the independence of the artisan; only a very few would reach the status of industrial.

In addition to the artisan, the journeyman, the industrial, and assorted wage laborers, other work situations were common by the twentieth century. Concerns such as the Railroad of the Sabana employed a wide range of workers, from highly skilled to untrained manual laborers. The more skilled wage laborers in that venture often referred to themselves as artisans, although they of course lacked the economic independence of the true artisan and should 2be compared to the skilled laborer in the United States' industrial setting. Domestic service and sewing were the dominant labor activities of women through the end of the century, when, as will be seen below, many began to enter low-skilled positions in industrial concerns.

Accurate descriptions of the composition of Bogotá's craft structure are simply not available. The 1851 census of Las Nieves reveals that masons, carpenters, cobblers, tailors, cabinetmakers, and blacksmiths constituted the bulk of the skilled trades. An 1881 guide listed sixty shoe shops, fifty tailors, a hundred or so carpentry shops, twenty printers, twenty-five blacksmiths, and an "infinity" of masons.[38] All these trades fit well within the spectrum of traditional crafts. The guide included no "modern" wage occupations filled by males, although females labored in cigar and match factories. A 1904 listing of trades represented in the Sociedad Unión de Industriales y Obreros included most traditional trades, along with brewerymen and electrical installers.[39] Trades participating in a 1914 workers' celebration were dominated by traditional crafts, but also included industrials and factory workers (from breweries, the electric company, glass factory, railroads, chocolate factories, and cement plants).[40]

Bogotá's occupational structure might well be compared to the "bastard workshop" described by Sean Wilentz in his study of nineteenth-century New York, albeit set in a far less dynamic economic environment. Metropolitan industrialization affected different trades according to their capacity to resist commercialization and rationalization in varied ways. Sweated trades such as clothing production rapidly lost their craft character in the New York setting. Similar trades in Bogotá faced increased pressure from foreign-made goods. In New York, certain transport and construction trades retained their fundamental integrity, as they did in the Colombian capital. Other crafts fell somewhere in between.[41] In both instances, production pressures forced craftsmen to adapt their own shops and work rhythms in order to maintain their financial well-being.

Public ceremonies, such as the 20 de julio celebration of Colombian independence or May Day, provided the opportunity for public manifestations of social solidarities. That artisans were an important collective force in Bogotá's social world is evident in public ceremonies and in expressions of class cohesion. A typical festive occasion in the early national period included events sponsored by the employees of the national and state governments, the military, hacendados, merchant groups, foreigners residing in the city, and artisans.[42] Similar groups participated in Holy Week (Semana Santa) activities throughout the nineteenth century. Not until the early 1910s did ceremonies depart from these patterns. By then, working sectors marched as wage laborers and artisanal workers in May Day and Independence Day parades, sometimes according to trade.[43] Quite significantly, artisan political organizations attracted large numbers of craftsmen during the same periods (1830s–60s) in which public ceremonies saw artisans represented as a collective entity. By the twentieth century, ceremonies reflected the increased divisions of the city's laboring population, such as the wage and craft workers in the 1910 centennial of Colombian independence.

Craft traditions set artisans apart from other social sectors. Certain work habits, such as taking Monday off ("St. Monday"), are commonly associated with artisanal and preindustrial labor settings. Evidence suggests that *hacer lunes*, as it was referred to in Bogotá, persisted through the last and into the present century. In 1867, the carpenter Rafael Tapias criticized this habit, saying that the "Bacchanalian excess" of the Monday celebration not only lost the artisan an estimated forty-eight pesos yearly, but also gave rise to heated political debate and violence.[44] Hostile responses from other craftsmen forced Tapias to add that his intention had not been to criticize anyone's work habits, but only to point out the loss of time and danger of mixing fun and politics.[45] Thirty years later, a leading artisan defended the tradition by commenting that, since artisans were their own bosses, the days they chose not to work were their own decision.[46] Early factory concerns encountered problems when managers tried to impose a stricter time regimen upon recently recruited laborers. One 1904 account noted that laborers rejected the industrial discipline; they wanted to enjoy their work and hacer lunes.[47] Even in the 1990s one hears reference to *el lunes de los zapateros* (cobblers' Monday).

Almost every petition to the government from artisans cited families and social worth as reasons that the government should support artisan interests. In most artisan families both men and women worked, as did children old enough to be apprenticed or earn some money. Apprenticeship began around age seven or eight and would last for six or seven years. At least one report in the 1860s admitted that artisans apprenticed more youngsters than business could sustain, but that the social obligations of shop owners outweighed purely financial considerations in agreeing to train new craftsmen.[48] A 1906 propaganda article against the sale of ready-made imported clothes is rooted in this theme.

> If the importation of these articles brings the paralyzation of work and with this misery to those homes [of craftsmen], the responsibility will weigh heavily upon us; remember the terrible words that your father used on many occasions when work was short and the situation hard and troubled: Oh! ready made clothes! These damned clothes steal the bread from my children! When will we see these men who import them [realize] . . . how impossible it is for us to earn our living and provide bread for our children![49]

It is impossible to isolate the artisan shop from the artisan home, either physically or socially. Together they served as the primary sources of social values and class consciousness. The language of artisan petitions, with constant joint references to home and work and to the artisan fate as a microcosm of national society, is the language of the artisan class.[50] It is on this base that class mobilizations rested.

The question of who spoke for artisans requires a final comment. An 1868 artisan newspaper observed that many masters had the "absurd idea" that they were the social superiors of journeymen.[51] Since most voices seeking to speak for the artisan class came from shop owners, a troublesome question central to this study must be asked. If masters saw themselves as unequal to journeymen, how representative, then, were their voices? No unwavering answer can be presented, but one of the arguments to be forwarded by this study is that one can, up to a point, judge the representativeness of artisan leaders both by their ability to successfully mobilize their subordinate counterparts and by their staying power as leaders. Artisans who were skilled and lasting advocates of their class interests were able to persist as leaders because they were more, rather than less, representative of those whose opinions are not available for historical examination.

## Economic Environment

Independence accelerated the pace of Colombia's integration into the world market, even while the more permanent features of that relationship were not defined until the early years of the twentieth century. Coffee's eventual position as the mainstay of Colombian exports came only after a series of disappointing failures after mid-century in export commodities such as tobacco and *cinchona* bark (*quina*, a source of quinine). Even with coffee's role as the country's primary export commodity and generator of capital, its development had an unequal impact upon various areas of the country. Due to its geographical isolation and the halting development of export commodities, the highland capital was only sporadically affected by the gradual development of an export-driven economy. Extensive portions of the central highlands did not benefit directly from the coffee boom of the late nineteenth century and exhibited traditional characteristics well into this century. These general economic patterns fuel the debate over the degree of economic continuity from colonial to national periods.[52] Recent literature indicates the persistence of colonial economic patterns until mid-century in most areas of the country, followed by the slow and uneven development of external relationships thereafter with many regional variations.[53] Most of the country was not integrated into the world market until well into the twentieth century. This slow pace of economic change meant that social structures would be only gradually transformed, which insured the continued presence of craftsmen in Bogotá's labor structure.

Colombian economic history and the policies that shaped it follow a generational rhythm. Independence leaders conducted themselves in ways that reveal their familiarity with colonial policies, with their experiences during the war for independence, and with the pragmatic fiscal needs of a young government. Economic policy did not rapidly depart from its colonial patterns until at least the mid-century, when a generation of politicians born during the national period wrestled control of the government from their elders. These leaders soundly rejected the country's colonial inheritance and imposed reforms based upon liberal economic principles and a belief in export-driven growth. The short-lived expansion of tobacco production in the Magdalena River valley, fueled by the abolition of the colonial tobacco monopoly and a receptive foreign market, appeared to validate the correctness of the reform program. However, by the 1860s tobacco profits plummeted and again a more pragmatic tone invaded the political elite. As a consequence, the shapers of the Constitution of 1886 returned the state to a more direct role in economic development, rejecting the laissez-faire orientations of the earlier generation of liberal reformers. The Regeneration government facilitated the rise of coffee by interventionist economic policies and helped to spur, in Medellín and to a lesser extent in Bogotá, the development of a nascent industrial capacity.

These economic turns and policy shifts affected the capital's artisan class. Policy makers, on the whole, retained many colonial programs during the so-called Neo-Bourbon period (1821–46), during which time the state continued to assume partial responsibility for economic development, policies largely favorable to craftsmen.[54] The fledgling government of Simón Bolívar, managed by Francisco de Paula Santander, did make several important policy changes, included the abolition of Indian tribute, elimination of fees on interprovince commerce, and removal of most applications of the *alcabala* (a sales tax), but none that affected artisans detrimentally. The fiscal needs of the republican government necessitated retention of various monopolies, including the lucrative tobacco monopoly, and tithes on production. Even those politicians who found these practices ideologically distasteful saw the necessity of preserving the more lucrative ones.[55]

The most reliable source of government revenue—tariffs—directly influenced the country's artisans.[56] Little difference in the level of tariff duties can be seen from the late colonial to early national periods, but in neither instance were rates extremely high.[57] Methods of assessment were altered and tariff schedules adjusted during the 1820s, but the essential degree of protection was not significantly altered. As tariffs were the largest single source of revenue for the government, few officials were willing to reduce the already meager fiscal base of the government. Even with moderate tariff reductions, however, and with the opening of Colombian ports in the 1820s, manufactured products far superior to earlier Spanish products entered the country in ever-increasing quantities.[58] José Manuel Restrepo suggested that the depressed conditions in the early 1830s stemmed as much from the introduction of foreign goods into national markets as from civil disorder.[59] Perhaps as a result, both the 1832 and 1833 tariffs afforded increased protection levels for domestic producers. Finance Minister José Ignacio de Márquez insisted that the latter schedule include protection, as well as revenue, as one of its formal objectives. In addition to customs duties, local and provincial taxes on imported goods added to the economic protection of the native producer.[60]

The Colombian capital served as the center of an upland market that stretched from Ibagué to the west and Bucaramanga to the north. Extreme geographical obstacles and poor roads limited commodity exchanges in the region to only the most valuable items— by weight. Bogotá, which had functioned primarily as an administrative center in the colonial period, produced goods consumed primarily in the city and its products did not circulate widely.[61] The Gran Colombian government had formally opened its ports to foreign commerce in 1824, thus legalizing the trade that had developed since the early days of the independence war.[62] Bogotá then became the distribution hub of various imported items.[63] John Steuart, writing in the 1830s, noted the presence of abundant quantities of British products, especially textiles, in Bogotá's marketplace.[64] Nevertheless, the state of the region's transportation network served to limit the quantities of foreign goods.

Economic stagnation contributed to the city's isolation. Only in the 1830s was the economy even mildly stimulated, most likely by the return of peace after the political crisis following Bolívar's death. The situation again became severe after the War of the Supremes (1839–42), the first partisan struggle of the century (discussed below). Judás Tadeo Landínez, a capitalist from Boyacá, helped sustain the government with loans during the worst stages of the war, as tariff revenues had been cut off and the government was in a desperate situation. With the very profitable results of his loans, Landínez invested heavily in sabana land holdings, spurring other investors to do the same. The ensuing explosion of speculation, sustained almost entirely by Landínez's funds, burst in December 1841, dragging himself and many other speculators into bankruptcy. Credit was in very short supply in Bogotá from 1842 to 1843 as a result of the speculation crisis.[65]

Government-aided industrial projects in the early national period offered the possibility of the transformation of the capital's economic structure. Many early republican leaders, especially those from the highlands around Bogotá, favored governmental support of private industrial ventures as a supplement to the region's agricultural and mining base.[66] The government would issue a monopoly for production of a certain item for a given number of years in a specified region, so that an industry might develop in a protected environment. Privileges enabled an iron works, china factory, paper plant, and factories for glass and textile production to begin operations, all industries that also enjoyed a certain degree of tariff protection.[67]

These early industrial efforts nevertheless fell short of their founder's expectations. The china factory began production in 1834 and reportedly had sufficient capacity to meet the needs of the entire nation by 1837. It operated through the end of the century. The Pacho Iron Works, granted a fifteen-year monopoly in 1827 and in production by the 1830s, proved to be an important factor in the regional economy, providing abundant quantities of lower-quality iron, which supported many spin-off industries.[68] Other ventures did not fare as well. A paper mill that began production in 1836 lasted only until 1849. The textile factory, which probably enjoyed the most protection under the tariff system, was producing good, inexpensive cotton fabric by 1838 that soon thereafter satisfied the needs of the Bogotá market. It was nonetheless bankrupt by January 1848, in part because of the credit crisis. The glass works privileged in 1834 proved to be a dismal failure.[69] Economic historians suggest that the disruptive effects of civil unrest upon capital and labor, a lack of sustained governmental support, and a market that was simply too small for consumer industries help to explain these industrial ventures. Their lack of success contributed to the governmental reorientation toward export agriculture that took place in the 1840s.[70]

The effects of these industrial ventures upon the capital's artisans were probably limited. Most factories employed foreign craftsmen and domestic unskilled laborers. On the whole, artisans labored under rather familiar conditions during the Neo-Bourbon period. Political unrest hindered their production, as did economic stagnation and the credit crisis. However, such had been the state of affairs for most of the generation since 1810. Aside from the few industrial efforts, neither the economic structure of the city nor governmental policies presented new challenges to craftsmen, although by the early 1830s some craftsmen voiced their concerns about the disruptive impact of foreign goods.[71]

Economic reforms during the Liberal Reform era (1846–63) threatened the relatively protected economic environment of the capital's artisans. Liberal reformers eliminated most remnants of colonial economic policy and redirected the nature of the state's intervention in favor of the production of export crops. The first reforms dealt with monetary and fiscal matters.[72] The reduction of tariff barriers followed in 1847, a move deemed fundamental to the emergence of an export economy. The 1851 tariff raised duties on certain finished products somewhat, but it did not seek deliberately to protect native industries.[73] The stated purpose of the 1861 tariff was to produce revenues through a three-tiered system of assessment based solely upon weight, a pattern for duties that lasted until 1880.[74] Other efforts to facilitate international trade included granting duty-free status to several ports and the removal of taxes on international ships using the Magdalena River, although revenue needs forced the government to impose a mild tax on international river transportation in 1856.

The decentralization of the nation's economic system in 1851 reflected the reformers' belief that the economy should be allowed to function without direct interference from central authorities. A 10 percent tithe on production (*diezmo*) was removed from church jurisdiction and given to provincial governments, as were revenues from stamped paper. In the same spirit, much of the rest of the state's fiscal apparatus was decentralized in 1850. At least initially, decentralization was a fiscal disaster. It was one reason for a 47 percent drop in national revenues between 1849 and 1851.[75] The demonopolization of tobacco production, begun in 1846 and completed in 1850, accounted for a considerable portion of lost government revenues. (Neither the salt nor liquor [*aguardiente*] monopoly was altered.) Liberal legislators anticipated that duties from increased production and exportation of tobacco would offset revenue losses from demonopolization. Tobacco production boomed in the Ambalema area under the direction of the Montoya y Sáenz firm and became the country's most important export commodity through the 1870s. While it is questionable that earnings from tobacco exports indeed compensated the revenue losses from demonopolization, the nation's economy was firmly reoriented toward the production of export crops.[76]

Bogotá's economic performance in large part paralleled the fortunes of regional export commodities and the level of civil tranquility. Weak exports and the disruption caused by the War of the Supremes, in combination with the Landínez bankruptcy, mired the city in the economic doldrums for much of the 1840s. The rapid expansion of tobacco production in the Ambalema region reversed this trend, leading to an economic upsurge that dominated the 1850s.[77] Unfortunately, the worldwide recession of 1857–58, coupled with the Colombian civil war of 1859–62, drove the economy into a deep recession that lasted throughout the 1860s—precisely when the tariff reductions of the 1840s and lowered transportation costs began to impact the city's craft sector. By 1863, complaints of general economic misery caused by the war abounded; it was said to have hurt artisans, though not to the same extent as unskilled laborers. A year later even many independent artisans were reportedly hard pressed to find work.[78] Miguel Samper's noted essay, "La miseria en Bogotá," graphically portrayed the city's depressed condition: "Beggars fill the streets and plazas. . . . The worker can not find constant employment, nor can the shop masters count on work; the property owner receives neither rent payments nor new rents; the shop-keeper does not sell, nor buy, nor pay, nor is paid; one sees the importer's wares undisturbed in his store and his payments asleep in his wallet; the capitalist does not receive interest nor the employees salary."[79] One artisan referred to the 1860s as the worst decade since the colonial period.[80]

Artisans frequently clamored for inexpensive credit. Since craftsmen often advanced the cost of the goods involved in production, they had to arrange loans from speculators at the prevailing rate of interest, which ranged from 2 to 5 percent per month. Moreover, during time of feared or actual civil strife, such as the months prior to General José María Melo's 1854 revolt, speculators withheld their capital and, consequently, evoked the wrath of artisans.[81] The only sources of credit until 1845 had been the church or money lenders. In that year the Province of Bogotá founded a savings bank (Caja de Ahorros) that survived until 1863. The bank made funds available to investors of all social sectors.[82] A branch of the Bank of London, Mexico and South America was established in Bogotá in 1864, but it survived only four years. The Banco de Bogotá began permanent lending services in 1871. The savings bank probably offered tradesmen the most reliable source of credit, as one of its objectives was to stimulate industry among workers and many of its depositors were craftsmen. Most of the banks founded in the 1870s favored loans to commercial concerns, but one, the Banco Popular, was designed to help smaller investors. Its shares sold for 50 pesos, an amount equivalent to perhaps one month's labor by a craftsman; numerous artisans were among the initial purchasers.[83]

The economy of the region in and around Bogotá slowly revived around 1870, due to a short-lived resurgence of tobacco exports and the first effects of coffee expansion. Favorable economic conditions lasted until the early 1880s, when tobacco's definitive collapse, a temporary decline in coffee prices, and civil unrest caused a three-year downturn, after which the capital entered a ten-year expansionary phase. Domestic price inflation, war, and fluctuating coffee prices in the international market precipitated a period of economic decline in the mid-1890s. After the War of the 1000 Days (1899–1902), the capital entered a period of growth that lasted, with a few short recessions, until the Depression.

Numerous small industries and factories developed in the capital in this era, although without a marked impact on the male labor force. Another china factory opened in 1870, as did the Rey y Borda match factory, which by 1874 employed over two-hundred women. One hundred and fifty women labored in that same year in a cigar factory.[84] A Cuban cigarette factory, La Estrella de Bogotá, founded in 1883, used imported Cuban tobacco, Spanish paper, Cuban cigar masters, and employed some thirty to forty Colombian women workers. La Equitativa chocolate factory, established shortly thereafter by Luis M. Azcueñaga, also employed mostly female labor.[85] These early industries were oriented, on the whole, toward the production of consumer goods using low technology and unskilled labor. They did not compete with skilled artisanal production, nor did they complement traditional crafts.

Tariff rates had not been lowered to a degree that rapidly undermined domestic crafts production, contrary to craftsmen's predictions.[86] In fact, the reorientation of the economy toward the external market ended the stagnation of the earlier period, which undoubtedly benefited many craftsmen, especially in construction trades. However, at the same time, the disruption of the ambience in which artisans labored altered the composition of the capital's craft economy. Foreign competition increasingly threatened marginal producers, especially in trades such as shoemaking, tailoring, and leather work. By contrast, lowered tariff rates had little effect on construction trades, which owed their prosperity (or lack of it) to general economic conditions. The depression of the 1860s was probably very important in determining which trades would remain competitive and which would be reduced in significance.

Rafael Núñez repudiated many of the more dogmatic tendencies of economic liberalism after he assumed the presidency in 1880 in favor of more state-directed developmental policies. A national bank, founded in 1881, emitted paper money, which, in periods of moderate emissions, stimulated the local and regional economies. However, illegal emissions in the 1890s helped to destabilize the economy in the critical years before the War of the 1000 Days.[87] Moreover, the paper money policy of Núñez and his successor, Miguel Antonio Caro, alienated many merchants who preferred the adherence to a metallic standard. Núñez favored protection of national industries and successfully pressed the passage of the Tariff of 1880, which, although it lowered the basic rate, protected tailoring, shoemaking, and furniture production through a 25 percent surcharge. Tariff rates were raised 25 percent by two legislative measures in 1885 and 1886. Industrial activity in the Medellín area expanded due to these tariffs, but they had less impact on bogotano industries. Fiscal needs drove tariff rates upward through the 1890s. President Rafael Reyes's tariff of 1905 further stimulated industrial growth, even though the tariff was primarily fiscal in nature.[88] This last measure again helped Medellín more than Bogotá.[89]

Bogotá's first major industrial complex, the Bavaria brewery, run by German-born Rudolf Kopp, introduced significant numbers of men into the factory system. Kopp used German technology and brewery masters and Colombian labor. His factory followed German industrial patterns, which by 1894 included workers' housing next to the brewery. Weekly wages in the enterprise were reportedly the highest in the city, supplemented by health insurance, loans, sick pay, and up to two liters of beer a day. In return for such benefits, Kopp demanded rigid industrial discipline from his three hundred male and female workers (1906). Indeed, Bavaria's managerial inflexibility sparked a series of conflicts over the pace of work and control of time, just as in most early United States industrial operations.[90]

New monopolies on cigar, cigarette, and match production provided yet another component of the Núñez government policy to spur industrial development while providing urban women with jobs. The Regeneration's moves to draw women into industrial labor evidenced some success after the War of the 1000 Days. El Rey del Mundo, a cigarette factory owned by the Spaniard Esteban Verdu, employed fifty women in 1904. Verdu also demanded strict discipline from his workers, who, according to one visitor to the plant, worked like "human machines." The same commentator noted that this "kept them off the streets." By 1916 some two-hundred women and fifty men labored for Verdu. In the latter year, however, heavy taxes on tobacco forced closure of Verdu's plant and those of several other cigarette manufacturers, even as workers sought to change the industrial work discipline under which they labored.[91]

## Conclusion

Colombian economic policies influenced the socioeconomic experience that sustained artisan political activity. Many Spanish colonial policies continued during the Neo-Bourbon period. After 1846, policymakers liberalized the economy to facilitate international trade and export agriculture. The Regeneration governments of the 1880s moderated this liberalism with the overt stimulation of internal industries and the establishment of protective tariffs, even while external trade remained the dominant economic priority. Post-1903 governments continued the policies of the Regeneration.

Artisans shared a common socioeconomic experience, especially during the first generation of Colombian independence, as they labored in an economic environment rather similar to that of the late colonial period through the Neo-Bourbon period and into the 1850s. Although it has yet to be proven statistically, it seems probable that the economic reforms of the 1840s and 1850s had, by the 1870s, undermined the cohesive economic and social traditions of Bogotá's craftsmen. Socioeconomic distinctions became more apparent during the last thirty years of the nineteenth century as some trades hurt by foreign competition went into decline and others, largely unaffected by governmental policies, retained characteristics similar to those of the earlier period. Practitioners of displaced crafts and those of stable trades lost many of the shared experiences that had earlier bonded the craftsmen, fragmenting, as a consequence, their social, economic, and political lives. It was during these years that separate trade labels began to identify craftsmen. Moreover, by the 1890s, the creation of limited industrial and transport concerns gave rise to a small but important "modern" wage-labor sector. Various types of workers formed the occupational structure by the 1910s, employing both traditional and more modern productive techniques in a mixed-labor system, in which each laboring class had its own social norms and, as a result, its own organized political expression.

The orientation of the country's economic structure toward participation in the world market slowly created a multifaceted labor force. One of its facets was much more influenced by policies that aided the development of an export economy and increased importation of foreign manufactured goods, policies which brought with them expanded transportation and commercial activities. Artisans affected by these policies lost their productive independence in a slow process of proletarianization. In rural areas, an agro-export labor force evolved to sustain the coffee economy. Other sectors of the economy were affected more by general economic conditions than by specific governmental programs, which sustained the growth of industrial, service, and informal workers (e.g., street merchants). Many trades continued to employ traditional productive practices throughout the period studied and retained their status as independent artisanal producers, even while the larger economic structure had seen radical change.

The transitions that redefined the artisan class are of particular importance for understanding artisan political activity. Both the credit crisis of the 1840s and the artisanal crisis of the 1860s prepared the way for intense political mobilizations by artisans. Significantly, both periods of activity occurred prior to increased fragmentation of the artisan sector. As a result, movements drew the participation of large numbers of craftsmen in defense of widely held beliefs. The same level of political activity would not return until the 1910s, when surviving artisans and emerging wage-laborers combined to initiate a new stage of political activity by Colombian workers, one that revealed quite distinct social ideologies.

# TWO

# COLOMBIAN POLITICAL CULTURE

T HE STRUGGLE FOR POLITICAL POWER AMONG MEMBERS OF THE
Conservative and Liberal parties defined Colombia's political
culture early in its national existence. Eduardo Santa claimed a
generation ago that Colombians are born with party labels on their
umbilical cords, a testament to the intensity of partisan identification.[1] From small towns to national society, partisan politics bifur-
cated Colombian society into patterns that have lasted for generations. This political culture shaped nineteenth-century Colombia
in both negative and positive ways. Partisan competition contributed to endemic political violence and repeated conflicts at the local, regional, and national levels. However, Colombia's modified
democratic tradition, one of the oldest in Latin America, is in large
part sustained by historical patterns of partisan mobilizations.
Strong party affiliations, coupled with deep regional identities,
meant that unlike most other Latin American nations, no Colombian group could monopolize power. The origins of the Conservative and Liberal parties, the extent of their programmatic divisions,
and the factors that shaped their nineteenth-century evolution are
subjects of oft-times intense debate.[2] Discussions concerning the
degree of influence of socioeconomic or regional variables upon the
formation of the parties are particularly heated. These points of
dispute relate directly to the interpretations of the political activity
of Colombian artisans.

A distinguished company of social scientists traces the origins of the Conservative and Liberal parties to the socioeconomic positions of their founders.[3] Luis Eduardo Nieto Arteta, the earliest leading proponent of this interpretation, asserts that reactionary social groups, which included large landowners and landowning religious communities, struggled to maintain colonial institutions in order to protect their privileged economic, political, and social positions. These groups coalesced by the late 1840s into the Conservative party to ward off the anti-colonial sentiments of merchants, artisans, slaves, and small agriculturalists. The efforts to reform remnants of colonial institutional structures, both in the 1820s and 1840s, eventually galvanized this latter group into the Liberal party.[4]

Charles W. Bergquist argues that long-term economic trends, interpreted through the lenses of dependency theory, fundamentally modify this landlord/merchant scenario, although it retains the primacy of economic interests in party formation. First in *Coffee and Conflict in Colombia* and then in *Labor in Latin America*, Bergquist maintains that economic interests, especially as they relate to the export sector, altered the development of social classes and their political trajectory. Bergquist focuses upon the late nineteenth-century period, when coffee emerged as the primary export commodity. In a retrospective analysis, Bergquist contends that agro-export and mercantile interests dominated the Liberal party from the 1840s onward. After that time, "diverging economic interests" that developed over the course of the nineteenth century, chiefly around the failure of tobacco, the rise of coffee production, and the persistence of traditional agricultural interests, shaped the distinct "philosophical and programmatic positions" of the Colombian upper class, divisions that he finds in competitive programs of political economy. Pro-export groups, in his analysis, suffered under the restrictive policies of Miguel Antonio Caro's fiscal and economic Regeneration, only to find political allies in the government of Rafael Reyes, which enacted policies that lasted until the Depression of the 1930s. Contending economic interests and ideologies are visible, according to Bergquist, in late nineteenth-century political strife, especially preceding the War of the 1000 Days.[5]

A growing chorus of regionalists takes exception to these interpretations. Both Helen Delpar and James William Park recount the multiple non-economic factors that helped shape party alignments,

most of which can be traced to regional differences.[6] These scholars utilize Frank Safford's thesis that access to institutions of
power at the beginning of the national period served as the primary
determinant of party alignment, an interpretation that is sensitive
to the geographical and social structures that underpin regional
power networks. Institutional power favored some regions over
others; proximity to colonial centers of educational, political,
or ecclesiastical power shaped a Conservative orientation aimed at
maintaining institutions that enhanced one's "life chances." Conversely, persons in those regions located at a greater distance from
power centers were more likely to be Liberal, and to favor reforms that would enhance their access to power.[7] Safford's work
effectively collapses the supposed distinction among merchants,
landowners, and professionals that sustains socioeconomic interpretations, pointing out that most elite members wore several occupational hats during their lives. Just as in early imperial Brazil,
Conservatives and Liberals came from the same social groups and
often took opposing stances on issues for reasons other than class.[8]

This concept explains the general lack of ideological conflict
between Colombian Liberals and Conservatives. In terms of political structure, few officials questioned the theoretically contractual
nature of government or the concept of popular sovereignty, although the extent of active citizenship caused some disagreement,
as did the degree to which strong central authority was needed to
offset the ignorance of the masses—or regional power seekers. No
one, at least after the decline of the *bolivariano* faction in the
1830s, thought seriously in terms of an aristocracy. Both parties
distrusted the military as an institution, but not to the extent that
they would reject the aid of military leaders favorable to their
cause. In general, economic policy generated few disputes in the
first generation of Colombian political life. Divergent appraisals—
realistic versus optimistic—of the government's fiscal situation actually stirred more debate than did the issue of which economic
orientation was proper for the state. Liberal economic reforms, begun in 1845 under the nominally Conservative Tomás Cipriano de
Mosquera, drew support from most congressional representatives, a
consensus that undermines the analysis of Nieto Arteta.[9]

Liberals and Conservatives separated only on the programmatic
issues of church-state relations and social welfare issues. According to Jaime Jaramillo Uribe, Conservatives tended to hold a corpo-

rate worldview that gave a fundamental social role to the church. Corporate philosophy subordinated the individual to the church, which both embodied and guarded universal morality. Traditionalists maintained that while morality was an inherent part of the human being, individuals could never rationally comprehend morality in its fullness. Religion did encompass its totality, and the church was to act as the guardian of moral knowledge. Liberals, by contrast, tended to adhere to an atomistic philosophy, holding that individuals could determine the morality of their actions without the aid of the church. These opposing philosophical systems led directly to disputes regarding the proper social function of the church. Closely related to this issue was the role of the Society of Jesus. Conservatives valued many Jesuits as luminaries who served to maintain and expand the proper position of the church. Education, as a corollary to this religious question, engendered considerable disagreement. Santander's 1826 Education Plan, based upon Benthamite teachings, was strongly opposed by those politicians later identified with the Conservative party both at the time and also when Santander tried to revive the plan in the government of New Granada. When Conservatives won the War of the Supremes (1839–42), Mariano Ospina Rodríguez promptly issued an educational plan informed by more traditional standards. Not surprisingly, the 1870 educational reform process caused a similar uproar.[10]

Liberals argued that educational institutions that imposed clerical authority hindered the individual from maturing to the point of sound decision-making. Not surprisingly, Jeremy Bentham's utilitarianism dominated the philosophical approach of the first generation of Liberals.[11] Second-generation Liberals were even more committed to an individualist ideology. José María Samper defined his interpretation of *dejar hacer* (laissez-faire) as "the aspiration to found the exclusive autonomy of the individual, limiting the action of the government to provide security, to repress violence against the law, and to impart justice."[12] Significantly, liberal economic and political philosophies, shaped by men of both parties, dominated the score of years after 1846, when the administration of Tomás Cipriano de Mosquera opened the Liberal Reform era.

Jaramillo Uribe's insights on the generational influences further illuminate nineteenth-century Colombian politics.[13] He asserts that the traditional or Benthamite mentalities that shaped the "independence generation" resulted in disputes over education and the church, although the desire to mold a united nation moderated these divisive issues. A second generation, nurtured on the writings of the Romantics and less prone to compromise, came to power in the late 1840s. The more avid Liberals of the day were labeled *gólgotas* in the early 1850s and Radicals after 1855.[14] Liberals dominated the political scene with few exceptions until the 1870s. Conservatives assumed the role of the not always loyal opposition. Several key leaders of the Liberal generation of 1849 underwent remarkable political transformations. Both Núñez and José María Samper began their political lives as avowed gólgotas, only to moderate their views in the 1860s. Together they led the Independent Liberals of the 1870s before proclaiming themselves Nationalists in the 1880s.[15] This movement away from idealist attachment to extreme liberalism paralleled the rapid decline of the political influence of the Generation of 1849.

The shortcomings of liberalism spurred a pragmatic backlash, which was evident in the third generation and in the 1886 Constitution. The adaptations by politicians after the 1870s bridge, to a certain degree, the analytical space between advocates of the socioeconomic and regional schools. Laissez-faire economic policy had not produced an export bonanza that would sustain economic development, nor had many individuals felt comfortable with the absence of the church as a social mediator. During the Regeneration, which began in the 1880s and lasted until the 1910s, coalitions attempted to produce an effective political structure that would prevent the bloodshed of the earlier years. The policies of first the National party of Rafael Núñez, José María Samper, and Miguel Antonio Caro, then of the *quinquenio* (five-year regime) of Rafael Reyes, and last of the Republican Union illustrate the increased tendency toward cooperation in this generation. (The fierce fighting of the period indicates, however, that coalitionists were by no means the sole political actors during these years.) Consensus slowly emerged among the parties concerning the need for a stronger central government and for direct state intervention in economic policy, especially to stimulate the expansion of coffee agriculture.

Just as the issues separating the parties were not wholly clearcut, some individuals are hard to place in either political camp. General José María Obando, identified as a *santanderista* liberal after 1832, split the ranks of those loyal to Santander in his 1836 presidential candidacy. Obando helped precipitate the Guerra de los Supremos by his support of small convents in 1839, only to be exiled upon his defeat. Returning as a Liberal hero in 1849, Obando nominally headed the moderate *draconiano* wing of the Liberal party, which contributed to a major revolt against radical reformist *gólgota* Liberals and Conservatives in 1854. General Tomás Cipriano de Mosquera was identified as a Conservative, but his 1844 presidential candidacy and subsequent administration shattered the emerging Conservative party. In 1857, Mosquera ran for the presidency as head of the National party and two years later led the Liberal revolt against Conservative rule. After the 1863 Ríonegro convention, he was at bitter odds with the Radical faction of the Liberal party. In 1867, Mosquera imposed a short-lived dictatorship upon the Radical congress and by 1869 was again in league with Conservatives. Both Mosquera and Obando were more personalistic than party-minded in their approach to power. Obando had extensive support among the popular sectors of Colombian society, especially in the southwest regions of the country, and a strong network of clients. The military bearing and populist orientations of both generals might merit their classification as *caudillos*, but of a particular Colombian variant. In any case, it is clear that any understanding of Colombian history prior to 1870 must take into consideration personalism and the appeal of certain military leaders.

Men such as Núñez frequently founded third parties to express their own beliefs more independently. However, most of the third, and occasionally fourth, parties generally drew upon both the membership and ideological stances of the dominant groups. As with the National party of Núñez, these alliances could become potent political forces in their own right. More frequently, as with Mosquera's National party, their impact was short-lived and their leaders quickly made their way back into the fold of one of the two parties. Third parties are an underappreciated component of Colombia's political culture. They frequently forced the dominant parties either to accept third-party leaders into their ranks, or to unite to repress third-party challengers in order to maintain Conservative/Liberal control of the political apparatus.

The struggle between the parties offered artisans and others a limited opportunity to gain a formal voice within the polity. Elites needed clients in their struggle for power. In rural areas, the pursuit of clientage led local bosses (both lay and clerical) to create self-perpetuating Liberal and Conservative enclaves that have existed to the present.[16] In larger urban centers, the establishment of clientage relationships fostered more competitive recruitment. Elite efforts to mobilize popular support for their party struggles first stimulated the participation of non-elites in the political process. Artisans and other middling social groups were, because of their status as voters,[17] the principal targets of parties and factions trying to expand their popular support. Patrons and clients operated in a two-way relationship, which occasionally allowed non-elites, such as artisans, the opportunity to articulate their particular interests.

Patron-client relations offered non-elites a certain degree of economic and social mobility under special conditions. The premier example is that of Ambrosio López, born in 1809 to Jerónimo López and Rosa Pinzón. Jerónimo was a tailor in the employ of the viceroy and Rosa made *chicha*, a maize-based low-alcohol beverage. Ambrosio acquired both skills. Apprenticed as a tailor, Ambrosio joined the military in 1823, serving for four years, during which time he claimed that the "progressive" Santander became his "protector." Ambrosio had a checkered career in the wake of the September 25, 1828, attempt on the life of Bolívar (allegedly masterminded by Santander), serving in the national guard and engaging in commerce—mostly in the production of aguardiente—during the 1830s. Ambrosio abandoned the progressive cause in the War of the Supremes to become a judge, *alcalde* (mayor), and captain in the guard during the Conservative presidencies of the 1840s. Ambrosio took an active role in the Society of Artisans, only to leave the organization in 1851. In the 1854 revolt by General José María Melo against the liberal constitution of 1853, Ambrosio supported Mosquera, for which he was rewarded with the position of director of waters in the capital during much of the 1860s. Toward the end of that decade, his skills in aguardiente production earned him a job at the Samper brothers' distillery, Los Tres Puentes. When he died in 1881, the *Diario de Cundinamarca* hailed him as a life-long Conservative, although at one time Ambrosio called himself a Liberal Conservative. Ambrosio's son, Pedro, became an important banker through his father's Samper connection, and his grandson, Alfonso López Pumarejo, served as president of the country in the

1930s.[18] Although Ambrosio identified himself as a tailor throughout his life, his rise is related to his political abilities and connections. First with Santander, then with Mosquera, and finally with
the Samper family, Ambrosio worked his way up the social ladder,
leaving his family well positioned. Ambrosio López's case is clearly
unique, but it illustrates the ways by which political clientage afforded the opportunity for social mobility.

In the early national period, due to Colombian political culture,
urban craftsman were more politically driven than their European
counterparts but less so than their equivalents in the United States
at that time. Artisans were at the forefront of the political struggle
for United States independence and continued to play an integral
role in urban politics until the middle of the nineteenth century.[19]
While Colombian artisans played a less significant political role in
their independence movement, the general acceptance of republican principles (though not always their practice) quickly integrated
craftsmen into the network of urban politics. The political activity
of craftsmen was significant particularly in the formative period of
the country's political culture. The same pattern is visible in other
Latin American nations to a limited extent. By contrast, the rejection of republicanism in Restoration Europe (save in modified form
in England) denied craftsmen a formal voice in European polities,
even while changing economic patterns subjected artisans to extreme pressures. The political role of European craftsmen tended to
be more explosive, especially in the uprisings of 1830 and the revolutions of 1848, and more directly linked to socioeconomic issues.

## Popular Recruitment and the Formation of
## Colombian Political Culture

The vision of a Gran Colombia that would maintain the unity
of Colombia, Ecuador, and Venezuela faded in the late 1820s, as
even Simón Bolívar's charismatic and powerful leadership proved
unable to hold pressures for regional autonomy at bay. Bolívar's
dictatorial propensity, moreover, generated powerful opponents
who, on the night of September 25, 1828, attempted to assassinate
the Liberator.[20] Although Vice-President Francisco de Paula Santander was never proven to have taken part in the conspiracy, he was
charged with the crime and sentenced to death, a penalty com-

muted to exile. Bolívar's death in late 1830 signalled the permanent collapse of Gran Colombia and, after months of civil war, the creation of the Republic of New Granada. Santander returned from exile in 1832 to serve as New Granada's first president.

The Granadian Constitution of 1832 established a moderately centralized system of government. Local and regional governments shared power with central authorities, but most policy initiatives came from Bogotá. Regional alliances played an important role in national politics, especially those of the Cauca and Cundinamarca. The formal authority of military leaders was reduced, but not their effective say in local or national affairs. The executive, legislative, and judicial branches shared responsibility for the management of government authority, but the executive retained extraordinary powers for use in emergency situations. All in all, the Colombian Constitution of 1832 was not so different from its predecessor of 1821, save perhaps that it affected a much-reduced territorial extension.[21]

President Santander's often harsh methods of rule and his appointees fomented considerable political divisions. Partisan camps developed when Santander attempted to impose General José María Obando as his successor in the 1836 presidential election. Obando's militarism and his alleged role in the assassination of Independence hero Antonio José de Sucre[22] alienated many in the political elite. These included José Ignacio de Márquez, whom Obando had bested in the 1834 vice-presidential election and who again opposed Santander's favorite. Vicente Azuero, a santanderista, also refused to support Obando and stood as a civilian option to the Caucano general. These factions reflected earlier divisions between followers of Bolívar and Santander, as well as the alignment of loyalties during the abortive dictatorship of Rafael Urdaneta following the breakup of Gran Colombia. Bolivarianos had lost most of their influence in that ill-fated effort, leaving the field open to persons loyal to Santander or those of more independent hue, such as Márquez.[23] Márquez polled more electoral votes than Obando in the 1836 presidential election, although not a majority, which, according to the constitution, meant that the final decision for Márquez was made by the congress.

These same factions redoubled their efforts in anticipation of the 1838 vice-presidential and congressional elections, which were held amidst controversy over the content of public education and the extent of religious influence in Granadan society. Here, for once, ideology entered the fray. Santanderistas from both the Azuero and Obando camps—the so-called *progresistas*—set aside their differences and prepared to oust Márquez loyalists. The latter's followers, the *moderados*, joined in an alliance with the church (in spite of Márquez's reputed anti-clerical attitudes). These political coalitions sought to enlarge their electoral base by the active recruitment of non-elite voters, which for the first time brought artisans openly into the political process.

Members of the church hierarchy organized La Sociedad Católica (Catholic Society) in May 1838 to forestall further encroachments into the terrain of the church and to amplify support for candidates sharing their ideological leanings.[24] The Catholic Society stressed the importance of morality and religion in both state and society, expressing the regret that many officials did not stress the "proper" basis of moral order. The Catholic Society recognized the virtues of President Márquez, but feared that the forthcoming elections would introduce men of "irregular conduct" into public office.[25] According to the Society's newspaper editors, proper education, together with votes for Catholic representatives, would prevent the "infection" of foreign and atheistic ideas from spreading through the nation.[26] The church's campaign to infuse political debate with Catholic ideology extended into other areas of the country. Catholic Societies operated in Cali, Pasto, and Popayán, where the debate took on an air of ideological contention that persisted at least until the Conservative insurrection of 1876.[27]

While the Sociedad Católica in Bogotá made no direct appeal to the artisan class, its mobilization efforts undoubtedly attracted many craftsmen. Progressives, on the other hand, appealed openly to artisans for political support. *La Bandera Nacional*, the political mouthpiece of Santander, Lorenzo María Lleras, and Florentino González, claimed that *moderado* electors were simply clients of the president who voted as they were told in order to assure their continued employment. Progressive electors, it was alleged, were by contrast independent "patriots" who lived without having to "beg" from the executive.[28] Moreover, pro-Márquez voters were said to include the rank-and-file of the military who would vote according to orders, since they could not read. Progressives published an electoral list of "honorable artisans and laborers" who "lived by the sweat of their brows," men who, the editors claimed, voted only for the good of their country. The leading progressives, however, did not include any of the potential artisan electors in their official electoral list, despite the appeal for the votes of the craftsmen.[29]

The election's results drove the two sides farther apart. Of the 1,481 votes cast in Bogotá, according to an unofficial tally, 1,356 went to moderates, 80 to progressives, and 45 to candidates judged to be neutral.[30] The victors noted that despite efforts to recruit artisans to the santanderista cause through the use of socially divisive language (terms such as *nobles* and *plebeians*), craftsmen had favored the administration with their votes. Moderates claimed that political societies made a positive contribution to the electoral process, even while their control of the election process raised accusations of fraud from the progressives.[31]

In the wake of the electoral defeat, progressives began their own aggressive political instruction of the popular sectors. The Sociedad Democrática-Republicana de Artesanos i Laboradores Progresistas de la Provincia de Bogotá (Democratic-Republican Society of Progressive Artisans and Laborers of the Province of Bogotá) was therefore founded on June 17, 1838, to instruct the "different classes of the state in the maintenance of their interests, in the knowledge of their public rights; moralizing their customs, showing them the true philosophic road to the good, and identifying their interests with those of the state."[32] Four membership categories defined the 189 founding members of this organization: full (*nato*), instructor, honorary, and corresponding. Full members had to exercise a profession or mechanical art, or be dedicated to agriculture in some manner. Other members were required only to profess democratic-republican principles and to conduct themselves properly. Some 123 persons, including Santander, accepted honorary memberships.[33]

Artisans had little control over the direction of the Society. Isidoro José Orjuela, a tinsmith, served as president of the organization, but upper-class progressives such as Lleras and Juan Nepomuceno Vargas engineered the Sociedad's programs and activities. Instructors of similar background, including Francisco Soto, Vicente Azuero, José Duque Gómez, Florentino González, Ezequiel Rojas, and Rafael Elisio Santander, endeavored to instill progressive political and social precepts, together with moral training, in its full members. Azuero, for example, professed that representative government was designed to further the common interest, not that of any specific group or family, and that democratic liberties were preeminently compatible with the church's value system.[34] Rojas expounded the utilitarian principle that happiness motivated human behavior. Correct conduct, Rojas explained, developed from the need to provide for the good of the family, or of those close to the individual. If one did not work or were lazy, hunger and vagrancy would plague both family and society. Work, on the other hand, gave the individual the means to pursue desires, provide for a family, and improve the general society. Rafael Elisio Santander, in his turn, tackled the knotty problem of reconciling progressive morality with the role of religion in society. His proposals suggested that the state sponsor such moral education with the aid of the church, though without intimating that the church should direct the program and without renouncing his own utilitarian convictions.[35]

The Democratic-Republican Society desired the "proper" social conduct of its members. Artisans and laborers were urged to celebrate fewer festivals and to complete promptly their contracted work. Craftsmen were warned on several occasions that gambling wasted both time and money and, since it added nothing to the general happiness (at least in the eyes of the utilitarians), should be abandoned. The initial editions of *El Labrador i Artesano* (the organization's mouthpiece), included articles pertaining to industrial education such as those describing new techniques for the manufacture of sulfuric acid and incombustible candles, and for applying copper plating. Occasionally employment opportunities for blacksmiths, masons, and carpenters to work on a church in Zipaquirá, for example, were brought to the readers' attention.[36]

The Sociedad's proprietors made concerted attempts to convince its members of the value of their political participation. The organization's intellectual leaders reasoned that since people were born with different talents and had varying degrees of wealth and comfort, equality before the law was crucial in order that all persons might satisfy their needs and desires without infringement upon the desires of others. Legislation alone did not guarantee such equality, according to the progressives; therefore, it became neces-

sary to educate the "inferior classes" in the area of political participation as a barrier against the establishment of an aristocratic government reminiscent of the colonial period.[37]

Such blatant efforts to inculcate progressive ideology in Bogotá's craft sector provoked strong opposition from members of
both the church and administration. One pro-government newspaper ran a fictional account of a debate in a craftsman's shop that
derided the progressive effort to mobilize artisans as political allies.
The owner of the shop had refused to join the Democratic-Republican Society, because he claimed that progressives sought only to
use artisans as a ladder for their electoral ambitions. If they had a
genuine interest in artisan political education, the fictitious craftsman asked, why had the effort only begun in 1838? Santanderistas
had dominated the capital's political scene since the early 1820s,
giving them plenty of time to support artisan interests. The article
suggested that the progressives' "unemployment" was the principal cause for their sudden interest in artisans, rather than any real
commitment to the needs of that class.[38]

After the June 1838 election, the Democratic-Republican and
Catholic Societies engaged only in political education. It is noteworthy that both groups tried to instill into their members principles of good citizenship with the end of ensuring order and social
harmony. Different ideological foundations guided their efforts, but
they shared a common objective. The Catholic Society of Bogotá
suggested that adherence to the dogma of the church, and submis-
sion of self to proper teachings, would achieve a moral social order
replete with proper liberty. Progressives, on the other hand, placed
their faith in the ability of people to determine for themselves
those actions that brought them happiness; a mutual understanding of useful actions would then guarantee social harmony and
prosperity. By either route, citizens would advance the welfare of
the society as a whole. Thus, neither set of educational messages
should be seen as subversive, or as purposely agitating social divisions.

An April 1839 petition to the congress, signed by 343 artisans,
suggests that the mobilization efforts by members of the church
had borne fruit. The petition called for a restriction of Benthamite
texts and other "impious books" in education so as not to corrupt
the good customs of the Colombian people. No ecclesiastical re-

form should be passed, according to the petition's authors, without the consent of the church. Missionary colleges should be established to proselytize among the heathen, and a seminary should be established for clerical education. The petition also asked that the Jesuits be allowed to return to the country. The petition attempted to convince legislators that the interests of the church coincided with those of the state; it thus called on congress to reverse many of the legislative measures instituted earlier by Santander and his associates since the time of Gran Colombia.[39] Although the precise relationship between partisan mobilization and the petition remains unclear, insofar as many of the signatories of the document were members of the Sociedad Democrática-Republicana, political boundaries seem not to have been firmly fixed among the tradesmen. It also indicates the influence of, and support for, the church among the city's craftsmen.

Rather than addressing the artisans' petition, in June 1839 the congress ordered several minor convents of Pasto closed. The subsequent *pastuso* revolt sparked the War of the Supremes, the first of the major civil conflicts of the nineteenth century. General Pedro Alcántara Herrán subdued the original rebels by August, only then to face General Obando's rebellion, which allegedly favored the protection of religion and federalism.[40] Not until September 1840 did the combined forces of Herrán, General Tomás Cipriano de Mosquera, and General Juan José Flores of Ecuador defeat Obando, who was forced into exile in Peru. In the meantime, other "supreme leaders" (*supremos*), generally those of a more progressive persuasion, declared themselves to be against the government. President Márquez responded to the third wave of insurrection by placing Vice-President General Domingo Caicedo in control of the government. By mid-1842, finally, a troubled peace returned to the country.

Artisans assumed what would become an all-too-common role in the nineteenth-century conflicts, that of soldier. The Constitution of 1832 had stipulated that the National Guard would support the Army in times of civil emergency. Only active citizens could serve in the Guard, so that artisans made up the backbone of its forces. Some sources indicate that three-quarters or more of the Guard was comprised of artisans.[41] Through Guard service, craftsmen supported the administration, but artisan support was also courted by progressives. When the northern provinces revolted in late 1840, progressives in the capital published several handouts that advised craftsmen that artisans had nothing to fear from a war that originated from the defense of religion. Artisans were urged to unite with the northern towns and demand an end to the fighting, a plea most seem not to have heeded.[42]

The war sharpened the political divisions that had first become visible in the 1830s. Personal antagonisms, wartime animosity, and ideological differences combined to define more clearly the alignment of political forces. Progressives, who constituted the foundations of the Liberal party, were either humiliated by defeat or were forced to bide their time until the advent of more favorable political conditions. With the death of Santander in 1840, Vicente Azuero in 1844, and Francisco Soto in 1846, a new generation of political actors would direct the progressive revival at the head of the Liberal party.

For the time being, however, moderates (now referred to as ministerials) ruled the country. They took advantage of their victory to reverse some of the legislative "errors" of the santanderistas. Their ideological preferences shaped the Constitution of 1843, which enhanced the power of the executive branch at the expense of the legislative, the judiciary, and local authorities. Suffrage requirements remained essentially the same.[43] Ministerials decreed that teachers could select their own textbooks, thereby weakening Santander's 1826 Plan of Studies. Bentham's *The Principles of Universal Legislation* was banned outright as a university text.[44] Mariano Ospina Rodríguez's campaign to purge New Granada of utilitarian and other "immoral" tendencies included inviting the Jesuits to return to Colombian soil to serve, in J. León Helguera's words, as a "corps of conservative shock troops."[45]

The hotly contested 1844 presidential election belied the apparent cohesion of the victorious camp. Ministerials who recalled the seeming ineffectiveness of civilian President Márquez supported Mosquera, whereas those ministerials who distrusted military men (especially Mosquera) sponsored the candidacy of Rufino Cuervo. Opponents of the government, while subdued, lent their support to General Eusebio Borrero, as did associates of the dissident ministerial Julio Arboleda. In the end, Mosquera polled 762 electoral votes, Borrero 475, and Cuervo 250, while numerous minor candidates received the remaining 177 votes. Congress was once again called to service, and opted for Mosquera, the clear preference among the voters.[46]

## The Society of Artisans

Mosquera proved a controversial president from the beginning. His authoritarian style alienated many potential allies, while his program of economic reforms served as the catalyst for the creation of the Sociedad de Artesanos de Bogotá. Lino de Pombo, as minister of finance, initiated widespread fiscal reform, transferred control of the government's Ambalema tobacco monopoly to private hands, repealed the tax on gold exports, and adopted a new monetary system.[47] Pombo's successor, Florentino González, rapidly accelerated the liberalization of the economy. González's hopes for Colombia's economic future, outlined to the Congress of 1847, included proposals for fiscal reorganization, further currency reform, and the lowering of import duties, especially those on textiles.[48] The long-sheltered artisan class would be forced to participate in more "productive" and "profitable" industries: "the cobbler will learn to lay bricks, the tailor to pole boats or to fish, the blacksmith to farm; and while they learn? And if they do not learn? They will succumb!"[49]

Artisans from both Bogotá and Medellín expressed their opposition to the proposed tariff revision through several petitions to the Congress, the most significant artisan-initiated political statements up to that time.[50] The 219 self-identified "artisans and mechanics" that signed the capital's petition claimed to represent the more than 2,000 families in the capital who would be hurt by the proposed legislation.[51] Nevertheless, the Law of June 14, 1847, passed with strong bipartisan support and opened the door to less-restricted trade, even though some congressmen expressed concern over lost revenues. The new tariff schedule reduced rates by about 30 percent, abolished all restrictive duties on transit, and combined previous multiple duties into a single tax levied at a maximum of 25 percent of an object's value as of January 1, 1848.[52]

Artisans then attempted to reverse the new law through political mobilization. Ambrosio López Londoño (tailor), Agustín Rodríguez (tailor), Dr. Cayetano Leiva, Francisco Torres Hinestrosa, and Francisco Londoño informed the *jefe político* (political boss) of Bogotá of the formation of the Sociedad de Artesanos in October 1847. The group was quite small at its inception, numbering only ten to fifteen principal members, all but two of whom were artisans.[53] The Sociedad declared that it would work to repeal the Law of June 14 and "to promote the advancement of the arts and other areas that can help our well-being." Membership in the Society was open to artisans, to aficionados of the trades, and to agriculturalists who, like the ideal craftsman, were envisioned to be independent small producers.[54] Specific goals of the organization included steady work for all members, obedience and respect for the government, and various forms of instruction for the membership, to include democratic theory, military skills, principles of justice, and religious training.[55] Members were obligated to pay a three *real* fee each month, aid needy members, and use the right of suffrage only with the advice of the Sociedad. Members were cautioned not to present discourses disobedient to the laws of the land or to censure legal authorities, and they were to avoid discourse of personal, political, or religious issues.[56] Despite the ban on political discussions, there is little evidence that the Society discussed anything else.

Opposition to the Sociedad developed immediately. The editor of the Catholic *El Clamor de la Verdad* refuted Ambrosio López's claim that the Society was designed to help an oppressed and threatened class, stating that the "secret society" would only serve as a machine for someone's electoral purposes. The editor commented that the group appeared to be an enemy of Christ, based on a reference by López to a banned book by Felicité de Lamennais.[57] López denied any secret intentions on the part of the organization, noting that the Society was entirely open and had only the laudable objective of uniting the artisans.[58] *El Clamor de la Verdad* then softened its editorial opposition to the Society, stating that its original objection had been only to Lamennais's book. The paper praised the openness of the organization but reminded artisans to be on their guard because of the upheavals of the times.[59]

Six months after its foundation, the Sociedad underwent a fundamental transformation. The Society's first director, Agustín Rodríguez, claimed that the Society had some three-hundred members by April of 1848, but reported that it was often difficult to meet the twenty-person quorum necessary for a meeting. The Society's focus upon the upcoming presidential elections, which it thought could favor artisans' interests, changed its character.[60] On May 4, 1848, it met to consider which candidate to back in the June presidential election, which paralleled that of 1836 in its importance for the eventual political culture of the country.[61]

Mosquera's undoctrinaire presidency had by now alienated many *ministeriales* and, by opening the Pandora's box of reform, his administration had splintered the party. At least four presidential candidates emerged from the divided ministerial ranks. Mosquera's vice-president, Rufino Cuervo, attracted the support of more moderate party members, but he did not appeal to conservatives, who instead favored Joaquín José Gori, who had led internal party opposition to Mosquera. Gori opposed the new tariff, primarily on the grounds that it would cause a large revenue loss for the government, and was consequently supported by many artisans. Two generals, Eusebio Borrero and Joaquín Barriga, also sought the presidency. The leading progressive, who had been at the group's forefront since the death of Azuero in 1844, was Florentino González. His service in the Mosquera administration had alienated potential progressive support, however, although it attracted ministerial moderates such as Lino de Pombo and Julio Arboleda.[62]

The nascent Liberal party had been unable to reorganize itself during the early stages of the Mosquera administration. They now, however, took advantage of the ministerial split to select war hero José Hilario López as a unity candidate.[63] General López calmed the fears of those remembering the ineffective peace-keeping efforts of Márquez ten years earlier. López was closely identified with the popular General Obando (who was still in Peru), but he did not share Obando's stigma of having revolted. López was, in any case, in the country and available for the election. Moreover, the general lacked a forceful personality, a trait young Liberals hoped to utilize. Quite significantly, in spite of the divisive nature of the campaign, the platforms of the various candidates did not differ in any major degree.[64]

Liberals sought to use the Sociedad de Artesanos as a potential platform for the revitalization of their party. Many spoke at the Society's meetings, where they promptly assumed a dominant role in its deliberations.[65] Some speakers presented the ideas of French thinkers such as the Comte de Saint Simon, Pierre Josef Proudhon, and Louis Blanc, or of the Revolution of 1848, news of which had just reached New Granada. This has led some historians to argue that the programs of the Sociedad and these French thinkers shared many common points.[66] (However, as discussed below, the young Liberals used socialism only rhetorically, while in fact favoring an individualist society with little or no state intervention.[67]) In addition, the Society listened to its guests' opinions on the various candidates. Francisco Javier Zaldúa spoke in favor of the progressive López; José de Obaldía praised Obando; and Ezequiel Rojas pledged his endorsement of López, claiming that the general would return Colombia to the legality of the days of Santander.[68]

The Society's election committees reported their findings to the membership on May 15, 1848. Francisco Londoño, now director of the Society, personally favored Gori, but a lengthy discussion led to an agreement to support López. The Society's adherence centered on his demonstrated capacity to preserve the peace of the country.[69] The Sociedad made no mention of López's political program, only that he represented liberal principles. Acting on a proposal by Ambrosio López and José María Vergara Tenorio, the Society reaffirmed its decision to work for López's election at a meeting on June 10, 1848.[70] It accordingly appealed to artisans of the Province of Bogotá, acclaiming López as a fighter for liberty, a soldier of the people, and a Catholic democrat. "Citizen General" López was said to favor elimination of laws that benefited only the privileged and speculators. The Society's cause, which was said to be that of the people, was triumphing in Europe and America and, with López, would triumph also in Colombia.[71] (The influence of young Liberals can clearly be seen in the language of this appeal.)

A vocal segment of the capital's craft community preferred Gori to López. A painter described López as too susceptible to outside forces and unlikely to sustain the dignity of the office. By contrast Gori, according to the painter, fit the role of a republican president: a dignified, experienced, and moderate man of laws, one who could direct the nation to rational progress. Moreover, Gori was not the candidate of Mosquera, an identification that all candidates sought to avoid in this election.[72] Artisans who supported Gori took issue with the Society's support of López, cautioning potential voters not to be misled by promises that López would repeal Mosquera's tariff legislation and that he would deny foreign artisans entry into the country. After all, as one handout reminded its readers, such powers were constitutionally reserved for the congress and not the president. Artisans were cautioned not to put faith in men whose interests were opposite to their own, men who, allegedly, ridiculed the artisans in private and who would abandon them when they were no longer needed. One handout ended with the prophetic phrase: "Time will disillusion you."[73] Artisan members of the Sociedad were allegedly being manipulated by outside forces, while the few craftsmen who did understand the situation were said to be resigning from the organization. Agustín Rodríguez, for example, who favored Gori, reportedly handed in his resignation as president of the Society, only to have it rejected.[74]

The Sociedad de Artesanos formally rebutted these charges. Its board of directors protested insinuations that artisans were unable to make political assessments by themselves. They could, and would, refuse to be misled by individuals who only wanted to divide and exploit the artisan class. A "great majority" of the organization's members was said to support López.[75] Interestingly, the Society's response used the word *members* instead of *artisans*—and said nothing about the defection of Rodríguez, who was at the time on the Gori electoral list.[76]

When the presidential election finally took place, no candidate obtained a majority. López led the national count with 725 electoral votes, Gori garnered 384, and Cuervo totalled 304; other candidates, mostly ministeriales, shared 276 votes. Once again, congress would select the president from minority candidates. Together ministerial candidates received the greatest number of votes, but the election clearly demonstrated the deep fissures in their ranks. López won 102 of the 242 votes in the province of Bogotá, Gori 95, Cuervo 27, and 18 votes were garnered by others. Despite the efforts of the Sociedad de Artesanos in mobilizing support for López, he fared worse in the capital than he did in its province; Gori tallied 31 votes, López 12, Cuervo 8, and Mariano Ospina Rodríguez 1.[77] These results clearly revealed the strength of the Gori candidacy in Bogotá, which, when coupled with various pro-Gori announcements in the press, suggests that artisans in Bogotá were not completely swayed by the Society's electioneering. The artisan alliance with the young Liberals who backed López was far from secure even at this early date. Nonetheless, the Society of Artisans had demonstrated its potential as a political action group, a role that would be expanded in the coming years.[78]

Meanwhile, political tensions rose in anticipation of the selection of the president by the congress on March 7, 1849. One paper claimed that a "certain" group of people was trying to spread the idea among the pueblo that an aristocracy existed in Colombia, and that it should be ended just as it had been in France. Artisans were warned of the motivations behind such propaganda and reminded that if craftsmen had not yet been elected to high office it was due to their lack of education, not to the system's rigidity.[79] Ambrosio López responded that artisans could see perfectly well that an aristocracy of politicians who lived off public monies did exist. Insulting the artisans' intelligence did not, López concluded, contribute to public tranquility.[80]

The Sociedad de Artesanos held meetings almost daily after mid-February 1849 to prepare an election strategy. The agreed-upon approach "was to frighten the weak [members of Congress] and do nothing more."[81] The Society approached the governor of the province in early March to request arms for its members so that they might serve as a standing militia, ready to defend the country's republican institutions at a moment's notice. The arms were denied to the Society, but it was reported that they purchased all the pistols, knives, powder, and ammunition in the capital.[82] While the credibility of this report is questionable, it does illustrate the anxiety aroused by the Sociedad and its plans for the 7 de marzo. Anxiety was not calmed when a group of artisans entered the congress on March 2 and shouted down Conservative speakers.[83] Such activities recalled to many minds the incident that had occurred a year earlier in Caracas, when a government-inspired mob invaded the Venezuelan congress, killing several deputies and members of the guard and bringing congressional resistance to President José Tadeo Monagas to an end. Fears of a *caraqueñada* led Mosquera to prepare for similar disturbances in Bogotá. The five-hundred-man Fifth Battalion was charged with maintaining order. On the night before the selection, cannons filled with grape-shot were placed at key intersections of the city.[84]

The 7 de marzo presidential selection is one of the most disputed in Colombia's history. Although Congress was not scheduled to open until 10:00 A.M., a large crowd came much earlier to the spacious church of Santo Domingo, where the selection would be held. First to enter were the artisans, next the *goristas*, then the *cuervistas*, and finally the students, who sat nearest the congressmen. The various sides were said to be about equally represented. A barrier of heavy tables separated the audience, estimated at 1,600

45

people, from the congressmen.[85] The session opened on time and the voting began. At the end of the first round of voting, both López and Cuervo had received 37 votes, and Gori 10, which removed him from the contest. In the second round, Cuervo improved his total to 42, López to 40, and 2 votes were blank. At this point many people in the crowd thought that Cuervo had won. The tumult that swept the audience was calmed only when José de Obaldía leaped to the top of a table, shouting "¡Todavía no hay elecciones!" (There are not yet elections). When order was restored, the third round of voting began. Due to insistent shouts by the audience, it took over two hours to complete. At its conclusion, López had 42 votes, Cuervo 39, and now 3 votes were blank. The last vote was that of Mariano Ospina Rodríguez, which according to traditional accounts read: "I vote for General José Hilario López so that the deputies will not be murdered." At this time, about 3:00 P.M., the spectators were expelled from the church. The crowd, now swollen to 4,000, waited outside in the rain. At 5:00 P.M. it was announced that the fourth round had resulted in the same tally as had the third, which, according to the Constitution, meant that the leader received the blank votes—General José Hilario López was president-elect.[86]

López supporters in the plaza were overjoyed. Celebrations among progressives lasted far into the night. The next day *El Aviso* praised the conduct of the crowd and proclaimed:

> *Long live the Congress of 1849!*
> *Long live the popular president!*
> *Long live the people of the capital!*
> *Long live the democratic artisans![87]*

The Society circulated a handout which proclaimed that the 7 de marzo would be remembered with the same patriotic enthusiasm as the 20 de julio; equality and fraternity had now joined Colombian liberty.[88]

## Partisan Mobilizations: The Democratic and Popular Societies

The 7 de marzo opened a new era for both Colombia and the Sociedad de Artesanos. Members of the López government were quick to appreciate the potential of the organization as a mobilizing force in the creation of the democratic republic, in the support of the Liberal party, and in the cultivation of liberal beliefs.[89] The Sociedad de Artesanos, now christened the Sociedad Democrática de Artesanos, became a tool of the Secretariat of Government, to whose head, Francisco Javier Zaldúa, it reported.[90] Chapters of the Democratic Society were established throughout the nation in an effort to support the 7 de marzo regime. Sixteen Sociedades were founded in 1849, twenty-one in 1850, sixty-six in 1851, and nine in 1852—a sequence that highlights the importance of the organization to the Liberal party in times of civil strife (the Conservative insurrection of 1851) and in support of the reform measures of 1849 and 1850.

A López election society in Cali became the first Sociedad Democrática established outside of the Colombian capital. The Society attempted to prepare Liberal newcomers for vacant government positions immediately following López's victory.[91] Juan Nepomuceno Núñez Conto, who had championed the cause of Cali's *ejiditarios* against local Conservatives the previous year,[92] remodeled the caleño society along the same lines as the Bogotá chapter in mid-1849. The new Democratic Society declared its existence on the 20 de julio and immediately undertook an aggressive campaign to recruit the local populace into the Liberal party and Democratic Society.[93] Contemporary authors, both moderate and Conservative, charged that "popular passions," expressing both racial and economic tensions, were freely vented in the sessions of the Sociedad.[94] Local Conservatives, who had dominated the Cauca provincial government through the 1840s, responded by the formation of the Sociedad de Amigos del Pueblo (Friends of the People). The Amigos del Pueblo and the Democratic Societies immediately clashed in street brawls, the most serious of which occurred on March 10, 1850. The Liberal governor, Manuel Dolores Camacho, though a decided friend and benefactor of the Democratic organization, so feared uncontrollable social violence that he banned meetings of both Societies.[95]

Beginning with the Society in Cali, Liberals in other provincial towns founded their own Sociedades Democráticas. By October, Societies from Cali, La Plata, Sogamoso, Cartago, and Facatativá had reported to the Democratic Society of Bogotá, which in turn promised to work with them. Ten other Sociedades had been founded by January 1850, when countrywide membership reportedly surpassed 10,000. Bogotá's chapter membership was said to number more than 2,500, and Cali's more than 2,000. The Democratic Societies thus became a national network dedicated to the reform principles of the 7 de marzo. Young intellectuals were sent throughout the country to address the various groups.[96] In all but a few instances, notably those of Popayán, Cali, Cartagena, San Gil, Socorro, and Bogotá, the Democratic Societies were simply chapters of the local Liberal party, which included government employees. In towns such as Cali, the Democratic Society also functioned as a means by which the popular sectors might express local grievances. The administration endeavored to employ this national organization in numerous ways. Perhaps one of the most significant uses in the long run was the Societies' relationship to the National Guard, the militia that supplemented the standing army. A September 1849 circular to jefes políticos throughout the nation instructed them to build a strong guard, composed of individuals loyal to the 7 de marzo.[97] These frequently were the "Democrats" of the towns.

Conservatives in the capital city established La Sociedad Popular de Instrucción Mutua i Fraternidad Cristiana (Popular Society of Mutual Instruction and Fraternal Christianity) in December 1849 to counter the growing power of the Sociedad Democrática.[98] In part, this body originated in mobilization efforts begun by the Jesuits after their readmission to Colombia in 1843. The fathers had founded an institute for artisan education and had established workers' congregations, designed both for mutual aid purposes and to introduce "proper" spiritual and temporal values. Some reports suggest that the meetings of the Jesuit groups drew upwards of eight-hundred participants in the late 1840s.[99] The Sociedad Popular was linked to the Jesuit congregations and to the Catholic Society.[100] Its founders observed that Conservative lethargy, inaction, and disunity had allowed the Liberals into power. In order to assert the will of the "majority party," the party had to unite, consolidate itself, and form associations.[101] The popular base for such associations would be the artisans of the nation. The connections between the Popular Society and the Conservative party were never hidden to the extent that they were between the Democratic Society and the Liberals. Although Simón José Cárdenas, the Popular Society's first president, was an artist, officers of the group included the

Conservative leaders José Eusebio Caro, José María Torres Caicedo, José Manuel Groot, Urbano Pradilla, and Mariano Ospina Rodríguez.[102]

The programs and ideology of the Popular Society are indistinguishable from those of the Conservative party. The Sociedad Popular announced that it hoped to pursue the perfection of public institutions, promote the country's progress, work for the triumph of principles based upon evangelical morality, and put into political power men of honor, patriotism, and morality. The first three objectives could only be attained upon the success of the fourth, so political efforts were to be the primary focus of the group's energies.[103] It planned industrial assistance by the creation of a monetary pool from which artisans could draw to purchase tools and books necessary to their trades. Such funds would also be used to assist poor artisans in the case of sickness and to reward members for virtuous actions. Educational objectives included teaching reading, writing, grammar, arithmetic, and geometry, as well as lessons on the government's structure, the constitution, and the rights and obligations of citizens. In order to strengthen the marital institution, a fund was to be created so that poor artisans could pay parochial costs and other necessary marriage expenses. Together these methods would serve to enhance the "principal bases of civilization"—the family, property, and instruction. Diffusion of these principles through membership in the Popular Society would insure the "legal triumph" of the Conservative party.[104]

The Liberal government immediately began a campaign against the Sociedad Popular, and eventually even used the Democratic Society as one of its tools of repression. As early as December 31, 1849, Governor José María Mantilla cautioned two members of the Popular Society, Francisco Cristando and Florentino V. Posse, that the government would use measures to repress the group if rumors about their collection of weapons proved true. Mantilla warned the Society's vice-president, Simón Espejo, on January 2, 1850, of potential reprisals if he continued to verbally assault the government. Espejo claimed that he would use his rights as a citizen to speak his mind. Mantilla then allegedly threatened him with exile.[105]

The political rivalry between the partisan organizations erupted into violence on January 15, 1850. A Popular Society meeting of that evening, said to have been attended by more than one-thousand persons (including Maríano Ospina Rodríguez, José Eusebio

Caro, and José María Baraya, jefe político of the city), was interrupted by the shouts of some thirty to forty Democrats in the crowd. According to Conservative accounts, Democrats soon left the assembly, shouting that a Conservative revolt had begun.[106] Liberals related that when the Popular meeting became disorderly, a Democrat in the crowd went to a concurrent regular meeting of the Democratic organization and informed them of the occurrence. That session broke up, whereupon some of its members requested arms from the governor to restore order. Others went to the Popular meeting. Finding calm amid their rivals, Democrats reconvened their own session to consider steps to counter the opposition movement. José María Samper proposed that the Democratic Society should petition the president for the expulsion of Jesuits and the dismissal of all Conservatives from public office. Martín Plata proposed that the National Guard be called out to prevent disruption of the public order. Both resolutions carried.[107]

Announcements covered the city walls on January 16, 1850, calling upon all "good Liberals" to meet at noon to present the petitions to the president.[108] López promised to review the petitions, but indicated no course of action.[109] The petitions were nevertheless a partial success. Three Conservative judges were removed from the Supreme Court, and General José María Ortega, Conservative director of the Military College, was dismissed along with several of his subordinates. The questionable legality of the firings so infuriated Lino de Pombo that he resigned his position as head of the Supreme Court.[110]

Two days later Vice-President Rufino Cuervo urged leaders of both groups to remain calm. He suggested that both Sociedades consider a ban on meetings until after the opening of congress in March so as to avoid further violence.[111] Public gatherings do, in fact, appear to have been curtailed in February, due to the cholera epidemic ravaging the city. In March, after the Democrats had resumed their meetings, the Sociedad Popular asked for permission to do the same. Police representative Plácido Morales gave permission for the group to meet, but only in the open air or in the Democratic meeting hall, not in their accustomed location. Simón José Cárdenas, the Popular's president, protested, stating that the Society need not ask permission to meet in the open and that restriction of its meeting place was unwarranted, as cholera was gone from the city. Morales stood by his decision and reprimanded the Popular leader for his arrogant attitude.[112]

Cárdenas himself came under attack in what became one of the more publicized personal controversies of the period. His February 16, 1850, visit to jailed Popular member Ignacio Rodríguez provoked a heated argument and Cárdenas's arrest. Cárdenas protested that he had been singled out for arrest simply because of his political activity for the Conservative party. The Conservative artisan leader harshly criticized jailer Camilo Rodríguez, alleging that he was unfit for public office because of a 1839 criminal conviction, whereupon Rodríguez promptly accused both Cárdenas and Popular member Juan Malo of libel. Cárdenas was found guilty and was sentenced to six months' imprisonment. To Conservatives, the trial was not concerned with libel, because Rodríguez did have a criminal record; rather, it was political persecution, which to them was characteristic of the 7 de marzo regime.[113] If so, it appears to have been effective, for by June 1850 the Popular Society had grown quiet under the press restrictions imposed by President López after the expulsion of the Jesuits in May of that year.[114] Governmental repression had effectively silenced the popular mobilization of the Conservative party, establishing a dangerous precedent that came to be characteristic of Colombia's political culture.

In 1851, there was a revival of the clashes between the Democratic and Popular Societies. The Popular meeting of March 11 resulted in the worst violence to date among these two groups. As Democrats tried to break up the assembly, gunfire was exchanged, killing one member of the Popular Society and seriously injuring several policemen. This incident served to revive demands for the suppression of the Sociedad Popular, which was forced to curtail meetings until May.[115] The Popular Society resumed its meetings with reorganizational sessions in every quarter of the city. Several disgruntled Democrats attended one session and suggested the formation of a *sociedad de la unión de artesanos* (union society of artisans) that would be dedicated exclusively to artisan interests and would not serve as a tool for the parties.[116] Nothing came of the proposal, as the Conservative rebellion of 1851 soon overshadowed events in the capital.[117]

The rebellion of 1851 stemmed from a complicated mix of economic, political, and social factors. Democrats in the Cauca valley initiated a series of attacks upon hacendados (many of whom claimed Conservative allegiance), claiming that landowner encroachment upon town lands (ejidos) justified the behavior. The early months of 1851 were so dominated by these actions that the period was given the name El Zurriago (The Whipping) to characterize the brutal nature of the attacks. Violent assaults upon landowners were especially virulent around Palmira, where attacks were made in broad daylight.[118] Conservatives claimed that the government sanctioned these actions, as force was seldom used to quell them—seemingly a valid complaint. The jefe político of Cali dismissed one case of the burning of a hacienda, saying that, after all, its owner was a "dangerous conservative."[119] This violence helped provoke the unsuccessful revolt, which quickly spread throughout the Cauca valley and into Antioquia. General Obando was named Chief of the South, while Colonel Tomás Herrera was given charge of the fighting in Antioquia. By mid-July, Obando had quieted the Cauca, but Herrera needed until September to suppress the Antioqueño revolt. The Democratic Society of Bogotá saw service in Antioquia as part of the National Guard and returned to Bogotá on December 9.[120]

## Conclusion

The years before the 1849 presidential selection stand as the formative period of Colombian political culture. Significantly, the Conservative and Liberal parties developed in response to regional loyalties, generational experiences, and questions of control of the reigns of government, not to essential class interests. Each party found it necessary to recruit non-elites to secure electoral allegiances, a process that in time engendered rigid popular identification with one or the other party. Partisan violence and manipulation of the electoral process almost immediately warped any sense of genuine representative government, even while appearances suggest a republican façade. At its extreme, partisan competition could lead to civil war; in normal times it festered social tensions. Although it is clear that the Conservative and Liberal antagonisms at the root of the twentieth-century La Violencia are to be found in the political scene of the 1930s and 1940s, the character of partisan contention was established in the repression, rancor, and popular recruitment associated with the 7 de marzo regime. Yet, partisan mobilizations allowed non-elites in some instances to express their class interests, making an alternative character for Colombia's political culture possible. In the mid-century liberal reform era, the policy contours of that polity—both actual and potential—would be determined.

# THREE

# ARTISAN MOBILIZATIONS IN THE ERA OF LIBERAL REFORMS

*The country progresses, we are told, and in truth luxuries
increase for certain classes, buildings multiply, merchandise
are abundant, and exportation increases . . . and in all the
principal streets we see an unaccustomed movement, but the
pueblo suffers scarcities and privations; everything becomes
dear to them, and their products or work do not cover
expenses; and the pueblo has to say: we do not want progress
nor English civilization, in so far as hundreds of people are
dying of misery under . . . the marble porticoes.*
— *"El artesano de Bogotá"*[1]

L IBERAL REFORMS IN THE MIDDLE YEARS OF THE NINETEENTH
century transformed Colombia's governmental structure, recast its economic infrastructure, and loosened its society from
many colonial restrictions.[2] Changes in economic policy during the
presidential administration of Tomás Cipriano de Mosquera (1845–
49) opened the reform period, which came to full flower under the
regime of José Hilario López (1849–53), and culminated in the
wake of the 1859–62 civil war. By the mid-1860s, Colombia had
completed the most sweeping set of reforms in Latin America, pro-
voking, as happened in other countries, oftimes heated reaction,
especially from the capital's artisan organizations.

The liberal ideology that sustained the reform era appealed to
broad segments of the Colombian polity, although it was by no

means universally accepted. In theory, advocates of liberalism believed that the efforts of individuals to satisfy their self interests, when unfettered by restrictive social, economic, or political policies, would best serve the interests of the public at large. The reformers therefore favored the individual over the group and laissez-faire over monopolistic economic programs. In social policy, this meant, for example, that few if any restrictions should limit speech, the press, assembly, or other areas of individual expression. Liberty of instruction was favored over church-sponsored educational facilities. The capacity of individuals to fulfill their potential, according to liberal theory, required that the temporal power of the church be curbed. In the political arena, direct expressions of the people's will were deemed preferable to indirect, filtered political expressions. Fewer suffrage limitations would enable more individuals to voice their political sentiments, thereby blocking the inordinate power of the few over the many. Smaller units of government, bound up in a federalized system of government, were seen as superior to powerful, centralized state regimes. Economic liberalism demanded the elimination of monopolies, reduced levels of taxation, private ownership of land, and the free movement of products across national boundaries in keeping with a faith in comparative advantages in the international exchange of goods. Slavery, anathema to both autonomous individual economic and social expression, was incompatible with liberalism. Liberals promised that "progress" and "civilization" would follow the release of individual enterprise and the abandonment of policies favorable to privileged social groups.[3]

In the adherence to the ideology of liberalism, Colombian reformers marched in cadence with much of the Western world. Liberalism followed the logic of the Enlightenment and the material advances of capitalism. Liberalism served as the "ideology of choice" for many designers of the new republican governments that hoped to keep pace with the progress they saw in the United States and areas of Western Europe, particularly in economic terms. Contrary to its own rhetoric, the ideology of liberalism did not produce a neutral state. It instead directed Colombia's political economy toward the economic structure of the North Atlantic, enhanced the development of export enterprises, and reduced the capacity of domestic manufactures, which were judged by many to be "non-competitive," to sustain accustomed levels of activity. Liberalism not only satisfied the particular interests of social groups that aspired to full participation in the export-import economy but it also attracted broad segments of elite society, without direct correlation to socioeconomic function. Liberalism's promised full participation in the social and political affairs of the nation appealed in particular to middle-level groups such as artisans, who envisioned that their abilities might be better served under that system of beliefs.[4] At the same time, domestic craftsmen opposed economic liberalism, which threatened their productive positions.

National leaders supported most reforms that drew upon the principles of economic liberalism; these reforms were therefore most comprehensive. As discussed earlier, many of the reforms, notably those concerning fiscal policy, had been proposed in one form or another since the 1820s, but most had been forestalled by ideological opposition or by pragmatic hesitation on the part of early leaders such as Santander by fears of the loss of revenue for governmental operations, a pragmatism not shared by the reformers of mid-century. Mosquera's economic reforms, which included tariff reduction, elimination of the tobacco monopoly, and a new coinage, elicited general bipartisan support, a consensus that continued after the Liberal victory of 1849, thereby reducing the significance of that election to the reform process.[5]

It is commonplace to attribute full responsibility for the reform impetus to the young Liberals. Indeed, the Generation of 1849, men trained under the educational system instituted by Santander and who became politically active in the full flower of youthful optimism, served as a primary catalyst for reform, yet they were simply the most visible advocates of reform. With the noted exceptions of the areas of reform dealing with the church, an essential consensus existed between politicians of both parties before 1852. The election of 1849 shaped Colombia's political culture, not its reform process. From that year, the Conservative and Liberal parties have dominated Colombia's politics, albeit not without significant third party challenges and considerable political strife. The election of 1849 also symbolized the liberalization of Colombia's political culture, with the appearance of political organizations with significant popular input. Equally important, the defeat of the Melo revolt in 1854 closed that political culture to only these parties, as Conservatives and Liberals came together to defeat a third-party challenge, thereby establishing the precedent for the twentieth-century Frente Nacional (National Front). Significantly, the 1854 challenge involved an unprecedented degree of popular mobilization; its defeat also established a tradition central to the country's political culture.

The Liberal regime of José Hilario López continued the economic liberalization of its predecessor, while attempting to redirect the nation's social and political orientation as well. Importantly, Conservatives controlled the 1850 Senate, which sponsored reforms that decentralized the nation's fiscal structure, abolished tariffs in Panama, reduced taxes on stamped legal documents (*papel sellado*), and allowed for the free export of gold. Subsequent congresses, dominated by Liberals in 1851, 1852, and 1853, opened rivers to foreign traffic, ended the death penalty for political crimes, declared absolute freedom of the press, finally eliminated slavery, hastened the elimination of corporate Indian landholdings (*resquardos*), abolished special religious rights (*fueros*), eliminated the church tithe on production (*diezmo*), and began political decentralization. The Constitution of 1853 culminated this first stage of reform by declaring the separation of church and state, allowing for civil marriage and divorce, extending the vote to all male citizens over the age of twenty-one, decreeing direct secret elections, allowing popular election of governors and many other officials, creating a more decentralized governmental structure, and weakening executive powers.[6] Robert Gilmore reminds the observer who might argue for the innovative character of the Liberal government that precedent for "every measure tagged with the 7th of March label can be found [in petitions made] between 1809 and 1840."[7]

This by no means suggests that Colombians gave 100 percent support to the reforms. Liberty of religious expression, if allowed, threatened the hegemonic position of the Catholic church, which was seen by many Conservatives to be the bedrock of morality, public virtue, and social stability. Separation of church and state, another liberal principle, ran counter to deeply imbedded traditions. Liberal anti-clericalism was thought by many to jeopardize religious leaders and imperil the very individuals who imparted the principles of harmonious social life. Significantly, many pro-church advocates warned that Colombian society was not sufficiently "civilized" to permit individuals free expression without the ominous threat of anarchism and disorder. Nor did all persons favor the elimination of slavery, which, in combination with the expulsion of the Jesuits in 1850 by presidential decree, incited the Conservative revolt in 1851. Moreover, the Liberal party splintered into a wing of younger, more radical reformers (gólgotas) and moderate reformers (draconianos). The latter group, men whose liberalism had been shaped as santanderista progressives, opposed the reduction of executive powers and the role of the military in government. Artisans of the Democratic Society in time joined with the draconianos in an attempt to curb the reforms, including tariff laws. Failure of that effort led to an artisan-military-draconiano revolt in April 1854 to halt the reform tide and return the country to previous constitutional norms. The movement was defeated by a Conservative/gólgota alliance in December 1854, thereby eliminating most organized opposition to the reform process.

With the draconiano challenge repressed, gólgota Liberals and Conservatives returned to the reformation of the country's political structure, an item not fully completed under the 1853 constitution. Although decentralization had ceded considerable autonomy to an expanded number of provinces (now thirty-six), the multiplicity of territorial divisions, coupled with uncertain governance structures, dictated the need for additional reform. Provinces were consolidated into "sovereign states," beginning with that of Panama in 1855. Antioquia followed in 1856 and six more states were added in 1857.[8] The Constitution of 1858 that created the Granadian Confederation ratified these territorial changes and established a starkly federalist system of government with eight sovereign states.[9] Radical Liberals (the name assumed by gólgotas after 1854) and Conservatives worked closely to frame that document.

The Radical/Conservative alliance did not last. The civil war of 1859–62, the only successful rebellion in the nation's history, ended in a Liberal victory and provided the opportunity for a final set of reforms, the most explosive dealing with church/state relations. Alleged clerical support for the Conservative rebellion led to the July 20, 1861, decree demanding governmental authorization of all church officials. Several days later, the Jesuits were once again expelled from the country. All corporate properties were disamortized and offered for public sale on September 9, leaving the church with physical domain over only its churches and chapels. Religious communities such as convents and monasteries were ordered abolished on November 5, at which time the government ordered the expulsion from the country of all those who resisted that decree, or those of July 20 or September 9. These edicts satisfied liberal anti-clericalism, the desire to eliminate corporate ownership of land, and the very real fiscal needs of the government, which reaped the profits from forced sale of church property. Archbishop Antonio Herrán's opposition to the disamortization decree earned him ex-ile.[10]

When the war had finally ended in late 1862, a constitutional convention met in Ríonegro to replace the Pact of Union that had united the country since 1861. Though plagued with disputes between pro-Mosquera and Radical Liberal delegates, the country's fourth constitution in twenty years was promulgated on May 8. The Constitution of Ríonegro created a federal union of nine states,[11] each of which held all powers not expressly given to the federal government. Liberal fears of Mosquera's executive ambitions resulted in a two-year, non-repetitive presidential term, a limitation that burdened representatives as well. Differences on the extent of wartime religious reforms aggravated the Radical/Mosquera coalition during the meeting, but all of the latter's decrees were incorporated into the constitution.[12] Before the convention closed, its delegates selected Mosquera as president until April 1864, when the first popularly elected president of the United States of Colombia assumed office.[13]

## Artisans and Liberal Reforms

Artisan mobilization against the liberalization of the economy began at an early date. Craftsmen from Bogotá and Cartagena requested the full prohibition of competitive foreign goods into the country in 1831, claiming that their economic misfortunes originated in foreign imports.[14] Five years later, fifteen bogotano artisans, including Agustín Rodríguez, who later became the first president of the Sociedad de Artesanos, alleged that low tariff levels were undermining the social and economic welfare of the country and its craftsmen, suggesting that the government was obligated to provide for the best interests of its citizens by a system of protective tariffs. A congressional commission to hear the petition agreed, but took no action to increase rates.[15]

Governmental policies designed to draw immigrants to the country also evoked considerable criticism. The colonial guild system had produced few masters and suffered from technological stagnation. Many in the government hoped to rectify that situation by the introduction of foreign craft masters, who would bring with them the latest productive techniques. Unfortunately, immigrant masters failed to improve the situation, with most preferring to make short-term profits and then return to their native lands. "Some Native Artisans" wrote in an 1843 article that the formal status of aliens under the laws of the nation gave them various advantages over their domestic counterparts. While native tradesmen were obligated to fulfill military obligations in either the Army or the National Guard, foreigners were exempt from that civic responsibility. Thus they did not lose work to military service and enjoyed more time to pursue their crafts. Moreover, foreigners were exempt from the multiple taxes that burdened natives. In short, foreign craftsmen were seen as a privileged class not burdened with the responsibilities, taxes, and risks implicit in the citizenship enjoyed by native artisans.[16] Moreover, most foreign craftsmen were said to have been unwilling to share knowledge of their trades with native artisans.[17] Similar opposition was voiced publicly by tradesmen in 1867, 1875, and 1887. Native artisans, however, willingly acknowledged the contributions of some foreigners in advancing the general state of the arts, particularly those foreigners who shared their skills with natives.[18]

While accusations against foreign craftsmen inevitably claimed that Colombian artisans produced goods of equal quality, petitions for tariff protection frequently requested that masters be brought from abroad to teach native craftsmen.[19] Such requests were common after the crisis of the 1860s, when they resulted in approval of a plan to bring foreigners to Colombia to teach mechanical arts.[20] In the end, such aspirations were not realized, although several Colombians were sent abroad in the 1880s to study industrial trades.

The most vocal artisan response to liberal reform came in reaction to tariff reduction. Bogotano craftsmen who founded the Society of Artisans protested that tariff reductions on "ready-made clothing, shoes, tools, and other manufactures" would damage the country's industry and disemploy thousands who "foment the national wealth" by manual trades.[21] Although the political mobilization to repeal the Law of June 14 quickly embroiled the Society in the heated 1848 presidential campaign, upward revision of the tariff rates remained foremost on the artisan political agenda. When the 1849 congress did not raise tariff rates, Bogotá's Society expressed confidence "that the wisdom of the Congress will weigh and meditate for the good of the country's industry in the most assertive and convenient manner."[22]

When artisans renewed their drive for tariff protection, the obstacles blocking their goals became clear. The Sociedad Democrática de Bogotá presented a petition in May 1850 to remind legislators of its faithful service to the ideas of the 7 de marzo, implying that tariff protection would be the just compensation for that support.[23] The petition called for increased tariff protection for all the country, or at least for the provinces of Bogotá, Mariquita, Neiva, Tundama, Tunja, and Vélez, supposedly the areas most affected by manufactured imports. Against those who argued that tariff increases would aid only a small sector of society, the artisan petition calculated that if each shop in the capital had twenty journeymen, then four-thousand workers and their families would be hurt by low tariffs in Bogotá alone. They estimated the population of consumers of foreign products at two-thousand. To them, these statistics clearly demonstrated that low tariffs favored a minority of the population, not the reverse as proponents of free trade insisted. The petition made clear that artisans were suspicious of foreign ideas as well as foreign products. The notion that worship of foreign ideas might help the nation materially was called the "*vanity* of theoreticians and the *greed* of speculators."[24] After several days of heated exchange among legislators, a debate that was monitored closely by the craftsmen, the bill died in committee.[25]

Quite significantly, Lorenzo María Lleras and Juan José Nieto, leading members of the emerging draconiano wing of the Liberal party, supported the rationale for higher tariffs. Lleras noted that he had studied the ideas of such proponents of economic liberalism as Say and Bastiat, yet, as head of the commission that had studied the plight of the country's artisans, he reported, "it makes me sick to see the conditions of the artisans." Lleras thus abandoned his economic training, realizing that what might work in other countries was not necessarily applicable in Colombia. Lleras insisted that Colombia provide for the welfare of its citizens, pointing out that in theory no duties should be levied and that the consumer should pay only the cost of the item plus transportation. Yet, if this were the case, how could the government function? Already revenue shortages had forced the government to cut back projects, reduce expenditures, and fire employees. Theory, Lleras concluded, did not override the pragmatic need for revenue, nor the government's obligations to its citizenry.[26]

Many of the same craftsmen repeated the request for tariff protection to the 1851 congress. Like previous requests, this petition focused upon the desperate economic situation facing artisans and their families. The artisan document argued that craftsmen cared more for social reality than economic theory, which dealt with nations as single entities, not as amalgamations of various classes and peoples. The authors of the petition pointed out that what might cause "advancement" for the whole nation did not necessarily help its separate parts. The artisans thus questioned the advice of those who felt they could remedy their plight by changing trades. According to the members of the Democratic Society, only agriculture and commerce provided real alternative employment and they lacked the necessary capital to become established in those fields. The artisans reminded legislators that their petition was not a party matter, but reflected the needs of a threatened social class.[27]

The inherent flaw in the artisan/student union supporting the national network of the Democratic Societies is revealed in the rejection of requests for higher tariffs. The Sociedad de Artesanos had been formed in reaction to liberal tariff reduction and, in keeping with the interests of its artisan membership, had made increased tariff rates its primary objective. Younger members of the Liberal party, invited into the group as a means of reaching that goal, had used the Artisan Society as an electoral force through which their own reform objectives and political ambitions could be met. The political liberalism espoused by the students and others appealed to members of the Society, as it promised the expansion of the polity to include the voices of previously excluded groups, such as artisans. After the 7 de marzo victory, the national extension of the Sociedad Democrática succeeded in mobilizing popular support for many reform measures and in bringing popular sectors into the polity. On the positive side, the students had influenced artisans to become more politically active, by which craftsmen had increased their self-consciousness. But artisans wished to negate the economic measures favored by the young Liberals and other politicians. Mobilization to win higher tariff rates vividly revealed the contradiction. Political liberalism enabled craftsmen to seek interests relative to their class, which included opposition to the tariff reductions demanded by economic liberalism. The flawed relationship did not last.

After the congressional rejection of the May 1850 petition, artisans in the Democratic Society became vocal opponents of the young Liberals in their organization.[28] The ultimate indication of the division is seen in the Liberals' accolades to Florentino González as a "man of progress" worthy of a cabinet post or of the vice-presidency.[29] The blacksmith Emeterio Heredia roundly condemned the suggestion, claiming that González was not a good Liberal and that his attitude toward craftsmen had been demonstrated in the tariff of 1847.[30] The conflict became so bitter that José María Samper was driven from the Democratic Society after he insisted that it support the tariff reductions undertaken by the government.[31]

Young Liberals, who were by now labeled gólgotas, established the Escuela Republicana (Republican School) on the 1850 anniversary of the attempted assassination of Bolívar, a move that symbolized their separation from the Democratic Society. The rector of the National University, Vicente Lombana, and the core of the gólgota activists founded the Republican School to provide reformers and intellectuals with a sounding board and base in which to examine their particular interests and ideas. Conservatives claimed that the objective of the Republican School was to defend the ideas of socialism, but this statement must be understood in the spirit of the times.[32] José María Samper, after he moderated his political opinions, rightly observed the character of gólgotan socialism, noting that "We were all socialists in the School, but without having studied socialism nor understood it, enamored with the word, with its political novelty."[33]

Artisans accelerated the lengthy process of making the Sociedad Democrática more representative of their interests in late 1850. This was in part made necessary by increased complaints about its direction.[34] For at least Ambrosio López, these appeals for introspection had the desired affect. His critical analysis of the Society's history, published in early 1851, concluded that leadership had been lost to imitators of the "red serpents" of the 1848 French Revolution. The embarrassed tailor recognized his own role in subverting artisan economic objectives (i.e., tariff legislation) in order to help the López campaign. The 1849 victory, he related, had not brought the true democratic institutions hoped for by the artisans, but an "oligarchy with the name of a democracy."[35] Worse perhaps than this for López had been the "red serpents'" attack on religion. He did not approve of the expulsion of the Jesuits nor of the attacks upon the Catholic church and its dogmas, which he saw as necessary for a just republic. The disillusioned López wrote that Conservatives were using their economic power to oppress artisans. Indeed, both Conservatives and Liberals offered the artisan only "worse misery." To López, the future was bleak: "Fellow disillusioned, beloved friends, there exists a strong opposition that strengthens every day, and I believe that the day is not distant that our affiliation will force a civil war among ourselves."[36] Artisans, as López saw it, had to reassert their solidarity. Only some military men and moderate Liberals could be trusted in this process. It would then be possible to fulfill the artisans' hopes "of protected arts . . . with our families living happily in the soul of a true Republic, where citizens are not denied their real rights."[37] For his slanderous publication, López was expelled from the Society.[38]

The blacksmith Emeterio Heredia, then president of the Society, refuted López's charges in his own publication. Did not Ambrosio like freedom of the press? And, he asked, what of Zaldúa's proposal in the Senate to create industrial workshops? As for the struggle to increase tariffs, Heredia reminded López of the support the artisan petition had received in the Chamber the year earlier. Surely this provided evidence of a republican government that was responsive to the needs of artisans. Heredia felt that a man of López's nature, who allegedly had reaped personal benefit from public appointments, a "conservative without principles," had no right to censure the Sociedad Democrática and the Liberal government without first censuring himself.[39] López responded that his charges had gone unanswered and that his expulsion was contrary to free liberal expression, proof of the influence of "red" Liberals in the Society.[40]

The López/Heredia exchange reveals the extension of publicly stated artisan concerns from an almost exhaustive attention to tariff rates to a variety of issues raised during the reform process. The Jesuit question, for example, drew artisan societies into one of the most polemic disputes of the era.[41] As reformers had focused their attention upon the order, José María Samper twice convinced the Democrats to petition for their expulsion.[42] President López resisted the strong anti-Jesuit pressures until May 18, 1850, when, citing the April 2, 1767, decree of Charles III that had previously expelled the priests, he ordered the Society of Jesus once again to leave Colombian soil. Two days later, some two-hundred artisans of the Popular Society guarded their exit from the capital.[43]

Liberal party divisions and the fractured artisan/Liberal relationship became more apparent after the Conservative insurrection of 1851. The carpenter Cruz Ballesteros renewed López's polemic in December of that year when he charged that craftsmen had been deceived by Liberal theory. Indicative of the insolent and unappreciative attitude of Liberals toward artisans, in Ballesteros's opinion, was their seeming disregard for the lives of artisans who served in the National Guard: the latter had been poorly clothed and fed and had been used as cannon fodder in the field. And, when they had returned to Bogotá, their compensation consisted of little more than Liberal speeches. Liberal theory and Liberal reality were two different things for Ballesteros.[44] The powerful blacksmith orator Miguel León followed with a similar attack in January 1852 against Manuel Murillo Toro, perhaps the most outspoken gólgota ideologue.[45]

## The Sociedad Democrática in Revolt

Artisans in the Democratic Society became increasingly alienated by the reforms after the defeat of the 1851 Conservative insurrection. Their antipathy paralleled that of the draconiano wing of the Liberal party, with whom they forged a durable alliance. Democrats formally adopted José María Obando as their presidential candidate on February 22, 1851. Obando, an enormously popular candidate with a lengthy Liberal vita, had strong support among both the lower classes and the military; and he lived in Las Nieves, where he frequently attended Society meetings. Obando opposed the gólgota reform platform, especially their plans for reduction of the military, although his campaign statements avoided serious discussion of the reforms.[46] For their part, gólgotas favored General Tomás Herrera of Panama who, while not as radical as most of his supporters, did favor some of their proposals, particularly those that offered Panama more regional autonomy and economic opportunity. Conservatives, subdued after the 1851 fiasco, presented no candidate, although they undoubtedly opposed the Obando candidacy.[47]

The conflict in the ranks of the Liberal party, which came at the apparent pinnacle of its power, is clearly understandable in that the rival factions no longer needed to maintain unity in opposition to the Conservative threat, which allowed ideological and programmatic divisions to become more apparent. In general, draconianos did not favor the more radical reforms that had been adopted in the last few years, especially questions of civil liberties, the death penalty, federalism, and the church.[48] Draconianos had supported the artisans' tariff petition, had not been in a hurry to expel the Jesuits, and did not fully support the anti-clerical legislation of the gólgotas; but they had not made a concerted effort on these issues. Additionally, draconianos, a substantial number of whom had military backgrounds, shared common class backgrounds with craftsmen. Significant percentages of the Colombian military hierarchy were men of lower-status groups socially and ideologically opposed by gólgotas.[49]

The status of the permanent army within the Colombian state reversed draconiano acquiescence to gólgota plans. To most gólgotas, a permanent army that consumed an excessive share of limited treasury funds was incompatible with republican principles that envisioned the spontaneous support of the people for the defense of a threatened government. Accordingly, gólgotas desired the permanent army's elimination, or at least its reduction in size.[50] This was absolutely unacceptable to the draconianos, many of whom were military men. Draconiano writers argued that the army-less utopia envisioned by the gólgotas would lead to anarchy or dictatorship, similar to what had occurred in France.[51] When the congress reconvened in March 1853, Florentino González failed in his attempts to curb the institution; the proposal to eliminate the permanent army was defeated 55 to 14.[52]

Obando defined the draconiano cause as he took office on April 1, 1853.[53] The president stressed the need for order, suggesting that radical reformers had destabilized Colombian institutions and society; he therefore pledged to halt the trend toward "anarchy." Draconianos presented a largely reactionary program against suppression of import duties, reduction of the power of the executive, moves to make education independent of the state, the proposed reduction in the power of the military, and the agrarian laws. They further claimed that special loans were needed to support social institutions such as hospitals, charity houses, national colleges, and public schools—all items of special concern to the popular classes.[54] Draconianos declared that their reaction was "for the good of the country: a reaction that assures the priesthood of its independence and rights; the laborer of the fruits of his work; the artisan the price of his industry; to all peace, order, and liberty . . . rights and social guarantees."[55]

Artisans took advantage of perceived executive support to press for reestablishment of a protective tariff. On May 17, they presented a petition to the Chamber of Representatives, allegedly pledging a caraqueñada if the request were not granted. After a brief discussion in the chamber, the petition was referred to the Senate, which, since it was controlled by González and the gólgotas, meant sure death for the proposal.[56] A violent fracas developed on May 19 outside the legislative chambers between artisans and gólgota youths in attendance, which caused many injuries to both sides, and the death of a black mason, Bruno Rodríguez.[57]

The May 19 incident divided the city along class lines. The combatants of May 19 were distinguished by their dress: the artisans wore their "official" red-and-blue ruanas and the gólgotas wore frockcoats.[58] The very names given to the two sides, *guaches* (a derisive label given to the artisans which implied coarse, vulgar people) and *cachacos* (fops), indicate class labeling. Artisan participants in the protests came from both political societies, evidence that class unity now overshadowed party affiliations—or perhaps that political alignments were now being determined on the basis of class origins. Gólgotas—mostly upper-class youths—and many Conservatives took the lead in berating the artisans, while the latter were increasingly linked with the draconianos, which included many military men of humble origin.

Publication of the liberal Constitution on May 21 did little to calm the political situation. To the dismay of many observers, Obando signed the document without protest. Artisans saw the Constitution of May 21 as a further indication of the erosion of order under gólgotan influence. Artisans had become increasingly alienated from the new order, as it ran counter to many of their own interests. In addition to their concern over the tariff question, they were uneasy over the weakening of both the church and state, and they were particularly distrustful of the groups responsible for the changes. For some, social divisions had become enmeshed with the reform controversy. One pamphlet supporting the artisans asked: "Who are the people? In the majority they are religious, Catholic, Apostolic, Roman, republican; who live by the work of their hands in order to earn the bread for their children and lazy masters; who are the people? The honorable veteran, the obedient and suffering soldier, the farmer, the poor merchant, the persecuted priest, all men, all citizens who work a trade; they are the people and not Gólgota."[59]

Tension gripped the city as the June celebrations of Corpus Christi neared. The barrio of Las Nieves was said to have become closed to cachacos.[60] Realizing the potential for conflict, Governor Nicolás Escobar Zerda ordered the jefe político of Las Nieves, Plácido Morales, to cancel the traditional bull run through the city, an edict Morales ignored.[61] On June 8, artisans and gólgotas engaged in a rock-throwing melee near the city's center. General José María Melo watched the conflict from his balcony, laughing as the guaches bested the cachacos. But when armed cachaco reinforcements arrived, he ordered out the guards. In their successful effort to clear the streets, a soldier, Isidoro Ladino, was killed. Later that day, Florentino González was attacked by a group of men in ruanas in front of the Peruvian embassy and beaten severely. Inevitably, gólgota sympathizers lambasted the authorities for their failure to curb the "government of Las Nieves."

A heated leaflet debate continued the exchange, though with less deadly results.[62] The most telling comment came from a "friend of the artisans" who accused artisans of running too readily from the fight against "aristocratic offenders." Its author concluded: "In this land democracy is an illusion, we are republicans in theory and slaves in practice. . . . We are called the sovereign people, but the day that we speak, a rain of stones falls upon our august sovereignty; what can we do to install a positive Democracy? Make our own valiant efforts, and not flee at the sight of the oligarchs."[63] The newly appointed governor of Bogotá, José María Plata, made overtures for civic restraint, a move that proved only a temporary respite.[64] The board of directors of the Democratic Society called upon its supporters to unite to end the chaos and restore the good name of the artisan, even while it promised the government Democratic support against "delinquents."[65]

Despite pleas for calm, cachaco Antonio París Santamaría was killed on June 18 by a group of men in ruanas. Nepomuceno Palacios was arrested and charged with the murder, as were Eusebio

Robayo (a blacksmith), Cenón Samudio, and E. Amézquita (a small trader). Palacios was sentenced to death for the murder and his accomplices were sentenced to jail. Palacios was garroted on Friday, August 5, in the Plaza de Santander, much to the dismay of artisan leader Miguel León.[66] Why, he asked, was Palacios killed so quickly when Bruno Rodríguez's cachaco murderer had not met the same fate? "Because he did not have the title of Doctor or gólgota!"[67]

Obando's standing among the artisans rose in July when he reorganized the National Guard, strengthening the positions of craftsmen within it.[68] This encouraged Democrats to seek cooperation with draconianos in the October elections, the first in Colombia under universal male suffrage as established by the new constitution. Emeterio Heredia and other artisans who would play active roles in the 17 de abril coup of the coming year participated in the elections on the side of the draconianos. Heredia stressed that recent reforms, based solely upon theory and backed by the "youths" (gólgotas), were the cause of the nation's current crisis, suggesting as well that a conspiracy between gólgotas and Conservatives existed to drive Liberals (draconianos) out of office. The expansion of the electorate, he related, offered artisans the opportunity to dominate the legislature and secure passage of legislation in their own best interests, but only if they remembered the "crimes" of May 19 and June 8 and voted as a unit.[69]

Conservative victories throughout the country underscored the deep Liberal divisions.[70] Although draconianos gained control of several provincial governments, the broadened electorate created by the new constitution benefited mainly the Conservatives. The elections gave seventeen senate seats to Conservatives, eleven to gólgotas, and only five to draconianos, while in the lower chamber twenty-five gólgotas, twenty-four Conservatives, and nine draconianos were selected by the voters.[71] In some instances, Conservatives and gólgotas cooperated (Florentino González won the position of procurador general with Conservative support).

Speaking for the draconianos, Lorenzo María Lleras observed that the October election revealed the existence of three political parties: Conservatives, gólgotas, and Liberals. Conservatives had failed to obtain power through revolt, Lleras wrote, so they appealed to "fanatics" and the superstitious masses in the name of religion. Gólgotas supposedly promised the masses a classless socialist utopia as their appeal, which, in his opinion, ignored social distinctions based upon merit. True Liberals, who were in control of the executive, recognized the social reality created by work and sought to guarantee the rights of individuals according to law. However, Lleras concluded, collusion between Conservatives and gólgotas now threatened the country's Liberals.[72]

The tri-part political division became increasingly violent after passage of the 1853 constitution. Tumults occurred in Popayán, Barranquilla, Sutatenza, and other towns.[73] Armories in Barranquilla and Cali were raided by Democrats and some six-hundred weapons were stolen in early December. Despite governmental condemnation of this action, reports claimed that the raids were officially sanctioned. A similar theft of arms took place in Chocontá, and public disturbances by supporters of the Democratic Society occurred in Santa Marta, Neiva, Sabanilla, Tunja, and Zipaquirá.[74] Obando's scheduled military parade on January 1, 1854, was anticipated by many to be the announcement of a coup. Rather, he took the occasion to praise and declare loyalty to the Constitution of May 21.[75] However, the mortal wounding of Corporal Pedro Ramón Quirós that night sparked a chain of events that many believe led directly to the Melo revolt four months later.[76]

The historical interpretations of the Quirós affair have been extremely contradictory.[77] Melo was charged with murder, with his trial eventually scheduled for April 17, 1854. In the meantime, Melo's alleged responsibility for Quirós's death was used by antimilitary elements in the congress to generate hostility against Melo and support for the proposed reduction in the size of the military. Obando requested funds for an army of 1,240 men from the congress that had convened in early February, a slight reduction from the previous 1,300–man force. Congress, however, offered to fund only an army of 800, including a reduced officer corps with no generals. This last clause was specifically directed at Melo. Debate on the topic dragged on for weeks, with neither side willing to compromise.[78]

The disarray of the Liberal party provided the incentive for a reorganization of the Sociedad Democrática on January 6, 1854. The meeting was held at Lorenzo María Lleras's Colegio del Espíritu Santo, where Lleras was chosen director over his objections that an artisan should head the organization. The Society formed a central board of directors to work for reorganization of the Liberal party as a whole. The board, which consisted of twenty-one persons, drawn from leading draconianos and artisans, directed letters to provincial capitals urging the formation of provincial boards of directors, which would in turn coordinate smaller district units. Each of the provincial bodies was to organize Democratic Societies in as many towns as possible; all of these groups were to follow the directives of the central body.[79] The reorganized Democratic Society was no more purely artisan in nature than it had been in 1850. Non-artisan draconiano Liberals held most of the important positions and were quite influential in its direction. Artisan political objectives were more closely in tune with draconiano than gólgotan goals, however. No division of interests could be seen in the draconiano/artisan organization in 1854 paralleling those of the gólgota/artisan relationship of 1850.[80]

The Democratic Society's March 20 petition to the congress demonstrated its expanded range of interests. The Sociedad requested abolition of imprisonment for debts as contrary to the principle of personal liberty. In a similar vein, it was proposed that a debtor should be liable for criminal punishment in the case of fraud, but if an "innocent impossibility" prevented repayment of the debt, he would be free to work after cession of his available goods. This proposal would prevent forced labor for non-payment of debts. Monetary reform was called for, including minting smaller coins for day-to-day use. The Sociedad wanted congress to approve a national road from Bogotá to the Magdalena. It also requested establishment of an industrial workshop for children of the poor and working classes so that they could learn new arts. Reforms were requested in military recruitment, making military service voluntary, with higher remuneration. The Society also proposed that service in the Guard be limited to national emergencies, and not include peacetime chores such as escorting prisoners. Such changes would prevent disruption of the members' occupations. Lastly, the Society wanted an end to compulsory free labor services demanded by municipal governments and the reconsideration of municipal taxes upon the poor.[81]

The fifth anniversary of the 7 de marzo[82] came amid rumors of an impending coup by the Conservatives, by the military, or by the military with the Democrats—or even by gólgotas and the military.[83] A circular of March 5, 1854, signed by Democrat Francisco Antonio Obregón, contributed to the general alarm as he called upon Sociedades Democráticas nationwide to arm themselves, so that they could meet force with force. Notices of a seditious nature were also posted on city walls: Democrats paraded through the city.[84] Under these circumstances, the Senate presented a request for one-thousand weapons to the governor of Bogotá so that "respectable" citizens could arm themselves. President Obando overruled the request, stating that he knew of no threat to order and that, if one did exist, the National Guard would maintain order.[85] Since Democrats dominated the Guard, this response did little to calm the senators' fears. Congress then passed a law on March 24 allowing the right to free commerce in all types of weapons, and the right to train with them and carry them. Obando vetoed the proposed law, saying that individuals already had extremely liberal access to weapons under the constitution—more liberal, in fact, than he favored. He reminded congressmen that under the proposed law even criminals would have the right to bear arms and denounced the proposal as a threat to the stability of the national government and public order. The bill was passed over his objections and became law on April 3, although congress did limit the privilege to those who possessed their personal liberty.[86] On March 28, the congress passed the project for reducing the size of the army and of the officer corps. Obando also vetoed this law.[87] Debate on the presidential veto was scheduled for April 17.

The movement toward civil disorder quickened in early April as leaders of the Democratic Society met in secret.[88] The first day of Holy Week, April 10, witnessed a brick-throwing melee between parading Democrats and guardsmen versus gólgotan youths. A more serious clash pitted guardsmen and artisans against gólgotas on April 14. Two days later, on Easter Sunday, April 16, after news of an uprising in Popayán reached the capital,[89] the Guard and armed artisans marched through the streets with signs that proclaimed "Long live the army and Democrats; down with monopolists!" Some four-hundred artisans gathered in the central plaza at noon in a noisy demonstration. Early the next morning, Melo initiated his coup d'état. He led his troops to the plaza, where some seven-hundred artisans waited. With a cry of "Down with the gólgotas," the coup against the Constitution of May 21 began.[90]

The 17 de abril coup had an inauspicious start. Melo, General Gutiérrez de Piñeres, Lino García, Francisco Antonio Obregón, Pedro Mártir Consuegra, and Miguel León urged Obando to accept direction of the movement, but he declined leadership. Obando's refusal to take command came as a shock to the leaders of the coup. Their first proclamation had confidently cited Obando as the supreme chief,[91] but his refusal to direct the coup spurred a rash of defections. Obando, Lleras, and José de Obaldía had made up the draconian political hierarchy, while Obando, José Hilario López, and Melo were its military leaders. Lleras issued a statement late on April 17 that "he had not made, nor did he accept the revolution."[92] Obaldía, who many thought was instrumental in persuading Obando not to lead the coup, sought refuge in the United States consulate. Melo announced that López, who had left Bogotá on April 4 for alleged reasons of health, favored the coup, but on May 2 news to the contrary reached the capital.[93] All major draconian political and military leaders save Melo thus rejected the attempt to sustain what was commonly seen as their cause.

Melistas cited the "pandemonium of anarchy" and the introduction of "foreign ideas" contained within the Constitution of May 21 as the reasons for the 17 de abril. Melo abrogated that document on April 27 and replaced it with the 1843 constitution until a national convention could meet to frame a new law of the land. Specific features of the 1853 constitution to be altered included: universal manhood suffrage, popular election of provincial governors, the reduction of executive powers, and various articles affecting the church.[94]

Membership in the National Guard brought craftsmen into the military affairs of the movement; "the artisans were organized in militias in order to sustain the army [which] constituted the firmest prop of the provisional government."[95] Artisans made up the majority of the Guard's common soldiers and many of its officers, including blacksmith Miguel León, tailor José María Vega, carpenter Cruz Ballesteros, cobbler José Antonio Saavedra, and Francisco Torres Hinestrosa.[96] León worked to help procure supplies for Bogotá in the months following the coup. Emeterio Heredia served as jefe político in Fusagasuga. Moreover, craftsmen produced much of the equipment, clothing, and weapons used by the melistas. Felipe Roa, for example, supplied two-thousand uniforms to the Regeneration Army.[97]

Yet, artisan participation in the 17 de abril coup has been overstated. Bogotano artisans were less active in the early military defense of the Melo regime than they were in its final stages. Melistas won two battles against constitutionalist forces in May that served to protect northern access to the city and to permit the Melistas to advance in that direction. By July, most of the eastern highlands were in their hands. Melo chose not to move out of that stronghold, despite major support in the Cauca valley, which revolted at about the same time as did Bogotá. Cali resisted occupation by constitutionalists for most of June, when some eight-hundred Democrats surrendered to José Hilario López. The north coast offered weak verbal support for Melo and practically no military aid. Only in Cartagena did serious mobilization take place, but it was promptly suppressed by General Mosquera.[98]

The constitutionalists' response to the Melo coup, while slow in developing, brought a rapid conclusion to the rebellion. Mosquera, General Antonio París, and General José Hilario López led the military effort which, by November 1854, had surrounded the capital. A constitutionalist congress had opened in Ibagué on September 22 under the leadership of Obaldía. Its first action was to denounce the 17 de abril regime and to name a commission to investigate the conduct of those involved in it, including Obando. On October 28, the congress closed its sessions and vowed that it would reconvene in the capital.[99] The battle for Bogotá was joined on December 4. By 1:30 P.M. of that day only the barracks of San Francisco and San Agustín resisted the constitutionalist attack. In Mosquera's final assault on San Francisco, Miguel León was killed, and José María Vega, along with Joaquín Posada, the editor of *El Alacrán*, were critically wounded. By 4:00 P.M. the fighting had ceased, when Generals López, Mosquera, and Herrán met in a fraternal embrace at the foot of Bolívar's statue in the central plaza. The attempt of the 17 de abril to wrest governmental control from the so-called anarchists had failed.[100]

The defeat of the coup was felt by the capital's artisans for years to come. As acting president, Obaldía extended a pardon—in principle—to common soldiers, but not to officers of the National Guard.[101] Governor Pedro Gutiérrez Lee's commission to identify those guilty of seditious or criminal activity was, according to one account, completely arbitrary.[102] Obaldía's "pardons" allowed prisoners to accept the pardon and serve four years of duty in the army in Panama, or be subjected to trial—in the circuit court of Panama, so as to relieve the burden on Bogotá's courts.[103] Exact numbers of those sent to the notoriously unhealthy lowland province from Bogotá either as "recruits" or for trial are impossible to determine, but it seems reasonable to conclude that the number totaled from three- to four-hundred.[104] Not all of these men went alone. Lorenzo María Lleras told of receiving a letter in May, which reported the deaths of twenty of the twenty-five women who had accompanied their husbands into exile. (The same letter reported the deaths of forty men in exile.)[105]

The judgment of melista leaders was not concluded until June 6, when Melo and several members of his cabinet were expelled from the country for eight years. Other major melistas were exiled for periods of four or more years. Numerous artisans had already been "pardoned," the terms of which varied from three years' exile for Agustín Rodríguez to one year's exile from certain provinces for others.[106] Despite Melo's claim of total responsibility for the rebellion, much of the blame for the coup was shifted to Obando, who underwent a grueling trial for his behavior during the coup. It was not until December 20, 1855, that the Supreme Court reached its verdict: not guilty of crime or treason, but, because he did not fight the rebellion, guilty of having failed to fulfill the responsibilities of his office.[107]

The terms of the pardons drew pointed criticisms from artisans. One leaflet proclaimed that "to exile a man for three years is not a pardon, nor is it forgiveness for his crimes." Moreover, the alleged pardons were said to have been unconstitutional, "because the Constitution does not give the Executive the faculty to impose penalties, nor to judge the degree of guilt of a criminal, nor to determine who are leaders or agents and who is not."[108] Gólgotas, in an obvious fence-mending exercise, noted that pardons were within the executive privilege, but that Obaldía's decrees had contained penalties, for which only judicial authorities had responsibility.[109]

The results of the 1853 elections, the first under a system of universal male suffrage, had demonstrated the strength of Conservative patronage throughout the country. Liberals—of both the draconiano and gólgotan wing of the party—had no choice but to reunite as quickly as possible if they were to have any realistic expectation of electoral victories. In Bogotá, Lorenzo María Lleras, among the many citizens arrested in December 1854, served as a central figure in the effort to recruit former melistas to the party. From jail Lleras joined those proclaiming the illegality of the pardons.[110] Upon his release, Lleras served as lawyer for the jailed artisan José María Vega's defense against charges of having participated in the "invasion" of the U.S. consulate in November 1854.[111] Lleras met with Manuel Murillo Toro and Rafael Mendoza in June 1855 to plan the party's political agenda, a meeting that attracted artisan support to Mendoza's August bid for the governorship of Cundinamarca. Murillo, in September, posted an eight-thousand peso deposit to guarantee Melo's prompt departure from Colombian soil.[112]

The presidential elections of 1856 signalled the partial reentry of bogotano craftsmen into the political arena. Conservatives presented Mariano Ospina Rodríguez as their candidate in that contest. Most Liberals united behind Murillo, while Mosquera launched himself as the candidate of the "National" party. Murillo opened his campaign with a statement of support signed by twenty-five notable melistas, including several artisans.[113] In addition, Lleras and the blacksmith Emeterio Heredia used the pages of *El Artesano* to appeal to the Liberal political tradition of artisans, claiming that tradesmen had had more independence under Liberals, an obvious pitch to artisan pride. Lleras reminded artisans of the attitudes shown by gólgota Liberals after December 4, contrasting it with the stances of Mosquera and the Conservatives. Mosquera, whom *El Artesano* labeled a "wild card," was portrayed as single-mindedly driving for personal power as a representative of the aristocracy of Popayán.[114] Mosquera, however, reminded artisans of the abuses craftsmen had suffered in their relationship with Liberals, drawing special attention to the question of tariffs. Mosquera's platform of restricted public intervention in religious matters, public works, and expanded educational opportunities and industrial training for the poor attracted public support of some craftsmen, notably Narciso Garai and Ambrosio López.[115] Both Mosquera papers, *El Ciudadano* and *El Nacional*, harped on gólgotan betrayals of artisans in May and June 1853, and in April 1854.[116]

It is doubtful that the electioneering had much impact upon the artisans of Bogotá. Ospina earned the victory with 844 electoral votes; Murillo trailed closely with 673 votes; and Mosquera finished a distant third with 380 votes.[117] In any case, melistas were again part of the capital's political scene. Leading melistas, including Ramón Mercado, Francisco Antonio Obregón, and Ramón Beriña met in late 1857 to reestablish themselves as a cohesive political voice.[118] A memorial service in honor of melista dead drew some 250 to 300 Democrats to a mass at the San Francisco church on November 30, after which a silent candlelight march with the portraits of Diego Castro and Miguel León wound its way to the city's cemetery. Outraged Conservatives insisted that the event constituted a threat to public order, a charge refuted by artisans. José María Vega charged that the government had harassed artisans and other melistas, citing several examples of alleged public abuses.[119]

Conservative fears increased when Lleras and Manuel María Madiedo founded *El Núcleo* in January 1858 as a draconiano mouthpiece.[120] While calling themselves Liberals, the editors described their Liberalism as "practically based," in contrast to the Radicals' theoretical Liberalism.[121] Draconianos presented a slate to the November 1858 town council election that included artisans Cruz Ballesteros and Emeterio Heredia.[122] Heredia was also nominated to the state assembly, a race that he lost, but one in which Conservative painter Simón José Cárdenas, the slandered former leader of the Popular Society, earned a seat.[123] Cárdenas's victory was marred by accusations of fraud from irate Liberals.[124]

The increased strength of the Conservative party under the system of universal suffrage had prevented the Liberals from regaining control of the national government. Liberals throughout the country were outraged by passage of two laws that challenged their control of state governments in 1858.[125] A series of rebellions, first in Santander in March 1859, and then in the Cauca under Mosquera, plunged the nation into civil war as Liberals abandoned the vote for the sword.[126] The eventual Liberal victory resulted in several safeguards against the Conservative majority in the Constitution of 1863. Suffrage laws reverted to state control, where increasingly powerful machines of both political hues limited voter eligibility. State governments in Cundinamarca and Santander became powerful Liberal strongholds, the foundation of the so-called Radical Olympus. The way was paved for a final wave of reforms.

The religious reforms of the early 1860s inspired deep antipathy among many craftsmen, beliefs that surfaced after the promulgation of the 1863 constitution. The pamphlet *Los derechos del pueblo*, for example, questioned both the religious reforms and Liberal political conduct. Liberal bosses, the author claimed, had long enticed the people with promises of rights, but he had come to question the value of those rights. Formerly free Catholic schools were now closed; disamortization had raised the rents of shops and stores; and social services once provided by the church were lacking. Moreover, suffrage had been restricted under the political machine created by Ramón Gómez in Cundinamarca, thereby precluding democratic participation. Conservatives were said to have been persecuted both economically and politically in spite of the alleged freedom of political expression. In short, the pursuit of rights had devastated the people, leading him to conclude that artisans had been deceived by Liberals so that the party might satisfy its own interests.[127]

Artisan supporters of the government countered these sentiments. One leaflet observed that as part of the people, the clergy, like laborers, artisans, and merchants, were subject to the same laws.[128] Cruz Ballesteros, who purchased a house and shop formally owned by the church from the government, claimed that disamortization had been necessary to strip the church of funds used to conduct war.[129] Yet the anti-clerical measures enacted during the civil war proved to be crucial for the final alienation of certain leading craftsmen from the Liberal party. "An artisan," who claimed to have been present in 1863 when General Santos Gutiérrez, recently appointed governor of Cundinamarca, entered the capital, noted that "the people now have liberty of the press, but do not know how to read or write." They had liberty of education, but free education had ended with the closure of church schools. Liberties existed, the craftsman claimed, but with churches closed, the people had no place to baptize their children, marry, or bury their dead: "In short, the people have all the liberties they do not need, and are deprived of the one indispensable freedom . . . that of worshiping the God of their fathers and to receive religion's sweet consolation."[130]

## Conclusion

Artisan political reactions to changes in the economic, political, and social policies of Colombia do not support the tendency to see the acceptance and promulgation of socialist ideas by artisans of the Sociedad Democrática. Both Conservative contemporaries and leftist writers of the present perceived socialist influences in the Society, albeit from different points of view. In either case, the socialism of the Societies has been misstated. Contemporaries applied socialist labels to their foes to undermine the group's appeal,

or used socialist rhetoric symbolically to express their own roman-
ticism. Modern writers have pointed to the socialist content of the
era's speeches and proclamations, as exemplified by José María
Samper, Manuel Murillo Toro, or Francisco Javier Zaldúa. While
socialist rhetoric is found in their writings, laissez-faire individual-
ism guided their reform projects.[131] An examination of the words of
Ambrosio López, Cruz Ballesteros, or Emeterio Heredia, representatives of the artisan movement, reveals a starkly different message.
Their words and deeds were directed against "socialists" such as
Murillo or Samper. Artisan leaders countered gólgotan economic
liberalism and judged their belief in political liberalism to be rhe-
torical.

It is also a mistake to focus exclusive attention upon the reactive nature of artisan political mobilization during the era of liberal
reform. Artisan political activity challenged the direction of elite
parties in a way that threatened their control of and aspirations for
the country. To that extent, artisans challenged the existing socio-
political order. Craftsmen in the Democratic Society apparently
took the rhetoric of the 7 de marzo seriously, as had artisans in the
Popular Society, the Catholic Society, and the Democratic-Republican Society. Political liberalism offered artisans a voice within
the polity. When faced with items that affected their interests, artisans mobilized, and sought to influence government policy. In the
face of such threats to their control, elites of both parties tended to
lay aside their differences, which were minor, and repress the
threats, as seen in the aftermath of the 17 de abril coup. The constitutionalist union of Liberals and Conservatives illustrates that
while parties did differ on the issue of the church's role in state and
society, they had far fewer differences on other issues, and none
concerning which social sector should direct the state.

If similarities are to be seen between the socialist reaction of
Parisian workers in 1848 and that of bogotano artisans in 1854, it is
because both responded to similar threats to their traditional social
positions and economic well-being; and they met a similar fate.
Capitalization and industrialization of production threatened Parisian workers directly and bogotano artisans indirectly. While the
reaction of tradesmen in these two countries took very different
paths, both sprang from similar circumstances. The eventual violent response of bogotano artisans to the reforms challenged elite

control of the Colombian state, but it must properly be labeled as reactionary radicalism.[132] Whatever the label, artisan political participation in this stage of the reform movement was significant; the same would be true of such activity in the following years, although the results would be quite different.

# FOUR

# ARTISAN REPUBLICANISM

T HE MOBILIZATION EFFORTS BEGUN BY ARTISANS IN THE 1840s reached their zenith in the Sociedad Unión de Artesanos (Union Society of Artisans), which articulated a forceful ideology of artisan republicanism that countered the dominant liberalism of the age. The experiences that shaped artisan republicanism can be illustrated by the use of the word *desengañar* as it related to craftsmen in the early reform period. Taken as a verb, desengañar means to disillusion or to disappoint; used as noun, it implies disillusionment, disappointment, or blighted hope. An 1848 broadside to "the Artisans of Bogotá" warned craftsmen not to support José Hilario López in the blind hope that he would prohibit the importation of foreign goods, raise tariffs, or offer artisans positions in his administration. The author of the tract cautioned that López's supporters had "opinions entirely opposite" to those held by craftsmen of the Society of Artisans and that "Time would disillusion you."[1] By 1851, Ambrosio López urged that the Society sever its relations with gólgotas who pursued reform objectives alien to those of craftsmen, in his proclamation entitled *El desengaño . . .* (The disillusioned). In it he claimed that artisans had been led astray from their original intentions and had to reassert their authority over the body.[2] Later in 1851, Cruz Ballesteros critically examined the "theory and the reality" of Liberal policies and Liberal attitudes toward artisans.[3] When Nepomuceno Palacios was executed for the

murder of cachaco Antonio París two years later, Miguel León released a stinging denunciation of the system of "justice" that
would so quickly reach a verdict on an artisan accused of a crime,
but allow a cachaco accused of the same act to walk the streets in
freedom. "His fate is our own," León asserted:

> You have already seen the contempt with which we have
> been treated, our petitions [to congress] are not given any
> merit, nor are we seen as competent of public behavior; be-
> cause these [characteristics] are visible only in our self
> esteem: because of this we are not paid what we are owed,
> we are not protected by work that should be given us; be-
> cause the principal contracts for clothes are brought from the
> exterior and not made in this country. . . . [D]o you want
> more desengaños! Prepare yourselves to recover the optimal
> fruits of your patriotism, of your honor and your suffering, in
> the reward of the gallows, or if not as dogs in the middle of
> the street.[4]

Over a five-year span, artisans had internalized their disillusionment to the extent that many craftsmen joined in the 1854 Melo
revolt to restore the country to the principles and institutions that
they thought served it best. Ten years later, after further reforms
and a major civil war, disillusioned craftsmen expressed their
thoughts in the pages of La Alianza.

Contrary to the widely held belief that peace would bring back
the economic prosperity that Bogotá had enjoyed before the war, all
accounts agree that the city suffered tremendous depression during
the 1860s.[5] Miguel Samper, in "La miseria en Bogotá," described a
city mired in economic decay, with high levels of unemployment
and a stagnant society. Samper, a dedicated Liberal, blamed the situation on the war, on the government's failure to fully implement
economic liberalization, and upon a myriad of social defects, foremost being parasitism upon public coffers. His generous and detailed analysis spared neither Conservatives nor Liberals, though
he singled out artisans as the leading example of public reliance
upon governmental support. Craftsmen had, according to Samper,
hidden behind protective tariffs and had refused to commit themselves to the arduous task of becoming economically competitive.
He suggested that craftsmen, rather than begging for economic protection, should improve their work habits, abstain from political
activity, and improve their arts.[6]

José Leocadio Camacho, the most vocal artisan leader in the last decades of the century, rebutted Samper's allegations.[7] The thirty-four year old carpenter agreed that artisans, as the first victims of the poverty Samper had described, deserved a central position in the analysis, but not as the cause of the malaise. Camacho asserted that before 1849 the working classes had been dedicated to their labors and had come together only for mutual protection. In that year they had been drawn into the political fray, to the detriment of their arts, just as their tariff protection had been lost. Camacho agreed that part of the solution lay in putting aside political passions for the sake of general well-being, but suggested that other social groups do the same, including elites. The tendency of the well-to-do sectors of the capital to show favoritism to artisans of their own political persuasion, despite the quality of the craftsmen's work, typified the intrusion of politics into daily lives. These political relationships, in Camacho's eyes, permeated sources of credit, social relations, and friendship, to the detriment of honesty, skill, or domestic virtue.[8]

Camacho staunchly defended the integrity, social worth, and political capabilities of the capital's craft sector. Artisans' practices, Camacho claimed, helped support those craftsmen suffering deprivation and hardship. Whereas Samper had argued against the acceptance of new apprentices, Camacho claimed that it was the social duty of the craftsmen to teach new skills and, more important, proper modes of conduct, lessons that outweighed simple economic well-being. Camacho called upon the nation to intervene in favor of the people's economic and social welfare, emphasizing that social reality should take precedence over theories of political economy.[9]

While Samper and Camacho debated ideological grounds for improving the city's condition, some craftsmen took practical steps to relieve the misery of the capital's working classes. Juan Malo organized a "commissary of national products" to serve as a clearinghouse for craftsmen's works. Artisans would bring their finished products to the clearinghouse, where consumers could purchase ready-made goods—as they could with foreign items—instead of waiting for a product to be ordered and fabricated. At the same time, the commissary would supply artisans with raw materials, paid for by commissions from products sold in the establishment.[10] The proposal, which resembles the producers' cooperatives proposed by the Farmer's Alliance in the United States in the late 1880s, while innovative, never fulfilled its founder's aspirations.[11]

Craftsmen, with the help of leading citizens, established a "Colegio de Artesanos" in 1865 to fill the void created by the anticlerical reforms of the early 1860s. The disamortized San Francisco convent became the site for a variety of instruction in areas ranging from reading, writing, and languages to morals, religion, political economy, and constitutional law. President Manuel Murillo Toro offered his services to the school, as did Archbishop Antonio Herrán, Lorenzo María Lleras, Teodoro Valenzuela, and José María Vergara y Vergara, evidence of the non-partisan character of the school. Students also enjoyed instruction in trades such as woodworking, tailoring, or shoemaking. While some artisans questioned the utility of geometry for students whose needs were in the area of practical education, the school was generally well received. Unfortunately it was poorly funded and was promptly closed.[12]

The school's collapse demonstrated that viable systems of education demanded government assistance. Its organizers requested that legislators consider supporting the school, or creating a government school of arts and trades to help educate working-class children.[13] Typically, nothing came of the request until artisan political support was needed, in this case when Mosquera and the congress were at loggerheads. A proposal from Francisco de P. Mateus supporting the project was approved in 1867, then set aside in the wake of the conflict between the executive and the congress.[14] This program gained sporadic support until it finally was implemented in the 1890s.

Political competition also evoked strong sentiments from the city's craftsmen. Former melistas took part in the various campaigns of 1863, mostly in favor of Governor Gutíerrez Vergara.[15] However, the artisan Agapito Cabrera warned craftsmen that they again stood in danger of manipulation by political magnates. Cabrera urged artisans to reject political mobilization and unite, for "when the powerful fight, the humble succumb."[16] An October 1863 parade involving large numbers of craftsmen demonstrated the support for Cabrera's position. The march's organizers proclaimed that after three years of war that involved artisans as soldiers, the time had come to speak as men of work—not partisans. Craftsmen, they claimed, faced catastrophic economic conditions brought about by the war and by an influx of foreign merchandise.[17]

Tariff protection, it was said, was the fundamental means to resolve the crisis. Anticipating the timeworn response that such legislation infringed on the liberty of merchants, the craftsmen alleged that legislation was properly "governed by morality." And,
since public authority was intended to protect and foment industrial activity, tariff protection, which forestalled negative social developments and sponsored positive economic effects, was the
proper goal of that authority. The artisans announced their intention to seek congressional assistance, but asked that merchants restrict imports voluntarily in the meantime.[18]

Camacho emerged in the midst of these discussions as both a
voice and symbol of the renewed struggle of craftsmen for self-ex-
pression and action. Camacho's newspaper, *El Obrero*, published
first in August 1864, declared that it would promote the "cause of
the workers" demanding independence from political bosses who
sought to manipulate them. Camacho wrote that antipathy toward
craftsmen was not confined to a specific party, but was characteristic of the upper classes, leading him to conclude that craftsmen
should be unified by their material conditions and should work
together, since they could expect help from no other social sector.
Ex-Democrat Emeterio Heredia challenged Camacho's early pas-
sive approach toward this goal, leading the editor to recommend
two tradesmen for Cundinamarca's assembly election and to assume a more forceful stance in his editorials. In the proposed candidacy, Camacho noted that while artisans should not necessarily
rule politically, their voices ought to be heard.[19]

*El Obrero* was hardly typical of artisan publications in the capital, which, although many had unusually high standards, seldom
addressed the issues of the day in so learned a fashion. Camacho
was a highly literate man, who certainly did not use the vocabulary
of the people. However, he did speak the language of his class,[20]
which undoubtedly accounts for his leadership role. Camacho argued that the government's refusal to adopt higher tariff rates was
central to the miserable economic conditions of the workers, as
was its failure to support the arts. The carpenter noted, further-
more, that the upper class did not honor work, as they neither
knew how to work nor appreciated its value. Improved conditions,
therefore, required appropriate governmental policies and changed
attitudes toward Colombia's artisans.[21] The issues raised in *El Obrero* and within the context of 1860s Bogotá—the rejection of parti-

san manipulation, the advocacy of artisan pride and self-help, and the support of independent political action—served as the ideological foundation for the Union Society of Artisans, the culmination of two decades of political activity by bogotano craftsmen.

## The Sociedad Unión of Artesanos

The Union Society struggled to win an independent artisan political voice in favor of craftsmen's interests during an extraordinarily turbulent period. The Society's leadership came from artisans who had been active in both the Sociedad Democrática and from those such as Camacho who emerged in the 1860s, although the latter were somewhat more vocal. A circular to politically active craftsmen, dated September 15, 1866, explained that the proposed society would be dedicated exclusively to autonomous political action and would use a newspaper, La Alianza, as its mouthpiece. (The organization was often also called La Alianza.) Antonio Cárdenas presided over the group's Board of Directors, with Saturnino González as vice-president, and Felipe Roa Ramírez serving as secretary. Other directors included Calisto Ballesteros, Ambrosio López, Genaro Martín, and Camacho.[22]

Approximately three-hundred artisans organized the Union Society in October and November 1866. Unlike the Democratic Society, only persons who practiced an art or manual profession could join the Sociedad Unión, and then only if they were deemed "honorable" by their peers and agreed to work for the guild's mutual obligations. These obligations included contributions to a mutual aid fund, subscription to La Alianza, preparation for yearly expositions, payment of membership fees, and a vow not to wear or possess foreign-made clothing or shoes. Further, members pledged to enhance educational opportunities—such as the Colegio de Artesanos—that would assist their fellow craftsmen. In the political realm, members were obligated to be independent, to denounce those persons seeking to manipulate the organization, and to vote for "honorable" men irrespective of party affiliations. Camacho was chosen to lead the Union Society toward these goals, to be helped by Vice-President González and Secretary Roa Ramírez.[23]

In keeping with the independent political stance of the organization, it proposed a decidedly non-partisan slate for December

1866 municipal council elections. Seven Unionists were included in the twenty-two names offered for members' consideration, a list that included Conservative Ignacio Gutiérrez Vergara, Liberal Ezequiel Rojas, Liberal Nicolás Leiva, and Conservative Manuel Pombo.[24] The Society proclaimed that it intended to press for various legislative initiatives, including the right to free education, decreased tax burdens, protection of the right to practice one's chosen faith, and tariff protection.[25]

Unfortunately for the Union Society, its organization coincided with worsening relations between Mosquera and the Radicals. When Mosquera assumed the presidency in May 1866, Radicals challenged several of his proposals, refusing, for example, to authorize a loan from England that the president had negotiated a few years earlier. After the close of the 1866 congressional session, Mosquera ordered the review of *manos muertas* (properties willed to the church) sales, expropriated additional church properties, and decreed that state militias be reorganized, a move similar to that which drove him into rebellion in 1859. Public opposition to these measures led Mosquera to submit his resignation and call for a plebiscite for a new executive, a move the congress refused to accept.[26]

The hostility between the executive and the legislature increased with the opening of the 1867 congress. Radicals secured control of both the senate and the chamber by forging an alliance with Conservatives against Mosquera. The congressmen attempted to reverse the president's expropriation of church buildings and to limit his capacity to intervene in state affairs. Mosquera, incensed at these challenges, thereupon declared his relations with congress broken, a move that was reversed only after strong pressure from his advisors and public opposition. The Pact of March 16 calmed the situation temporarily, but did little to resolve the fundamental differences between the congress and the executive.[27]

Partisan maneuvering inevitably involved efforts to mobilize the capital's artisan class. Several disturbances in the congress were blamed on the craftsmen.[28] Mosquera reportedly met with a delegation of twenty artisans in an attempt to secure their allegiance. The Radical daily newspaper praised workers for having resisted political manipulation, even though some artisans appear to have been swayed to the president's side.[29] In particular, José Antonio Saavedra, a cobbler who had been active in the Democratic

Society and who was still a colonel in the National Guard, had been brought to Mosquera's attention the previous year as an avid defender of the president's programs. A confidant informed Mosquera that Saavedra was very influential in "la clase del pueblo" and could be brought to the general's side "forever" if he were treated in a "convenient manner."[30] The precise nature of the relationship between the two men is unknown, but it certainly grew stronger, as Saavedra helped to organize a Democratic Society to defend the president in early March. The Sociedad Unión condemned this move as contrary to the best interests of craftsmen.[31]

The conflict between the president and the Radicals led to Mosquera's abortive coup d'état on April 29.[32] The Union Society urged its members to stay away from involvement in the coup, in spite of Mosquera's open appeal to artisans through Saavedra and the Democratic Society. A delegation from the Union's board of directors met with Mosquera, seeking the release of Conservative newspaper publisher Nicolás Pontón, who had been arrested in the coup. Mosquera refused to release Pontón, referring to him as a threat to public order, but the chief executive promised to respect the liberty of the press for those who conducted themselves "properly." The Society criticized the forced recruitment of tradesmen into the National Guard, even while *La Alianza* noted that Saavedra had treated his men well in the Guard. The Society urged that artisans stay in their shops until the presidential adventure was terminated, which the army accomplished in late May.[33]

The Colombian historian Indalecio Liévano Aguirre claimed that artisans supported the 29 de abril coup with the same enthusiasm as they had had in backing the revolt of Melo thirteen years earlier. Liévano cited the behavior of Saavedra as evidence of this allegation, but did little else to prove his claim.[34] Although Saavedra was extremely active in the coup, and continued to agitate craftsmen in support of Mosquera,[35] the actions of this single cobbler and those artisans who may have joined him compares poorly to the widespread support for Melo in 1854. By contrast, abundant evidence indicates that artisans refused to participate in the threat to public order.[36] The Union Society attested that if Liberal artisans had joined the coup as they had thirteen years earlier, then it would have been very difficult to restore constitutional order. That they did not was, the Society claimed, "in large part due to the Society of 'La Alianza.'"[37]

However beneficial to the cause of peace La Alianza might have been, the coup attempt shattered the unity of the organization. Immediately after Mosquera's fall, a rumor circulated through Bogotá that "notable" citizens were collecting funds to ship artisans en masse to the *llanos* (eastern grasslands) in order to still their voices. The Union Society and the government denied the truth of the rumor, at the same time downplaying allegations that secret meetings of discontented tradesmen were taking place.[38] In late June, artisans from both parties represented in the Society, including Emeterio Heredia, Cruz Sánchez, Calisto Ballesteros, Ambrosio López, Genaro Martín, and Tomás Rodríguez, declared that they would not be agitated by those trying to disturb the peace and promised to do all in their power to maintain peaceful conditions.[39]

The Union Society struggled for survival. *La Alianza* ceased publication from June 14 until August 1867, and then from early September until late November. The Society elected a cabinet of unity on July 20 and when publication of the paper resumed in August, the struggle to restore the alliance of workers "against the league of lazy exploiters of the people" emerged as its dominant theme. Doctor J. Peregrino Sanmiguel noted that partisan politics had taken root in the Union Society, leaving it with only a handful of members, which, in his view, forced the organization to reform itself in order to broaden its appeal. One proposed measure was the establishment of a school of arts and trades to train craftsmen; another was to extend the Union Society throughout the nation; and the last was to admit foreign craftsmen and non-artisan supporters such as Sanmiguel to the Society.[40]

The electioneering surrounding the selection of a constituent assembly for the State of Cundinamarca contributed to the Society's problems. The political machine created by Ramón Gómez after 1861, condemned by Camacho as corrupt and self-serving, had been temporarily overthrown along with Mosquera, allowing the opportunity for an important political change.[41] The Society proclaimed the elections to be a splendid opportunity to effect desperately needed reforms and urged that its members select progressive young men as representatives who could end sapista domination of the state.[42] (The clients of Gómez—"*el sapo*," the toad—were called *sapistas*.) Electoral slates formed by both Conservatives and Liberals included only one name in common, José Leocadio Camacho, evidence of either his political importance, or the parties' recognition of the need for artisan votes—or both.[43] The Conservative slate won the contest, polling about two-thirds of the 1,400 votes cast statewide; Camacho's vote total was second highest of the candidates.[44] In the constituent assembly, which rewrote the state's constitution, the artisan leader sat on the election committee. Elections were held later in the year for other state and national offices, including the governorship, which was won by Conservative Ignacio Gutiérrez Vergara, delaying Gómez's return to power. Numerous artisans were forwarded by two Conservative factions and the single Liberal slate, and Camacho was elected as an alternate to the national congress.[45]

Cruz Sánchez initiated steps to reorganize the Union Society in November. A gathering on November 18 redesigned the group's charter to reflect the proposals of August; membership was opened to non-artisans and emphasis on educational aspects of the group was increased. A general membership meeting on December 5, said to have been attended by over four-hundred artisans and their supporters, marked the formal reintegration of the Society.[46] Eight-hundred people approved the new charter in January 1868, when Saturnino González was chosen as the Society's president and Antonio Cárdenas as its vice-president.[47]

Both the Union Society and its paper presented a more aggressive character after its reincorporation. Camacho continued as one of the paper's editors, but he was now joined by Venezuelan-born printer Manuel de Jesús Barrera, whose editorial style added a new dimension to the paper. Moreover, outside writers, notably Manuel María Madiedo, now contributed to La Alianza on a regular basis. The Society's goals, a 10 percent tariff increase on competitive foreign goods, a reduction of state taxes on books used for public education, free schools for children of both sexes, and an end to the active political role of clerics, were proclaimed as it renewed its activity.[48] The worsening economic situation of the capital city was indiscriminately blamed on the expensive governmental apparatus, usurious capitalists, a lack of coinage, frequent wars, monopolist control of the capital's food supply, and floods of foreign imports.[49]

The Society petitioned the congress on March 14, 1868, for higher tariff rates. The request sought an increase of duties on competitive foreign merchandise and lowered tariffs on raw materials used in the production of national goods. Some 250 names were included on the petition, which supposedly represented 3,000 more in the Society's offices.[50] The Chamber of Representatives rejected the petition on April 3, 1868. The Society's paper related bitterly that three of its commissioners had presented their case with decorum and humility, in stark contrast to the disruption that had marked the submissions of previous petitions. It was clear to Camacho and Barrera, however, that the representatives had the same amount of respect for moderate behavior as they had for turbulence. As elections for new representatives were approaching, the Society reminded its members that only those people who had supported their appeal deserved artisan votes.[51]

Political activity stirred the city in anticipation of the May 1868 election for state legislators. The Society's board of directors presented a slate of Alianza candidates, which included both artisans and their supporters.[52] The Union Society faced organized competition for the artisan vote however, for in late March a group of about 150 men had reorganized the Democratic Society with Saavedra as president, *mosquerista* Eliseo Payán as vice-president, and Joaquín Calvo Mendivil as secretary.[53] The May 3, 1868, election revealed broad support for the mosqueristas, but the Conservative list did well also. Saavedra was elected to represent the barrio of Catedral, while Conservative printer Nicolás Pontón was chosen to represent the town of Mosquera. "El Sapo," Ramón Gómez, also returned to the state assembly. Camacho, who was listed in both Alianza and Conservative slates, drew sufficient votes to serve as an alternate. No other artisans were so honored and the independent Alianza slate drew only 114 votes.[54]

The fragile unity the Union Society had achieved in the months after its December reorganization collapsed in the wake of this electoral contest. Numerous members of the Society's board of directors, led by Rafael Tapias and Francisco Olaya, resigned in protest, alleging that the Society had abandoned its independent character to form an open political alignment with our "worst enemies." (The enemies were not named.) The protesters promised to return to the organization when it returned to its original path.[55] The establishment of a Popular Society in the Egipto barrio in June revealed the full depth of political divisions within the artisan class.[56] As expected, the Society strongly denounced the dissidents, claiming that it had always been politically oriented and, if it had changed, it was to become even more representative of the tradesmen's interests by ridding itself of influences such as that of Tapias, whom Calisto Ballesteros called a slave of "those who wanted to keep workers in obscurity."[57] The Society accused the men, especially Tapias, of having violated both the letter and the spirit of the organization and expelled them on May 21, 1868.[58]

Following these rifts is not an easy task, but they illustrate the difficulties of maintaining artisan solidarity in the face of partisan electoral pressures. The Democratic Society, with Saavedra and Payán as solid supporters of Mosquera, represented the political ambitions of the *caucano* general. The Popular Society, much less influential that the Democratic Society, did not include the names of artisan supporters, making its relationship to the craftsmen's political spectrum impossible to determine. The Union Society, if it had a political inclination, favored more independent members of the Conservative party. While a core of the Union Society's members remained true to their original non-partisan objectives, the organization itself underwent noticeable changes. These in part reflect the influences of Barrera and Madiedo, which suggests that Tapias's protest may have been at least partially valid insofar as Madiedo had used the pages of *La Alianza* to engage in several polemics.[59] Tradesmen's contributions were significantly more aggressive after the December reorganization as well however; Madiedo was not solely responsible for its more militant character. It is likely that the Union Society's experience, combined with the worsening economic situation, contributed to the new political stance. In short, the multiple currents that the Union Society sought to avoid engulfed it after May 1868. Many artisans continued their efforts to unify their class, but others seemed to think that their goals could only be reached by more direct support for Mosquera or the Conservatives. The only political faction that artisans did not support were the Radicals, the gólgota heirs who would dominate the nation's political machinery until the 1880s.

The Society's board of directors attempted reunification in July.[60] The directors officially protested preparations for war that were being undertaken in Cundinamarca and vowed that the Society would do all that it could to avoid civil conflict.[61] Unfortunately, the Society's fragmentation had not ended, for in early August, Cruz Sánchez criticized the same preparations for war as president of the Supreme Directive Body of the newly founded Union Society of Artisans. Sánchez apparently began this group in order to return to the non-partisan alignment professed by the original Union Soci-ety.[62] Initially, La Alianza praised the goals of what they referred to as the Supreme Society, observing that they were the same as its own. Soon, however, *La Alianza* informed its subscribers that cor-respondence was being sent to the wrong society because of the confusion between the names. The matter came to a head when, on August 24, 1868, Sánchez was expelled from the Union Society for not returning Society property, for violation of its constitution, and for founding an antagonistic group with the Society's second name.[63]

Signals of the approaching conflict in Cundinamarca led the Union Society to circulate a petition in which the tradesmen pledged their solidarity to prevent war and their unwillingness to serve as cannon fodder unless upper-class citizens were also called to service.[64] At the same time, Liberal artisans actively supported their party in anticipation of looming conflict.[65] The Union Society warned that principles were not being disputed, only "men, sal-aries, and power." The last issue of *La Alianza*, dated November 7, 1868, noted that it would resume publication when the crisis had passed. Three days later the Conservative state administration was overthrown by the Liberal federal authorities. There is no evidence of the Union Society's operations after that date.[66]

## Artisan Republicanism

Gareth Stedman Jones notes in his discussion of Chartism that "it was not consciousness (or ideology) that produced politics [in England], but politics that produced consciousness."[67] Colombian politics in the era of liberal reform produced artisan republicanism, a non-elite consciousness rarely documented in nineteenth-century Latin America. The phrase *artisan republicanism* comes from Sean Wilentz, who documents its changing character in New York City in the generations after the United States' independence. Wilentz comments that artisan republicanism "helped mold [craftsmen] as a social group and offered some real basis of solidarity between masters, small masters, and journeymen." Changing patterns of production, seen in the increasingly divided labor force, coupled with "the artisans' fight against political subordination," trans-formed the original character of that ideology by mid-century, lead-ing, in his assessment, to a working class ideology.[68] Economic, political, and social experiences produced artisan consciousness that sustained their ideology.

The ideology articulated by bogotano artisans in the late 1860s drew deeply from experiences in the years since independence. Craftsmen perceived that their shared values and common interests emanated from their function as skilled and often independent laborers. Many artisans expressed the opinion that although the rich of society did not appreciate the artisans' social role, craftsmen felt a pride *de ser artesano* (in being artisans) and strove to protect their social positions. However, the path of economic development chosen by government leaders since the 1840s had allowed foreign products to undermine the once-protected niche of the craftsmen, a threat that stimulated their political mobilizations. Political involvement during the reform period had produced the widely held sentiment that partisan politics were exploitive and not in the best interests of craftsmen. Political strife, especially the recent civil war, had evoked deep hostilities against the senseless sacrifices that artisans and others had been forced to make. Together, these factors created an artisan class with a clearly formulated ideology. The ideology is visible in most documents presented by craftsmen to the public or to political functionaries during the reform period, although it is most clearly articulated in the pages of *La Alianza*. Numerous artisans contributed to the elaboration of this ideology, which was both idealist—with clear notions of the proper function of society and government—and critical of current practices.[69]

The concept of an ideal republic—the nation—constituted the heart of artisan republicanism. The ideal republic, for José Leocadio Camacho, consisted of a collective social organism in which symbiotic elements acted together for the good of the whole. Thomist conceptions of a universalist, corporatist state clearly shape this notion, although it lacks the cohesive role of the church.[70] Instead, social elements and citizens served to keep the nation in balance. A nation contained no distinctions of nobility or inferiority, because all persons shared equal virtue at birth. After birth, stratifications developed in response to positive social contributions—such as virtuous work—or negative manipulations—such as force of arms or bossism (*gamonalismo*).[71]

Craftsmen developed the concept of the nation from their own vision of a just society, which was composed of congruous social elements, foremost being the producers and consumers. The artisan position within the nation came from the work that was central to any society. Luciano Rivera alleged that craftsmen constituted the industrial and artistic core of society. A harmonious nation, however, could be tainted. While artisans, according to Rivera, were dedicated to honest work, the fruit of their labor was enjoyed by "self-centered" and "inhumane" wealthy persons.[72] Work and production were positive social contributions; those who consumed without producing drained society and violated the curse God laid upon Adam. The Union Society's editors did not limit their definition of producers to manual laborers, however; they also included merchants, lawyers, and farmers, all of whom contributed to the productive process. Camacho illustrated the "proper" function of property in his allegation that workers produced by their labor and skills, while consumers caused capital to circulate. Camacho claimed that the poor worker had the obligation to work and produce, while the rich should consume and stimulate the arts. Together, when property's social function was fulfilled, neither the rich nor the poor abused their role; a balance then existed between producers and consumers. (Camacho lamented that such was not the case in Colombia.)[73] La Alianza, as a union of producers, was for Ramón Jiménez the route to the creation of this ideal republic.[74]

Republican social well-being required a moral foundation. Moral restraint bridled the passion of absolute liberty, contributing to self-control and virtuous behavior. Human shortcomings necessitated religious guidance, but republican society required freedom of intellectual expression unbound by a moralizing church. A good republican society, according to *La Alianza*, balanced moral and intellectual forces, curbing moral fanatics who denied others' rights while avoiding the vain scientificism of unrestrained rationalist expressions.[75] Together, love of God and love of humanity produced *sociabilidad*, the proper basis of society.[76]

The family and educational institutions diffused these principles through society. Children learned morality and traditions, as well as the craft by which they contributed to society, in the family. One craftsman related that the father instructed children in proper morals and the knowledge of traditions, and also made sure that they learned a craft, so as to ensure their independence.[77] Camacho added that teaching proper social conduct was the responsibility of the mother.[78] Education assisted the family in teaching citizens to distinguish between crime and virtue and in fostering an awareness of their rights.[79] Various craftsmen wrote that good citizens needed both moral and intellectual training, although the former was absent under the present system of government. Mariano González alleged that the current system of education served only to perpetuate the position of the wealthy and to prepare them for the political struggle.[80]

The interests of the nation could only be served by a republican form of government. In order for the social contract to function in a republic, government should be properly elected, be representative, and alternate the parties in power. Ambrosio López, a veteran of twenty years of political activities on the behalf of craftsmen, wrote that the people were obligated to delegate much of their individual liberty to the government so that it might govern for the nation; they should support the government by taxes, labor, and, if necessary, blood. In return, citizens should expect peace and order, and a government that respected law, safeguarded property, provided instruction, and protected the nation. Civic instruction, in López's mind, fostered the republican spirit and protection extended to industry. For López, the social contract was complete when both nation and government fulfilled their respective obligations.[81]

Artisans judged that several changes in governmental policy were essential for the desired republic to become a reality. Free, popular education was needed to sustain both freedom and "popular sovereignty"; technical training would support the improvement of arts and social independence.[82] While republicanism, for the craftsmen, demanded that citizens pay taxes so that the government could forward the interests of the nation, Camacho wrote that the existing tax structure of the federal, state, and district governments demanded a heavy tax burden, but none of the government bodies looked after the nation's interests. Taxes upon sales, shops, and production helped to decimate industry, which Camacho saw as the backbone of the nation. For him, and for Felipe Roa Ramírez, several changes would improve the situation: sponsorship of immigration of skilled craftsmen, government-protected industries and training programs, expositions to honor native arts, rigorous suppression of contraband, and the removal of direct taxes upon the consumer. And, fundamentally, free trade, the "crude and open war against workers of the country," had to be abandoned in favor of industrial protection.[83]

Leaders of the Sociedad Unión found the never-ending struggle between the Conservative and Liberal parties to be the government's most grievous shortcoming. The Union Society's desire to avoid the multiple ramifications of partisan manipulations was a logical sentiment for men who had come to political maturity within the context of the Democratic and Popular Societies. According to the Union's ideology, parties should represent the various interests of the nation in its fullest collective extension. However, both parties fought for power and control of the government's treasury so as to enrich themselves at the public's expense. Political bosses sought the support of the people only at election time or their arms in times of conflict. These manipulations led one writer to refer to parties as a "social gangrene" that permeated the judicial and legislative process, thus obstructing justice and good laws. The alternative to these incessant struggles was genuine bipartisanism, a system whereby the parties regularly alternated in power, a solution proposed by Felipe S. Ojuela and others that antedated the twentieth-century's national front by ninety years.[84]

The newly created federalist structure of the national government attracted the criticism of various authors. Agustín Novoa argued that Bogotá suffered from the burden of three governments—district, state, and federal—and yet had gained no profits from decentralization. He thought that a return to centralism would end regional conflict and would create a government that worked for the nation. The federal congressmen, Ambrosio López observed, met yearly, collected their salaries, and did nothing positive. Camacho proposed that if a federal structure were to be maintained, congress should meet once every six years, see to the needs of the government (including electing a president who would also serve for six years), and then retire.[85]

Partisan struggles caused, in the opinion of the editors of *La Alianza*, the civil strife for which craftsmen and the poor had paid so dearly. Artisan republicanism accepted the obligation of citizens to defend the country, but not to sacrifice their lives or property in partisan struggles. Craftsmen made up a disproportionate percentage of the Army and the Guard, services that were supposed to be voluntary. However, the authors claimed that artisans and the poor were forcibly recruited, while the rich could pay to avoid service. Camacho, nevertheless, reminded his readers that all social sectors suffered from war; the poor and workers died in battle or lost their jobs, while the wealthy lost their capital to forced loans, in addition to their crops, businesses, credit, equipment, and animals.[86]

Craftsmen in the Union Society of Artisans were not only exceptional critics of the liberal reform governments, they anticipated many of the changes undertaken by the Regeneration governments of the 1880s and 1890s. Laissez-faire individual conduct or government policies were, according to the ideology of artisan republicanism, socially irresponsible. Insofar as nations were conceptualized as social entities, a government that cared for a nation's well-being required attention to the needs of its component parts, a system of education that nurtured the whole (with religious influences), and a centralized political organism. Craftsmen understandably emphasized their own industrial concerns, which, for them, were justified at the national level because of the central role of producers to society. Many of these same ideas are visible in the Regeneration's restoration of the church as the foundation to Colombian society, the return to centralism, and the government's support for economic development, though clearly not from the same ideological orientation as that of the artisans.

It is important to consider how the artisan republicanism of 1860s Bogotá compares to the ideologies of other Latin American craftsmen in the same period. Numerous students of labor history posit that productive function is a determining factor in the definition of ideology, a hypothesis that can be tested by the examination of comparable producers in different settings. Or, as others would maintain, do distinct social, economic, and political environments create distinct ideologies? Put in the language of a recent scholarly exchange, does structure or experience serve as the dominant molder of the history of artisans?[87] Unfortunately, the resolution of these questions is hindered by a lack of scholarly inquiry more than by the absence/presence of other artisan ideologies.[88] Whereas labor historians have delved deeply into the thought and behavior of twentieth-century workers, sustained examination of nineteenth-century craftsmen is limited. Still, the questions cannot be begged.

Artisans in other areas of Latin America reacted forcefully against many of the liberal reforms. In Peru, artisans rallied in the late 1840s against the liberalization of tariff laws and then took full advantage of political liberalism to become an electoral force in the 1850s. Both tendencies were blunted however, driving craftsmen to direct action against imported goods in late 1858, by which time political doors had been shut as well. In Peru, as in Colombia, concerted action against economic liberalism resulted in economic defeat and a narrowed range of political expression.[89] Similarly, Chilean artisans protested economic liberalization, while, at the same time, they found themselves being used as political puppets by elite parties.[90] In these and other countries, evidence suggests that alternate ideologies sought to counter the dominant liberal mode.

## Conclusion

The political activity of artisans in the 1860s shared many features with that of earlier years, but it also had several significant differences. The most important similarity was the continued appeal to and use of tradesmen by political parties in their pursuit of power. This was clear after the defeat of Melo, when gólgotas quickly forgot their differences with melistas and draconianos in order to rebuild the Liberal party to counter Conservative strengths. Artisans, by their positions as losers in the Melo coup, were unable to assert their objectives autonomously within the reunited Liberal party, but their potential power was evidenced by the tenacity with which gólgotas pursued them. Orthodox Conservatives, the obvious beneficiaries from universal manhood suffrage, saw less need to pursue the artisan vote, and made fewer appeals to tradesmen. The civil war of 1859–62 had momentous consequences for bogotano artisans. The war reinforced a feeling of political exploitation among craftsmen, as once again they were used as cannon fodder, only to be forgotten when the battles ended. Moreover, anti-clerical decrees alienated many tradesmen, who felt that the church's capacity to fulfill its social responsibilities were crippled by Mosquera and his followers, and that their ability to live a good Catholic life was threatened.

The postwar economic depression compounded the negative effects of the war. Artisans suffered not only from economic disruption because of the war, but also because the earlier reforms were affecting the bogotano marketplace in a much more significant fashion than in the 1850s. Lowered transportation costs, along with reduced tariffs, caused economic dislocation in many trades. These factors, combined with the effects of war, resulted in economic misery at all social levels, but perhaps was worst in the artisan sector. The impact of economic dislocation upon artisan mobilization in the 1860s had its parallel in the 1840s. Just as the credit crisis after the War of the Supremes and plans for reduced tariff rates acted as the stimulus for the founding of the Society of Artisans, so too did economic crisis spur organizational efforts in the 1860s.

In the face of economic misery, wartime abuses, and political disillusionment, artisan political activity underwent a major change. The Sociedad Unión represented a far more independent and mature political movement than had any previous artisan organization. Earlier groups had shared many of its aspirations, but none synthesized artisan interests into a clearly expressed ideology. The Union Society sought to reject the system that used tradesmen as both political and economic tools, and tried instead to assert both the value and potential power of united artisans within the political process. Its eventual failure does not belie the importance of the sentiments expressed within the Union Society. The socioeconomic system that had isolated craft production was now on the wane; artisans fought with increasing desperation as the political economy of liberalism gained potency. In the years that followed the disintegration of the Society, the decreased need of the parties to mobilize artisan voters and the fragmentation of the artisan class combined to create a very different environment in which tradesmen expressed their interests.

# FIVE

# MUTUAL AID, PUBLIC VIOLENCE, AND THE REGENERATION

T HE SO-CALLED RADICAL OLYMPUS ESTABLISHED IN 1863 BEGAN to collapse from the start. Obandista, mosquerista, and Radical cooperation did not survive the civil war. The federalist system of the Constitutions of 1858 and 1863 ensured that the increasingly divided partisan camps would engender near-constant military struggles. Shifting partisan alliances fostered endemic conflict, including major civil wars in 1876–77 and 1884–85. These alliances culminated in an Independent Liberal/Conservative coalition that spawned the Regeneration government of Rafael Núñez in 1886. The Constitution of 1886 strengthened the Colombian state and restored a centralist system of government to the country, with a strong executive, and numerous other "conservative" changes, notably a formal recognition of the Catholic church's role in Colombian society. Yet, the new government could not halt partisan violence, which included the War of the 1000 Days (1899–1902), the worst civil war of the century.

Economic conditions were equally unstable. The national economy recovered only slowly from the 1859–62 civil war. The collapse of tobacco prices in the 1870s left the government with serious fiscal problems. Export diversification sparked some hope that the policy trajectories of the liberal period might prove appropriate, but neither quina (from which quinine was extracted) nor indigo nor coffee seemed able to support a stable export economy.

Various presidents who had earlier supported the "dejad hacer" (laissez-faire) school now experimented with interventionist policies, though with little success. The Regeneration government, by contrast, assumed a decidedly interventionist stance in the realm of political economy. Again, the success of the Regeneration in sponsoring economic development was notable only in the long term.

A variety of craftsmen's organizations gave evidence of the increased differentiation of the artisan class in the last thirty years of the nineteenth century. Mutual aid societies, representing the efforts of artisan elites to look after their own material and social welfare, appeared in the early 1870s. Other artisans were left largely to their own fortunes, which, during periods of economic stress, contributed to outbursts of direct action in anger at socioeconomic injustices. In the political arena, the pre-election mobilizations that had been widespread in the reform era continued, but even these became less frequent as the years passed. Absent completely were large organizations such as the Union Society, which required a cohesive artisan class. This transitionary period saw old patterns of mobilization characteristic of a more homogeneous artisan experience give way to public expressions of a fractured and divided artisan class.

## The Industrial Society of Artisans

The Sociedad Industrial de Artesanos (Industrial Society of Artisans) promptly filled the institutional vacuum created by the collapse of the Union Society.[1] The Industrial Society sought the non-political objectives of the Sociedad Unión, including industrial education, efforts to bring new technology to the country, and government support for industries.[2] Many of the Union's activists, including Ambrosio López, Felipe Roa Ramírez, Fruto Ramírez, Rafael Tapias, and Ramón Ordóñez Torres—now the directors of the Industrial Society—had previously been alienated from one another by political issues, but had few qualms about cooperating in pursuit of goals that would enhance their economic positions.

The Industrial Society operated during the presidential administration of Eustorgio Salgar (1870–72), who undertook the first steps toward an interventionist policy on the behalf of industrial development, measures normally associated with the regimes of Núñez.

Indeed, as Helen Delpar points out, few Radicals, least of all Salgar and his successor, Manuel Murillo Toro, continued to support the economic liberalism of the 1850s and 1860s. In many regards, the pro-industrial policies of the Regeneration germinated in these administrations.[3]

These patterns became apparent as Luis B. Valenzuela criticized public officials in 1870 for their seeming lack of concern for the nation's poor industrial condition. The Sociedad Industrial seconded this allegation and pledged to pressure public officials to support industrial development. Representatives of the Society met with newly elected President Salgar in April of that year.[4] Society spokesman Rafael Tapias reminded the president of the craftsmen's repeated petitions for tariff protection, urging that he take steps to redress the plight of the country's industrial classes. Salgar reportedly told the craftsmen that he would do what he could to bring about better industrial conditions, a promise kept in part when the government announced plans for an industrial exposition, which Tapias claimed to be a result of the Society's pressures.[5] The Society urged craftsmen to prepare pieces for display.[6]

Reactions by local craftsmen to the invitation were not uniformly positive. An open letter by "many artisans" suggested that systematic government protection would have been better than periodic prizes for good craftsmanship. It pointed out that the exhibition was intended primarily for producers of agricultural exports and not tradesmen, who could not afford the time required to prepare an exhibit. Moreover, the craftsmen alleged that many of the sponsors of the exhibition were personally guilty of seeking low costs rather than high quality when they made purchases locally, a practice that rewarded "semi-artisans" and not skilled craftsmen.[7]

The Salgar administration helped establish an institute for artisan industrial education, a project that later matured under the Regeneration. The National University's Instituto de Artes i Oficios opened in March 1872, with Salgar present. The Institute offered classes in geometry and chemistry, which some artisans thought should be supplemented with desperately needed industrial training. Seven hundred persons received various types of education in the next three years, even while protests were raised in favor of more practical training: "it is necessary to found model shops, a machine gallery, and an industrial museum."[8] An 1872 petition suggested that Colombian workers wanted to improve their skills but simply lacked the opportunity, and that foreign engineers and masters should be brought to Colombia from Europe to train native craftsmen, a move they claimed would improve not only industry but also public order.[9]

President Murillo followed Salgar's interventionist footsteps by ordering the establishment of a school of arts and trades in 1874. Such a school was not, however, established until the Núñez administration, when two executive decrees enabled several Colombian craftsmen to train with European masters. These craftsmen were, according to the original plan, then to train Colombians in three model shops,[10] although only one was ever established. Several craftsmen, including José Leocadio Camacho, selected five youths to be trained abroad in industrial arts.[11] The School of Arts and Trades, an outgrowth of these programs, began operation in 1891. Six years later the school had exposed 621 students to various sorts of industrial training.[12] President Rafael Reyes extended this program throughout the nation between 1905 and 1908, but his focus was geared more toward general education than industrial training.

Murillo's meeting with a commission from the Sociedad Industrial produced markedly different results than had Salgar's. The Society's spokesman, Felipe S. Orjuela, an ex-Alianza member, presented the craftsmen's wishes for active governmental support, commenting favorably upon Murillo's intention to provide credit for industrial ventures. (Murillo had proposed the reduction of the nation's debt burden by recognizing the real value of government bonds as opposed to their nominal value, with the balance to support industrial projects—such as railroad development.) Murillo saluted the Society's acceptance of his plan, noting that the high cost of capital was indeed hurting the country's laborers. The president then sparked a heated public debate by relating that many Colombian capitalists had proven unwilling to invest in industrial development, thus forcing the government to take up the slack.[13]

This policy departed markedly from Murillo's earlier attitudes. Murillo, like his gólgota counterparts of the 1850s, had believed that the power of the market, especially the agro-export sector, could sustain the nation's economy. Murillo now supported the construction of the Railroad of the North to enhance regional development, especially that of Santander.[14] *El Tradicionista*, founded by Conservative Miguel Antonio Caro, expressed outrage at Murillo's comments. The paper charged that the changed credit rules were economically unprincipled and smacked of "socialist" economic policies. Moreover, according to Caro, Murillo's pro-labor stance allegedly sponsored "class antagonisms" comparable to those of the 1850s.[15] The Industrial Society denied that it had espoused "socialism" in its meeting with the president, while it maintained its public support for the president, especially his plans to push completion of the Railroad of the North, because it would expand the nation's commercial network.[16]

Even while the Industrial Society seems to have become an important agency in support of governmental industrial policies, it disappeared from public view in 1872. The reasons for this are unclear. Many of the group's members soon became prominent in various mutual aid societies, the first of which was formed shortly after the April encounter with Murillo, which suggests a transfer of organizational energies to the new group. The Society's role in the shift in Radical industrial policy, in any case, merits recognition, especially in light of the artisan relationship with the Regeneration administration.

## Mutual Aid Societies

Latin American mutual aid societies are not well studied. Moreover, historians' assessments of these widespread organizations vary widely. Gerald Greenfield and Sheldon Maram, in their authoritative *Latin American Labor Organizations*, relate that nineteenth-century mutualist groups paralleled earlier craft bodies that "provided social and cultural benefits for their members." They did not, however, have a "strong sense of class consciousness vis-à-vis either capitalists or the state, nor did they express a sense of solidarity with a more broadly viewed working class."[17] Charles Bergquist offers a somewhat more sympathetic view, especially insofar as members of mutual aid societies "learned" how to protect themselves "from natural and man-made forces beyond their control." Bergquist, though, downplays the valuable role of artisans in Chilean mutual aid societies, suggesting that wage laborers brought class consciousness to them.[18] While many historians cite mutual aid societies as some of the initial mobilizations of wage laborers,[19] most tend to dismiss mutual aid groups as relatively unimportant, often linking them to church social welfare programs or elite political movements with little worker autonomy.[20]

While these are meritorious positions, much of the literature on mutual aid bodies fails to appreciate the collective efforts of craftsmen and others to provide security in the midst of changing economic and social conditions through mutual aid organizations.[21] Mutual aid societies helped artisans, immigrants, urban wage laborers, and lower- and middle-sector persons to look after interests of crucial importance to their collective welfare. Almost all such institutions collected funds to help members in times of sickness and to help with burial expenses. Many undertook educational endeavors or sponsored lecture series. A *caja de ahorros* (savings bank) was a common mechanism to assist members.[22] While mutual aid societies only seldom entered the political arena, which most likely accounts for the lack of scholarly attention to such societies, their social functions merit serious examination.

In most instances, artisans formed the nuclei of the earliest mutual aid societies. In Mexico City, for which a healthy literature exists, artisans developed mutualist organizations as trades proved unable to fully satisfy accustomed social security, especially in the years after 1850. Although many historians focus upon the anarchist-influenced mutualist societies of this period, most organizations had no such relations.[23] Instead, "the proliferation of artisan societies was the manner by which [artisans] confronted the process of pauperization and demoralization."[24] Throughout Latin America, mutual aid organizations first appeared in the 1850s, 60s, and 70s, suggesting that craftsmen relied upon their own initiatives to protect themselves from the decline of their industries as external economic forces more directly affected national economies, a not unexpected outcome given the self-reliance of that social sector.

Quite important, the founders of mutual aid societies were usually more successful craftsmen, the *dueños del taller*. The abolition of guilds in the early national period had ended the formal relationships among masters, journeymen, and apprentices, which, when coupled with the economic stress of the years that followed, increased the social and economic differences between these levels of artisanal workers. Non–shop-owning craftsmen slipped more quickly into a semi-proletarian status, whereas shop owners could survive as independent craftsmen for a much longer period.[25] Masters established mutual aid societies to preserve as much of their welfare as possible; non-masters, as will be shown, found other avenues of expression.

Bogotá's first mutual aid society, La Sociedad de Socorros Mutuos (The Mutual Aid Society), was formally inaugurated on July 20, 1872, when eighty-three men, most of them artisan notables identified with the Conservative party, pledged to cooperate for their collective benefit. The organization aimed to help members in case of illness or death. From the two-peso entrance fee and ten-centavo weekly dues, as well as special donations, the Society built an initial savings account of two-thousand pesos. In addition to needing fiscal responsibility, each potential member had to be approved by the Society as being of sound moral character. The Mutual Aid Society was not exclusively intended for artisans: about one-half of its 148 members two years later earned their living from other than a skilled trade, and included merchants, lawyers, and musicians.[26] Although non-artisans held important positions within these bodies, they increasingly concerned themselves with labor issues. Speeches by members extolled the virtue of work, the need for protection of Colombian industry, and the contributions of artisans to Bogotá's society.[27]

The Mutual Aid Society served as a model for similar groups. Sixty-nine men founded a Sociedad Tipográfica de Mutua Protección (Typesetters' Mutual Protection Society) in 1873 with the objectives of mutual aid, self-improvement, and the enhancement of the typographic art. The moral improvement of its members was emphasized in its initial report: "We ought to be aware that our mission is not limited simply to being mechanical workers who produce in order to satisfy the dietary needs of ourselves and our families; we recognize the necessity of nurturing our spirit, mainly by cultivating and developing our intellectual faculties, because this will yield the most positive benefits for our association and will affect our social position."[28] The positive moral behavior required of members speaks of the artisan self-image, and was a characteristic present in most descriptions craftsmen made of themselves.

Mutual aid societies were the most stable organizations in which artisans participated throughout the latter years of the century. Two of the more important mutual aid groups, the Mutual Aid Society and the Sociedad Filantrópica (Philanthropic Society, founded in 1879) merged in January 1889 so as to provide better services to their more than three-hundred members, who had capital estimated at over eleven-thousand pesos.[29] The Sociedad de Seguros de Familia (Family Insurance Society), an offshoot of the Mutual Aid Society, was established one year later to extend financial aid to the families of mutual aid members.[30] A Tailors' Society was founded in September 1899 with the assistance of the Typesetters' Society and a Shoemaker's Society the following month.[31] Such organizational strength, which emanated from an alliance of more elite craftsmen and their social peers, while generally apolitical, could occasionally serve as the basis for surprisingly radical action.

## Urban Violence

Artisans participated in two major outbursts of urban violence, one in 1875 and the other in 1893, that link socioeconomic stress with partisan politics. Insofar as the riots depart from more common forms of expression in nineteenth-century Bogotá, their explanation is required. The answer is related to the absence of broadly based artisan mobilizations comparable to the Democratic or Union Societies, through which numerous craftsmen could find political expression. In the score of years after the War of the Supremes, political parties came into their own as institutional entities. Electoral mobilizations were quite important during these years for the parties' ability to turn out voters, including artisans, on election day. By the 1870s, however, parties had developed permanent directories that made these groups less essential. Individuals by this time identified themselves with a particular party not only on the basis of contemporary appeals, but also on the basis of familial traditions. Also, as suggested earlier, the artisan class had remained fairly homogeneous through the 1860s, which made the mobilization of large numbers of craftsmen possible. After the crisis of the 1860s, social distances between craftsmen increased and some leaders lost touch with the mass of artisans. Prominent craftsmen organized in more exclusive mutual aid societies, leaving the artisan rank-and-file with few political outlets. Direct action, or urban violence, a new form of political expression, reflected the divisions of the class more than its unity.

The first of these tumults, the *pan de a cuarto* riot (quarter-peso bread riot) of January 1875, developed after a coalition of bakers combined with Joaquín Sarmiento, the city's most powerful miller, to drive up the price of wheat flour and bread by over 20 percent. While wheat bread served only to supplement the corn-based *arepas* consumed by most individuals, it was nevertheless an important part of the popular diet, especially in the smaller loaves used with meals or snacks.[32] Equally as important, the combinations symbolized monopolistic behavior, which contradicted many people's notions of proper economic practices. Early in 1875, the same bakers ceased production of lesser quality loaves that sold four for two-and-one-half centavos, a move that caused hardship and unrest among the popular sectors of the city.[33]

Partisan groups sought to take advantage of tense social conditions for their own political purposes. It appears that university-level Radical Liberal students dissatisfied with the moderate Liberal state government distributed a poster on January 22 demanding "War and death to those who make us hungry!"[34] The poster called the pueblo to demonstrate against the injustice the following day, a cry that drew thousands to the Plaza de Bolívar. The crowd soon moved from the plaza to the nearby residence of President Santiago Pérez, who listened to their demands of government action against the *panaderos* (bakers), only to dispassionately reply that such actions would be illegal in a country with free industry. Angered at his refusal to take action, the crowd stoned more than thirty shops and houses of the offending monopolists. Injuries in the riot were limited, but several properties suffered heavy damages. Shortly thereafter, the price of wheat and bread began to drift downward.[35] In the wake of the riot, bakers insisted that high flour prices had forced the prices up—not their purposeful collusion.[36]

The fundamental causes of the riot lie in societal reactions to the reformulation of the city and nation's economy. The price of flour and bread had been regulated by the government in colonial times, a policy abandoned with the establishment of an independent government shaped by liberal theories of political economy. However the laws might have changed, the demand that the president intervene to lower prices suggests that support for the old system, which was akin to a "moral economy," persisted in the popular mind.[37] The pan de a cuarto riot questioned the legitimacy of the ideology of liberalism. Indeed, the unorthodox editor and political commentator Manuel María Madiedo noted at the time: "Economic and social harmony are nothing more than the old question of rich and poor. . . . It is an error of belief that this can be put in equilibrium by 'free trade'; because between the poor that *live by the day* and the rich that *can live years without working, free trade* always hurts the one in need."[38]

The partisan manipulation of popular passions expressed in the bread crisis reveals much of the character of nineteenth-century Colombian politics. Both factions of the Liberal party, the Radicals and the Independents, sought to use the riot for their own purposes in anticipation of the year's presidential election. Liberal supporters of Aquileo Parra and local university students attempted to draw the city's influential artisan sector into the debate over the riot's causes by invoking the memory of the Democratic Society and its stand against economic exploitation of craftsmen. This tactic was intended to draw craftsmen away from Núñez and perhaps to forestall collusion between the leading Independents and Conservatives. This move failed when craftsmen of all political orientations, including José María Vega, Práxedes Bermúdez, José Antonio Saavedra, and José Leocadio Camacho, issued two public declarations. Both letters expressed their sympathy for those suffering in the current crisis and criticized individuals who would exploit it to their own ends in the name of artisans, while at the same time they condemned the monopolistic practices of the bakers.[39]

Although no comparable unrest took place in the 1880s, standards of living for many bogotanos began to decline toward the end of the decade, in part due to the fiscal policies of the Regeneration.[40] Pressures on wages resulted in widespread complaints about high prices and rents.[41] In this context, José Ignacio Gutiérrez Isaza penned a series of articles in late 1892 that attacked the moral habits of the capital's working classes. Gutiérrez singled out artisans as particularly notorious in their misuse of alcohol and for that vice's deteriorative effect upon familial well-being.[42] Artisans of the Philanthropic Society, the "elite" of their class, protested the account as slanderous and thereby contrary to the 1888 press law, which prohibited inciting one class against another. The Society, on a resolution offered by José Leocadio Camacho, insisted that Gutiérrez retract his allegations and that the government castigate the author. Neither demand was met. These protests led to verbal attacks by workers upon Gutiérrez in the streets, insults that escalated into a violent confrontation in front of Gutiérrez's house on January 15, 1893, between police and a crowd made up of artisans and workers. The police arrested numerous protesters before high-ranking government officials successfully calmed the crowd.

The riot erupted the next day. A delegation of artisan leaders appealed to acting head of state General Antonio B. Cuervo to release those protesters arrested the previous night and to impose the press law against Gutiérrez. Cuervo refused. Incensed at the government's unwillingness to enforce its own laws, many in the crowd reassembled at Gutiérrez's house, which was now defended by a large contingent of police. The guard fired upon the people, killing at least one craftsman. Similar confrontations then broke out throughout the city. In the hours that followed, the mob attacked all but one police station in Bogotá. Many stations were ransacked, with police archives the primary targets. The homes of several government officials also came under attack, as did the women's prison, where some two-hundred women accused of prostitution were liberated. Cuervo imposed a state of siege and called out the regular army, which restored order by mass arrests of persons caught on the streets. The police and Army detained an estimated five-hundred people. Some forty to forty-five people were killed and an unknown number injured in the tumult.[43]

The causes of the riot are complex. The dramatic increase in food prices and rents undoubtedly aggravated social tensions, but the crowd did not attack facilities associated with foodstuffs as it had in 1875. Instead, the mob first focused its fury upon the offending author. Gutiérrez's slander of the city's artisan class had touched a fragile nerve among craftsmen who were under increasing pressures from foreign imports and other forms of economic change that together helped to undermine their productive and social status. The protest by artisans and the mutual aid societies represented their attempt to defend the heretofore positive public image of the craftsmen. Quite important, the apparent approval given by elite artisans in the Mutual Aid Society to other workers and "popular" sectors to apply pressure on Gutiérrez opened the way for other tensions to be vented.

The crowd's anger against the city police originated in the effort of the Regeneration government to reorganize the police force. Several years earlier steps had been taken to "professionalize" Bogotá's police force by the importation of a French agent to supervise and oversee the reorganization of the corps of police. Juan María Marcelino Gilibert not only had personally alienated many in the capital for his seeming inability (or lack of desire) to understand bogotano ways, but also his measures more significantly had redefined the relationship between the capital's populace and the police. Traditional patrolling patterns were disrupted (with the introduction of uniformed, armed officers), a crackdown on downtown street crime and prostitution was begun (activities that had previously gone relatively undisturbed), and policemen were recruited from outside the city (which tended to separate the police's and the people's social experiences), all in the effort to instill Gilibert's own vision of proper urban order.[44] The 1893 *bogotazo* was most fundamentally a reaction to this reform of the police department, set in motion by the apparent sanction of direct action by influential artisans and based in the city's unsettled economic and political conditions.

The government not only made numerous arrests during and shortly after the riot, it also suppressed the Philanthropic Society as having instigated the tumult. Camacho protested the government's decree, saying that it was ill-founded. He petitioned Vice-President Caro to allow the Society to resume its meetings. The petition was approved, but only when permission to meet was obtained in advance and, even then, a representative of the police had to be present to monitor any "subversive" discussions.[45]

In April 1893, after martial law had been lifted and calm had returned to the city, the carpenter Félix Valois Madero founded *El Artesano* in an attempt to improve the tarnished image of the artisan class. Valois Madero filled the pages of his paper with articles pertaining to craftsmen, on such topics as the Model Shop and the artisan's right to determine his own hours of work. *El Artesano* was combative, engaging in polemics with Miguel Samper and Carlos Holguín, and with other papers. Its central thrust was political unification of the artisans to create "compact workers' guilds . . . [as] the life of industry, of progress, of national wealth, and of politics."[46]

During the eleven months after Valois Madero began publication of the paper, he emerged as one of the most visible figures of the artisan class. It is questionable, however, that the artisan public image improved as he had hoped. In March 1894, police informants told authorities of a workers' conspiracy to overthrow the government; on March 11, Madero and numerous others were arrested on that charge.[47] In the shop of Bernadino Ranjel, agents reportedly found some six-thousand leaflets with the slogans "Viva el trabajo," "Viva el pueblo," and "Abajo los monopolios" ("Up with work," "Long live the people," Down with monopolies"). At the same time, in Facatativá, authorities confiscated some five-hundred rifles and ammunition to match. Many of those arrested, including Madero, were tried under the Law of the Horses, found guilty of planning a movement of an unspecified nature against the government, and sentenced to several months' imprisonment. For the rest of the decade, the government's fear of conspiracy resulted in close supervision of all organizations that offered the potential base for collective action.

## Local, State, and National Politics

National politics tended to take a back seat to state and local politics under the Constitution of 1863. Artisan electoral organizations operated within a distinct environment that favored their participation in local and state politics, but less frequently in national campaigns. Most city councils after the 1859–62 civil war included at least one elected artisan member, a pattern that continued well into the twentieth century. As we have seen, José Antonio Saavedra, a cobbler whose political career dated from the days of the Sociedad Democrática, was often part of the Liberal party's council slate; José Leocadio Camacho served as his Conservative counterpart. Craftsmen also took part in other municipal services. Antonio Cárdenas, one of the founders of La Alianza, served as supervisor of the city's marketplace in 1870, and Calisto Ballesteros, also active in La Alianza, collected taxes for three years.[48] Artisans frequently served as night watchmen (*serenos*), and, in a reorganization of Bogotá's police force early in 1870, both Emeterio Heredia and Ambrosio López, longtime artisan notables, were among the craftsmen called upon to watch the blocks where they lived. The reorganization in question was followed by citizen complaints of arbitrary police conduct, which forced the council to name a commission to investigate the charges and (while it was at it) to look into allegations of fraudulent tax collections. Artisan Tiburcio Ruiz, who would become president of the resurrected Democratic Society in 1875, was one of the men named to the commission.[49]

The presence of tradesmen on the city council in no way assured an adequate response to the city's needs. Repeated complaints centered on garbage-filled streets, poor water service, high taxes, and high food prices. Citizens expressed the opinion that monopolists periodically cornered a particular item in the city market and drove up its price, calling on the council not only to stop such monopolies but also to put a ceiling on prices. As the decade of the 1870s wore on, complaints by citizens increased, leading to a reform of the council by Cundinamarca's state legislature, which paved the way for more effective city government in the 1880s.[50]

Artisan political support was not solicited during the presidential election of 1869, a somewhat surprising turn of events given the heated competition for their votes in earlier years. The low profile of craftsmen was even more unusual given that many of the same actors and political forces that had earlier been closely associated with artisan mobilizations were involved in the 1869 contest. Radical Liberal Eustorgio Salgar won the election despite an alliance (liga) between mosqueristas and Conservatives in favor of the exiled General Mosquera. Quite significantly, the liga, which was engineered by Conservative Carlos Holguín, signalled both an era of cooperation between dissident Liberals and Conservatives and the continued inability of the Liberal party to heal its divisions.

State elections, which during the early 1870s often decided whether the sapo forces of Ramón Gómez would control the state government of Cundinamarca, often resulted in violent confrontations. Sapista candidates won the 1870 state elections amid widespread allegations of fraud. Passions were so elevated that when the Cundinamarcan congress was seated, numerous disturbances marred its sessions, leading in the end to a coup that unseated Governor Justo Briceño in favor of anti-sapo Cornelio Manrique. Various artisans were presented as candidates for the resulting constitutional convention by newspaper editor Manuel María Madiedo, including Manuel de Jesús Barrera, José Leocadio Camacho, Felipe Roa Ramírez, and Rafael Tapias, indicating that the political relations forged in the Sociedad Unión persisted for some time.[51] Artisans of all political persuasions praised the coup but warned against threats to the public order that could result in their call-up to militia service.[52] Allegations of fraud also marred the May 1874 election for delegates to the state congress, a contest that resulted in widespread confrontations.[53]

These electoral incidents may well have been influenced by increasing tensions between the two wings of the Liberal party (Independents and Radicals). The antagonisms between the two factions would, in 1885, bring the period of Liberal rule to an end. Despite the momentous consequence of the division in the Liberal ranks for Colombian history, Helen Delpar notes that "no author" has identified the "interests and principles" that set the two factions apart before 1882, an indictment that includes political economy, regionalism, or the socioeconomic standings of the two camps.[54] At the time, as Independent Liberals declared their support for Núñez as their standard bearer in the 1875 presidential election, they claimed that Radicals had practiced oligarchic domination of the party, which excluded other voices and ignored regional interests. (Delpar observes that Independents opposed Radical anti-clerical measures in 1877, which facilitated their eventual alignment with the Conservatives.[55]) Mosqueristas, representing the interests of the Cauca, agreed with these allegations and consequently declared their support for Núñez's candidacy. Radicals chose Aquileo Parra to follow Pérez in the presidency.[56]

In Bogotá, preparations for the August 1875 elections began early and brought artisans directly into the fray. Artisan leader José Antonio Saavedra, a personal supporter of Parra, helped arrange an organizational meeting of the Democratic Society on April 17—by now a symbolic date for artisans. Some four-hundred persons, mainly described as artisans, showed up for the meeting, but, to Saavedra's dismay, most were Núñez supporters. The crowd warmly greeted José María Samper's message in favor of Núñez. Parra partisans "serenaded" nuñista Eustorgio Salgar that evening, while nuñistas jeered at President Pérez.[57] Partisan groups thereafter paraded through the streets almost nightly in support of their preferred candidates. The potential for violent confrontations led "many artisans of the capital" to call for an examination of the craftsmen's role in the campaign and urged them not to be misled by political peddlers (*traficantes en política*) such as Samper. They were reminded of La Alianza's principles and urged not to become tools for people who would not serve their interests.[58] Manuel María Madiedo's newspaper seconded that call, as did others.[59] Most incidents had ended by late May, but election day produced confrontations among voters, agitators, and the Guard, in which at least five people lost their lives (including four guardsmen).[60] The violence led to nullification of Bogotá's votes. Nationwide, neither Parra, Núñez, nor Conservative Bartolomé Calvo won the requisite number of states; congress thus chose Parra the victor in February 1876.

Conservatives in the Cauca valley and elsewhere saw the rupture in the Liberal party as an ideal opportunity to redress some of their grievances, especially those on religious issues.[61] Conservatives revolted in the southern Cauca in March, hoping—in vain—to draw Independents to their side. Liberal artisans who had been bitter enemies the previous year now closed ranks in support of the government, a stance that mirrored the behavior of Liberals throughout the country.[62] The reunited Democratic Society of Bogotá offered its services in defense of the country's public order. The Mutual Aid Society, whose artisan members tended to be Conservatives, issued a circular that urged each member to calm passions whenever possible.[63] The plea came too late, as once again artisans were recruited for war; of the 1,035 men who filled the 4 militia battalions and 1 squadron from Bogotá, all but 95 were skilled laborers.[64]

The defeat of the Conservative insurrection allowed divisions among Liberals to come to the fore. Independent Julián Trujillo had been selected as a unity candidate for the presidency during the war, a contest he won without opposition. Disputes between Independents and Radicals plagued Trujillo's regime. Animosities between Trujillo and the Radical-dominated congress peaked in a May 1879 incident that pitted members of the Sociedad de Juventud Radical against those of La Sociedad Liberal Independiente.[65] The violence of May 6 and 7 between Independent and Radical supporters resulted in shots fired in the chamber of representatives, at least one death, and extreme violence in the streets.[66]

Considering the May agitations, the August presidential elections were surprisingly calm. Núñez accepted the Conservative party's support in his bid against Radical candidate General Tomás Rengifo. Many of the Independents who had been associated with the events of May and Conservative artisans active in the Mutual Aid Society undoubtedly worked for the Núñez candidacy, as they worked closely with the *costeño* during his later presidencies. Indeed, the Núñez organization was quite successful, for the election resulted in an impressive victory for Núñez, giving him not just the presidency, but also control of the congress, while in Bogotá Independents and Conservatives wrested control of the municipal council from the Radicals for the first time since the 1860s. Only two states remained under Radical control when Núñez took office in April 1880.

Núñez and the Independent Liberals espoused economic and political principles that attracted artisan supporters. The emerging alliance between Independents and Conservatives seemingly offered an alternative to the partisan system that had spawned the conflicts and waste of resources so frequently criticized by craftsmen. Consequently, Núñez enjoyed a personal following among artisans that often cut across traditional political boundaries. Perhaps more important, Núñez favored an innovative reformation of the country's economic orientation that included implementation of a protective tariff system to foster industrial development, creation of a national bank to provide investors with credit, and support for public works projects to improve the nation's infrastructure.[67]

Artisans expressed their wholehearted support for these measures, especially tariff reform. Leaflets implored congressmen to support the plans and not to listen to "exploiters of the poor . . . who have no God other than gold and only their wallets as their country." (Liberals all, one presumes.) One document suggested that the proposed tariff reform, along with the National Bank and the increased power of the national executive, formed a "trinity" that could save the country. The signers added that "if these are not passed, we do not know what type of a regeneration will be offered to the Colombian people, or that one will be given."[68] Miguel Samper spoke in defense of laissez-faire principles in opposing both the proposed tariff and the National Bank, urging that the congress not abandon the liberal economic route taken some thirty years earlier.[69] The congress approved a tariff bill that raised basic rates on most finished products including footwear, clothing, and wooden furniture, and gave the president discretionary power to impose a surcharge on selected items.[70] It legislated the establishment of a National Bank with a monopoly to print and circulate notes, a policy that became the focus of considerable controversy in the years that followed.

Why did Núñez reverse the long-standing tariff policy? Ospina Vásquez suggests that the political support that the reform would win from craftsmen and others concerned the president more than any strict economic plan.[71] Bushnell seems to agree with this assessment, but notes Núñez's desire to improve the economic security of craftsmen and thereby foster "creation of a stable middle-class of citizens."[72] Liévano Aguirre holds that economic nationalism not defined by an unbending commitment to free-trade liberalism and an appreciation of Colombia's industrial needs propelled the reforms.[73] While it is difficult to ascertain the president's motivations with any certainty, it is clear that the 1880 tariff at least favored carpenters and joiners, trades practiced by several of his leading artisan supporters.[74] A realistic appraisal of the capital's (and nation's) industrial situation certainly would have recognized the potential returns from protection of trades such as cabinetmaking that had proven themselves competitive; other considerations would have underscored the political advantages of the move. In any case, Núñez's tariff stance and his support for the National Bank signalled his abandonment of liberal economics that had begun some twenty years earlier.

The capital's tradesmen praised the new tariff. Camacho noted that: "If our country . . . had protected its industry [earlier] by stimulating its crafts, the monster of empleomanía would not have been fed. The factories of crystal, paper, and cloth have decayed in Bogotá because the spirit of 'foreignism' has prevailed. If this same antipathy [toward national industry] had prevailed in France . . . it would now be a 'political' country like ours, but a slave to England or the United States."[75] Two years later, when Radical Francisco Javier Zaldúa had succeeded Núñez in the presidency, his Secretary of Finance, Miguel Samper, attempted to lower rates to their previous levels. Artisans of all political allegiances urged the congress not to change the existing tariff. One petition noted that some trades, most notably carpentry, had improved greatly under protection. The petitioners continued that secondary industries such as wood supplying had also profited, demonstrating the positive multiplier effect, which disproved the notion that protection favored the few.[76] The two branches of congress failed to agree on the proposal to reduce rates, and thus the 1880 tariff remained in effect. A proposal of a similar nature the following year met the same fate.[77]

The loss of power to Núñez forced Radicals to undertake steps to consolidate their power and to avoid future losses. Colonel Ricardo Vanegas founded the Sociedad de Salud Pública (Public Safety Society) in Bogotá on December 4, 1881, to help reestablish the Liberal regime and to combat reactionary threats. By early 1882, the Society claimed 382 members as it prepared for the city's municipal elections. Conservatives charged that political violence was part of the Public Safety Society's tactical repertoire, an allegation that seems true, especially in light of assassination attempts on Independents Daniel Aldana and Ramón Becerra. After the September attack on Aldana, public opposition to the group's use of violence caused the Zaldúa administration to distance itself from the organization. By December it was no longer active. The Society did revive momentarily for the 1883 presidential election in which Núñez stood against Liberal Salón Wilches with the support of Conservatives.[78]

Radical Liberal leaders feared that they would lose their domination of the political process if such a coalition were to be made permanent. Many prepared to rebel. The failure of quinine as an export product and falling coffee prices heightened political tensions.[79] Radicals judged that the economic crisis would produce popular discontent as they launched the insurrection in 1885. Federal authorities hesitated to suppress the spreading unrest until December, when Núñez appointed Conservative General Leonardo Canal to muster a reserve force to supplement the Colombian Guard. Liberals in other areas of the country then joined the rebellion; Independents and Conservatives were victorious on the battlefield by August 1886. Now, at last, the stage was set for a restructuring of the government under the rubric of the Regeneration.

## The Regeneration

The construction of Colombian constitutional order has always been crisis responsive. Partisan strife and economic instability preceded the constitutions of 1843, 1863, 1886, and 1991. Armed conflict between the contended partisan camps directly preceded all but the 1853 and 1858 constitutions, although the 1851 Conservative revolt and the Melo coup of 1854 facilitated the passage of even those documents. The domestic political and economic crisis of the 1880s stimulated the initial construction of the Regeneration state, but the failures of the Liberal regime of 1863–85 dictated its shape. Federalism and two-year presidential terms had engendered almost constant partisan conflicts. The near-religious devotion to laissez-faire liberalism and faith in export agriculture had also been ill-founded, as market forces subjected much of the Colombian economy to a debilitating boom-bust cycle. The inability of the federal state to foster essential development projects, such as railroads for the transportation of coffee, further restricted conditions for economic growth. These weaknesses had been the source of criticism since 1863, so that the transformation of the Regeneration "represented the culmination of a developing trend rather than an abrupt practice."[80]

Núñez and Miguel Antonio Caro were the intellectual architects of the Constitution of 1886, which swept aside most of the economic, political, and social principles of mid-century liberalism that had shaped the earlier constitution. Caro, who became the protagonist of the Regeneration, came to the government as one of the most gifted intellectuals of his day. The Bogotá-born leader, the very antithesis of a liberal thinker, staunchly defended Hispanic traditions in America, believing that centralized authority and Catholic precepts formed the ideal basis for society.[81] Caro supported the National Bank because it could counter individual-led, profit-motivated enterprises. In time, he expanded its paper-money emissions, believing an elastic monetary system to be critical for further economic expansion and more favorable to the country's populace than gold currencies, which he thought favored only the wealthy.[82] Núñez supported many of these policies, though perhaps from a more pragmatic than philosophical perspective.[83] Núñez believed, for example, that Catholicism was necessary to maintain social order in the country, even though his own adherence to that ideology has been questioned.[84]

The Regeneration transformed Colombia's political and economic structures, creating a constitutional order that has proven to be one of Latin America's most stable.[85] The Constitution of 1886 returned a strong centralized state to Colombia by establishing a government that replaced once sovereign states with subject departments. Under the new regime, the president had strong control over departmental authorities and extensive powers to be used in the case of internal emergencies. The Council of Delegates, which drafted the document, allowed a six-year presidential term, an honor first afforded to Núñez. A national army was created while regional armies were outlawed. Civil liberties such as the right to possess arms and absolute freedom of the press were restricted. Suffrage requirements were raised somewhat and prerequisites for holding public office were raised substantially. In keeping with policies begun earlier by Núñez, the central government's economic function was enhanced, including the exclusive right to print paper money. The state's economic policy remained strongly oriented toward exports, although it also sponsored policies favorable to industrial development.[86] Roman Catholicism once again became the official state religion and, though tolerance was granted to all Christian sects, the church's precepts governed public education. The church was thus restored as the agent of social cohesion that it had been prior to the liberal reform era. And, although it was not part of the constitution, a concordat with the Vatican, signed in December 1887, reflected the conservative orientation of the new constitution.[87]

The National party replaced the alliance of Independents and Conservatives. It dominated the national government until the War of the 1000 Days, though not without opposition. José María Samper and future president Rafael Reyes viewed the National party as the hope by which the country could rid itself of the evil of partisan strife.[88] In fact, that utopian ambition was realized only when Núñez was in Bogotá and in direct control of the government, something that never happened after August 1888. Highland Conservatives, especially Caro, profited from the absence of Núñez; the power of Independent Liberals within the National party eroded continually from the first days of the new constitution.

José Leocadio Camacho praised the bipartisan character of the Núñez government. Given Camacho's long-standing advocacy of the reduction of partisan conflict, this was certainly understandable, but substantive moves by the government could also be seen to favor artisans. These included support of the Taller Modelo (Model Shop); the tariff reform; and the creation of the Instituto de Artesanos, decreed by the president in February 1886. The Institute had the education of craftsmen and their children as its fundamental objective and was teaching some five-hundred students by the end of 1886. The government allowed the church to determine what curriculum would be used. While it was an obvious success in exposing students to the values deemed proper by the church, it did little to advance the industrial knowledge long sought by artisan leaders.[89]

Núñez had, of course, won much support from craftsmen by his earlier sponsorship of protective tariffs. These loyalties carried into the post-1886 period. Carpenters had fared especially well under the 1880 tariff; in 1887 leading practitioners of that trade praised the administration for its support of national industries.[90] Some observers, to be sure, thought that protection fostered poor workmanship, particularly in the carpentry trade: one commentator noted in 1886 that wooden furniture had decreased in quality while increasing in price under the higher tariff.[91] Rafael Tapias, a carpenter whose public defense of artisan interests dated from the 1860s, refuted the charge, stating that consumers were at least partly responsible for shabby workmanship because they frequented lower-skilled craftsmen in search of reduced prices and refused to pay for the quality demanded by the commentator. Tapias added that masters had to pass on rising material and living costs.[92] Félix Valois Madero, a carpenter who would play a significant political role in the 1890s, voiced many of the same defenses.[93] This polemic also served as an organizational stimulus for the capital's carpenters, who formed the Guild of Carpenters and Cabinetmakers on January 24, 1887. Valois Madero presided as president of the guild, which totaled about 150 members, many of whom had been active in Bogotá's political scene since the 1860s.[94]

Many earlier objectives, most notably the Model Shop, were finally met in the 1890s, although not necessarily because of artisan pressure. The measures undertaken by Núñez in 1881 to train a few craftsmen abroad matured in 1890 when Juan Nepomuceno Rodríguez, a mechanic who had acquired foundry skills in Europe, was named as director of the Taller Modelo. Located on the Plaza de Nariño, the shop was in operation by 1892, although it was not fully funded until 1896. Rodríguez trained craftsmen in several foundry skills and undoubtedly made a positive contribution to the capital's industrial expansion in those years.[95]

Two other ventures were undertaken during the same period to teach industrial arts in the capital. The Instituto Nacional de Artesanos (National Institute of Artisans) was reorganized in 1893 so as to place more emphasis on practical arts, though without fully abandoning theoretical training. By December of the next year, the Institute had graduated almost eighty students.[96] Artisans seemed to have been generally satisfied with the Instituto, but the same was not true of the education offered by the Salesian fathers after their arrival in Bogotá in 1890. In the latter part of that year, the Instituto Salesiano was founded to offer lower-class youths courses in carpentry, weaving, and shoemaking. The Salesian Institute came under attack immediately for "robbing" jobs from adult craftsmen and for undermining the "proper" method of apprenticeships. One of the slogans reportedly heard in the 1893 riot was "Down with the Salesians," and similar attitudes were expressed throughout the decade. Valois Madero in particular criticized the Institute, which led Miguel Samper to respond in its defense, a debate reminiscent of Camacho and Samper in the 1860s.[97] (Samper's defense of the conservative social program of the Institute is noteworthy in light of his devotion to economic liberalism.)

As the decade of the 1880s drew to a close, it became clear that socioeconomic pressures were of far more immediate concern for artisans and the lower classes generally than political issues. Prosperity had followed the end of the 1885 rebellion and the increase in coffee prices on the world market, but by early 1889 complaints of rising food prices were common. Most sources blamed *revendedoras*, women who would gain a monopoly of foods in the market and then charge exorbitant prices. Public outcry forced the mayor to take action to limit speculative practices, and by June most prices were reportedly back to normal. However, prices again skyrocketed in the second half of 1890, more likely because of the inflation caused by Regeneration monetary policies than revendedora monopolization. Whatever the cause, high food prices, as well as exorbitant rents, seriously threatened Bogotá's lower classes in the 1889–92 period.[98]

State-sponsored housing projects constituted one proposed remedy for the increasing pressure upon the poor and working classes. Camacho had suggested such measures in 1889, a stance seconded in early 1892 in the pro-government *El Orden*. The paper recommended that the government undertake construction of housing for workers in Bogotá and other major cities. The plan stipulated that recipients of the housing should be practitioners of a trade who could purchase the building at a low rate of repayment.[99] Congress discussed such legislation a few months later, only to draw criticism from adherents of the dejad hacer school who claimed sarcastically that state-supported housing should be made available to all needy social sectors not just to workers. Moreover, they argued, lower-priced housing in Bogotá would only serve to attract more migrants to the city, thus worsening crowding and sanitary problems.[100] In the end, the congress took no action; not until fifteen years later did the government actively sponsor such projects.

The presidential election of 1891 shattered any remaining unity of the National party and set events in motion that led to Colombia's last nineteenth-century civil war. Núñez let it be known that he would serve as titular president for the 1892–98 period while he remained in Cartagena; the vice-president would continue to be the country's de facto head. He hoped that the party would unite behind a single candidate, but both Marceliano Vélez and Caro contended for the open position. Vélez, an *antioqueño* who opposed the Regeneration's fiscal policies and the reduction of his department's political authority, would in time become the champion of the Historical Conservatives, who were juxtaposed to the Nationalists led by Caro. Núñez guarded his silence until September 1891, when he declared Caro his preferred running mate. Vélez then bolted the party and ran as a dissident presidential candidate with José Joaquín Ortíz. Liberals either cast their votes against Caro or continued their policy of electoral abstention. The only visible indication of artisan preference in Bogotá was *El Taller's* predictable support for Núñez and Caro.[101] Of the 5,000-odd legal ballots cast in the capital, 3,357 went to the Nationalists; the rest favored Vélez.[102] Throughout the nation, the voting returned an easy victory for the Nationalists.

The division of the National party undoubtedly pleased Liberals on both pragmatic partisan and ideological grounds. Various forms of political repression by Regeneration authorities had prevented that party from recovering its losses after the 1885 rebellion. A press law prohibiting slanderous statements proved quite effective in silencing opponents to the regime and the so-called Law of the Horses curbed loosely defined "political crimes." Liberals presented their own candidates for the May 1892 congressional elections.[103] In May 1893, Liberal chieftain Santiago Pérez released a platform that signalled his hopes for the party's future operations. The return to laissez-faire economic and liberal social policies along with an end to political repression dominated the Liberal agenda. Historical Conservatives shortly thereafter issued a similar document. The Caro administration at first allowed Liberals the freedom to pursue their political reorganization, but in August 1893, amid fears of bipartisan conspiracy and lingering effects of the January riot, Liberals throughout the country were arrested, their newspapers closed, and the party's treasury confiscated.

The renewed repression by Caro forced divisions within the Liberal party to the fore. As early as 1892, War Liberals, whose ranks would eventually include Eustacio de la Torre Narváez, Rafael Uribe Uribe, and Benjamín Herrera, had favored a more militant policy. Santiago Pérez, the leading Peace Liberal, supported by Salvador Camacho Roldán, Aquilo Parra, and Nicolás Esquerra, assumed control of the party, however, thereby briefly curbing the militants.[104] Liberal militants responded to the repression (and the exile of Pérez) by preparing to revolt against the government. The party divisions, however, meant that the January 1895 revolt that began in Cundinamarca and was supported in Santander was put down with relative ease by the government.[105] Numerous artisans were arrested in the opening days of the rebellion in Bogotá, although there is little evidence to indicate widespread support for the insurrection among that class.[106]

Both parties were hopelessly divided as the presidential election of 1897 neared.[107] A sharp decline in the world market price for coffee exacerbated the situation and weakened the capacity of the Caro regime to perpetuate itself. Indeed, the National party, whose strength had been centered in the bureaucracy and military of the Regeneration state and in the country's economic prosperity, had lost considerable power. Caro was the preferred Nationalist candidate, although the constitutionality of his candidacy was questionable. In the end, a bizarre nomination process akin to musical chairs resulted in eighty-three year old Manuel A. Sanclemente and José Manuel Marroquín at the head of the Nationalist ticket, Guillermo Quintero Calderón and Marceliano Vélez as the Historical Conservative slate; and Miguel Samper and Foción Soto as the Liberal candidates.

The election of 1897 represented a crucial turning point for Liberals. While militants had not won wide support in their 1895 revolt, the legitimate participation in politics counseled by moderates had also proven unsuccessful. Part of the moderate effort in preparation for the presidential election, which was engineered by

Aquileo Parra, had been to incorporate leading craftsmen into the party's departmental administrative body. Typesetter Alejandro Torres Amaya, chocolate manufacturer Enrique Chaves B., and Pompilio Beltrán, one of the youths sent to Europe for crafts training, were brought into party affairs in this manner and were Liberal electors in the 1897 election.[108] Presumably they helped to organize the December 1897 pro-Parra demonstration in front of his Chapinero home that drew an estimated six-thousand people.[109] They certainly were active in organizations of Liberal artisans in the months after the elections. Liberal electors tallied the most votes in the capital, easily outdistancing the Nationalist and Conservative slates.[110] In the country as a whole, however, Nationalist control of the political machinery resulted in their return to office. The Liberal party's showing in the election raised the hopes of the moderates for the future. But for the militants, it steeled their resolve to oust Nationalists from the government by force of arms.

As Liberal party functionaries prepared for war, Liberal craftsmen founded the Club Industrial Colombiano in December of 1898 to unite individuals of "democratic and republican" persuasions.[111] Some commentators identified this group as being in the camp of militant Liberal Rafael Uribe Uribe, an alignment that, if true, could indicate its function was to mobilize craftsmen's support for the coming conflict. Further indications of widespread preparations could be seen in the installation of similar clubs in the towns of Sogamoso, Popayán, and Barranquilla.[112]

In the months after Sanclemente replaced Caro as executive, the Regeneration government suffered further reverses and the economic crisis worsened. The War of the 1000 Days, or the Three Years' War as many called it at the time, began in October 1899 and lasted until November 1902. Although Liberals attempted a standard strategy that pitted regular forces of their side versus regular forces of the other, the fighting soon degenerated into guerrilla warfare. Liberals planned that their army in the department of Santander, supplied through Venezuela, would defend that region from Conservative attack while guerrilla bands in other regions would inspire the tide of popular opinion to shift against the government. Conservative naval forces blunted the Liberal effort to seize control of the Magdalena River in the first week of fighting and delivered a humiliating defeat to the Liberal army in the vicious battle of Palonegro near Bucaramanga in May 1900. Thereafter, the "gentlemen's war" gave way to bitter, indecisive conflict between small bands of Liberal guerrillas and government forces, who were assisted by their own guerrillas. The most sustained struggle occurred in present-day Huila (then the department of Tolima) and in Cundinamarca, the Cauca, and Santander, although very little of the country escaped the conflict. The war did not end until Liberal chieftains in 1902 signed the treaties of Neerlandia, Wisconsin, and Chinácota.[113]

Substantial disagreements surround the origins of the war and its relationship to the political economy of the Regeneration. Was it a "typical" nineteenth-century civil war? Or did the conflict have more in common with La Violencia of the twentieth century? Did a relationship exist between the paper money policy of the Regeneration, the development of the coffee economy, and the war, or, put more bluntly, did contending political economic ideologies provide the catalyst for the war? Charles Bergquist and Marco Palacios (among others) claim that the Regenerators, especially Caro, articulated a political economy that merchants and planters deemed detrimental to both the health of the emerging coffee industry and the nation's economy. Opposition to paper currency in general, and the large emissions of the early 1890s in particular, fueled enormous public controversy which sustained, according to Bergquist, a fragile alliance between Liberals and Historical Conservatives, largely because of their relationship to the coffee economy. The crux of the issue, then and now, was whether paper emissions stimulated or undermined the expansion of coffee. If the reliance upon paper currency had hurt coffee exporters, the primacy of competitive notions of political economy as a factor in the war must be considered. If, on the other hand, Regeneration fiscal policies did not destabilize the coffee economy, then perhaps the war was more akin to earlier conflicts.

These questions are not easily resolved. Adolfo Meisel and Alejandro López, in a summary of the paper money debate, conclude that the release of paper money, in conjunction with external inflationary tendencies, stimulated domestic inflation and exacerbated the nation's financial deficit. Costs of living rose quite dramatically in Bogotá at this time, fueling the complaints of artisans and others. Coffee prices in both England and the United States rose steadily after 1887 and peaked in 1895. The real adjusted price of coffee in that year, discounting inflationary effects, was near its highest point in fifteen years. The decline in the nation's economic performance after 1896 and the subsequent reduction of the government's fiscal base, according to Meisel and López, owed more to the sudden collapse of coffee prices than to the deflation of the peso due to the emissions of paper money, as charged by anti-paper critics.[114] Unfavorable economic conditions undermined the national government, leaving it vulnerable to partisan strife, just as had happened in the later 1850s, mid-1870s, and mid-1880s.

In spite of the convincing parallels between the platforms of the Historical Conservatives and Liberals in the 1897 presidential election, no alliance could be forged on the basis of economic ideology between the two camps. Conservatives of both Historical and National hue allied—albeit with real tensions—to combat Liberals. Gonzalo Sánchez, a leading scholar of contemporary Colombian political violence, identifies the conflict as a partisan civil war that balanced out "the internal rivalries of the ruling class."[115] So, too, does Carlos Eduardo Jaramillo, although he offers suggestive evidence of the inability of partisan leaders to keep social tensions in check during the long conflict.[116] Finally, Malcolm Deas asserts that few similarities link the conflict to the twentieth-century La Violencia. Instead, it had much in common with the partisan, elite-led conflicts correlated to economic stress that typified the nineteenth century.[117]

Whatever the scholars might conclude, the war proved to be the most debilitating of the century's conflicts. The various political and mutual aid societies in which bogotano craftsmen had participated seem not to have been drawn physically into the contest, though they suffered from its ravages along with the rest of the nation. While the war was fought primarily in rural areas, urban inhabitants suffered from reduced food supplies, severe price inflation, stagnant economic conditions, and susceptibility to recruitment as soldiers. The economic situation did not markedly improve with the end of the war in 1902. Throughout that year and the next, public and religious groups set up charity kitchens to deal with continuing shortages of food and the lack of money to purchase that which was available at high prices.[118] In September 1903, a group of industrials, artisans, and workers argued in a petition to the chamber that the peso's depreciation, combined with heavy taxes, had made their lives miserable. The petition reasoned that the congress could improve the situation by lifting taxes on consumption which, it argued, further reduced their already low living standards.[119]

The devastation of the war convinced many leaders that the time had come to resolve partisan differences in a manner other than fighting. The separation of Panama from the nation in 1903 with the assistance of the United States shocked Colombia and prepared it for fundamental political change. In any case, as the war ended, the capital's labor movement entered a new stage, one that served as a transition between nineteenth-century artisan mobilizations and activity by twentieth-century wage laborers.

# SIX

# THE EMERGENCE OF THE MODERN LABOR MOVEMENT

T HE DIVERGING FORTUNES OF BOGOTA'S ARTISANS IN THE LATTER years of the nineteenth century and the appearance of larger-scale manufacturing industries increased the complexity of the city's labor structure. The often conflicting interaction among artisans, industrials, and workers shaped the labor movement and its relation to politics during the first score of years in this century. The labels *artisan, industrial,* or *worker* carry connotations that vary depending on the context. In this chapter, descriptive labels by which actors described themselves are used, except when otherwise noted. The obvious conflict of interest among these different laborers was one that organizations grappled with at length; it was a leading factor in the evolution of groups representing workers in the 1910s. In any event, it is safe to say that in Bogotá, as in other cities with a complex laboring population, artisans—either as independent or skilled workers—played a central role in the labor movement.[1]

## The Union of Industrials and Workers

Political stability heralded the renewed mobilization of bogotano artisans. A 1904 circular from craftsmen in Popayán to their counterparts throughout the country precipitated a petition drive to seek higher tariffs from the national congress. The circular claimed that only concerted action could stem the flood of imports that had followed the end of the fighting.[2] Owners of small shoe-making shops in the capital, who called themselves artisans, seconded these sentiments in a complaint against U.S. imports by Colombian merchants who, they claimed, worshipped the "corrupt dollar." Juan Ignacio Gálvez observed that the proposed legislation would increase the tariff on manufactured items, reduce it to a minimum on raw materials used for internal production, and remove it altogether from machinery.[3] In this context, Gálvez called for the formation of a non-partisan workers' party to coordinate the petition drive.[4]

An estimated two-thousand people attended an organizational meeting of the Unión de Industriales y Obreros (Union of Industrials and Workers) to prepare Bogotá's petition drive in June 1904. Emeterio Nates, a shoemaker, presided over the session, which was attended by General Rasprilla of the National Police—undoubtedly to avoid repetition of events of years past. Those present overwhelmingly supported the initiative begun by Popayán's artisans. It was resolved that a newspaper directed by Gálvez should be the Union's mouthpiece, an honor Gálvez accepted only when José Leocadio Camacho agreed to work with him so as to demonstrate the non-partisan nature of the organization.[5] At the Union's formal foundation on June 8, 1904, Camacho became president of the Union; Nates, vice-president; and Jesús González F., secretary.[6] Spokesmen from twenty-five trades listened three days later to Camacho, now seventy-one years old, as he urged the unification of Bogotá's workers for the betterment of all persons involved in industry.[7]

The Unión's petition drive culminated in the presentation of signatures from Bogotá, Popayán, and Cali to the congress in early October. The Union undoubtedly thought that the proposal stood a good chance of being accepted, as President Rafael Reyes had included tariff reform as part of the fiscal package he presented to the congress when he took office. That stance, and his less partisan approach to politics, accounted for a march organized by the Union of some 2,500 workers past the president's house late in October.[8] However, despite the organized effort in favor of higher tariffs and the support of the president, congress adjourned without enacting the desired legislation. In his telegram to the caleño supporters of the bill, Camacho protested the insensitive attitude of the congress, while reaffirming the Union's hope for tariff protection.[9] President Reyes's penchant for personal control and his support for state-directed development soon overrode congressional antipathy. Reyes issued an executive decree raising tariffs in January 1905 in order to "protect national industries," a move Ospina Vázquez claims "put teeth in" the industrial protection begun some twenty-five years earlier by Núñez.[10]

There is no record of the Union of Industrials and Workers' re-action to the new tariff, as the association appears to have lost momentum and organizational unity after the petition drive. The Unión represents a transitional workers' group, evidencing both old and new characteristics. Clearly the Union drew upon past leadership (Camacho's) and dealt with issues faced in earlier pe-riods (e.g., tariffs), but, at the same time, its very title reflected the widening division of the working population. It also represents the first time that a bogotano group tried to form a popular mobiliza-tion consisting of workers from markedly different labor settings. Moreover, tentative moves to coordinate workers' groups from other areas of the country presaged future developments. While some of its leaders were well known, many were new actors who would dominate labor organizations over the next fifteen years. The five years following the Union's eclipse, however, were times of relative quiet, as the Reyes *quinquenio* (1905–9) did not provide the proper climate for politicized labor organizations.

Reyes had emerged from the war relatively unscathed by the bitter partisan struggle. Although a Conservative, he favored the cooperation exemplified by the National party over the antago-nisms of traditional Liberal and Conservative politics. His absence from Colombia during the war years made him an attractive presi-dential candidate in 1904, favored by some old Nationalists and by most of those Liberals who enjoyed the opportunity to vote. His-torical Conservatives and other Nationalists backed Joaquín F. Vé-lez, an equally, if not more, qualified candidate, but one who in the end lost a notoriously corrupt election. Reyes entered office ready to put into practice the "scientificism" he had observed in the Mexico of Porfirio Díaz and to take charge forcibly of the nation's development, for which protective tariffs were only one aspect of his program. Others included the reorganization of the country's beleaguered monetary system, improvement of its infrastructure, and promotion of export agriculture. Reyes also undertook substantial political reforms, most notably in bringing Liberals into his government to break the deadly partisan cycle of the nineteenth century. The president's antipathy toward congress increased during the first months of 1905, leading him to dismiss that body, convene a National Assembly in its stead, and force a four-year extension of his term in office.[11]

Conspiracies plagued the early quinquenio. Reyes's bipartisan inclination, combined with lingering resentment concerning the fraud that gained him office, alienated some Conservatives to the point that they prepared to assassinate him on December 19, 1905. The conspiracy was discovered, however, and its planners were arrested and put on trial. Men of similar persuasion fired upon the president's carriage on February 10, 1906. The assassination attempt inflamed Reyes and led him to complete the assumption of dictatorial powers begun the previous year.[12]

Although it was not immediately apparent, a feared third attack on the president aborted another effort to organize Bogotá's workers. Two newspapers sympathetic to workers' issues had begun publication in late 1905. The more radical of the two, *El Faro*, printed by the Liberal artisan Alejandro Torres Amaya, praised artisans' "natural goodness" and called for strong governmental action to improve their material conditions. The newspaper article spoke of an apocalyptic uprising of displaced individuals in assertion of their rights.[13] The editors of *El Yunque*, the more moderate paper, had been active in the Union of Industrials and Workers and now forwarded its concerns, such as the need for tariff protection and educational reform favorable to workers. The paper insisted that industrials and workers should continue to close ranks politically, so that when elections were held in 1908 they could "break the bonds" of partisan politics by electing their own representatives.[14]

A third alleged conspiracy brought to an abrupt end the efforts of both *El Yunque* and *El Faro*. The conspiracy was said to involve a plan to cut electrical wires to the city and undertake a movement against the government. Military authorities subverted the supposed plan, arresting large numbers of artisans, workers, and others. *El Faro* became involved in the incident when it published a petition asking permission to hold a public rally in support of the government, which some in the administration considered a subterfuge. The government denied the request, termed the paper a danger to social order, and arrested its editors. The capital's press in the following days offered conflicting accounts as to the degree of worker involvement in the alleged conspiracy, which the government in the end admitted did not exist. Nonetheless, since editors of both newspapers were arrested and sent to military colonies or to prisons in other areas of the country, the nascent effort ground to a halt.[15] The incident brought on an era of close governmental supervision of politicized workers' groups that ended only when Reyes was driven from power.

Although organizations with openly political ends could not operate during the remainder of the Reyes administration, numerous mutual aid societies, characteristic of earlier years, provided the basis for future political mobilizations. For example, the August 7, 1907, meeting of the Mutual Aid Society—Bogotá's oldest—was attended by representatives from the Sociedad Filantrópica, the Sociedad de Amigos de Paz, the Sociedad de Caridad, the Sociedad de Impresores, the Sociedad de Carpinteros Unidos, and the Sociedad Unión.[16] Four of the societies had been founded prior to the war, but the others, along with some not present, had been established after its conclusion. Most of these groups cooperated in the creation of the Unión Nacional de Industriales y Obreros in 1910.[17]

As might have been expected, mutual aid societies had struggled to survive the War of the 1000 Days. Typical, perhaps, was the experience of the Mutual Aid Society. Economic dislocations cost the body its office, furniture, archives, and much of its capital. Not until 1905 did it formally reorganize; within two years the Society had started a savings bank for its members and resumed its position as the largest organization of its kind in the capital.[18] The 1889 merger between it and the Philanthropic Society seems not to have survived the war, as the latter group was reorganized as a separate entity in 1906.[19] The Typesetters' Society, which had been active politically before the war, also experienced much hardship. Nonetheless, it, too, was revived by 1905, but with a less partisan stance. According to a press report, abandonment of its partisan past drew most members of that trade into the Society. Typesetters recognized their obvious status among the city's working population; the group noted in 1906 that "the typesetter is now, more than ever, conscious that he is in the workers' vanguard" and therefore should be obliged to work for peace.[20] The Society was given juridical status in November 1906, even though it had been organized nine years earlier. (This underscores the shortcomings of employing juridical recognition as a conclusive measure of the numbers of labor organizations, a method used by Urrutia Montoya and others to identify workers' groups, albeit with acknowledgment of its weaknesses.[21])

The church appears to have been closely associated with many mutual aid societies founded after the war. The Sociedad de la Protectora, established in 1902, was probably the first such body. Its members were described as "industrials" and "artisans" who pledged to mutually protect one another and to pressure the government to control the high prices of foodstuffs.[22] Two similar organizations, the Sociedad de Caridad and the Sociedad de la Cruz, were functioning by 1907.[23] A final church-supported mutual aid society, the Sociedad de Santa Orosía, began to operate in January 1907. It too appealed principally to workers and had certain connections to prewar groups, as Félix Valois Madero was its first secretary. By 1909 the Society had almost five-hundred members and substantial funds. The Santa Orosía Society, perhaps more than any church-affiliated society, cooperated actively with non-religious groups of the same nature.[24]

While the preceding societies had clear mutual aid objectives, the elite Sociedad Unión (Union Society), founded in April 1907 by Eduardo Boada R., had a more openly political nature. The Union Society attempted to bring all social classes together under the theme "Amor al trabajo," but loyalty to the "honor" of work was hardly its sole concern; many of its members were active in the fledgling Republican movement in opposition to Reyes.[25]

The semi-authoritarian regime of Reyes quieted direct opposition for three years after the 1906 assassination attempts. In early 1909, however, the president was forced to reconvene the National Assembly in order to ratify the treaties his government had negotiated with Panama and the United States to settle the conflict resulting from the loss of the isthmanian department. The terms of the proposed treaties favored both the U.S. and the now-independent department, and they did not reflect the feelings of most of the assembly's members or much of the nation. Opposition leader Nicolás Esguerra disavowed the assembly's constitutional power to ratify the treaties, insisting that according to the constitution, only an elected legislature could approve international agreements. This bold rebuff of Reyes's wishes helped to further discredit his regime. Faced with student-led demonstrations in the capital on March 13,

1909, Reyes delegated power to Jorge Holguín, who promptly declared a state of siege. Reyes reclaimed control the next day, but the opposition of the previous days had broken his political authority. Shortly thereafter the president called for congressional elections and set about preparing to "normalize" the political process.[26]

Medófilo Medina has amplified the role of artisans and workers in the 13 de marzo by characterizing them as the "popular sector" at the front of the first great urban protest of the twentieth century.[27] Such a claim is exaggerated, as it seems most likely that the demonstrations on the 13 de marzo represented a popular seconding of the sentiments expressed in the assembly against the treaties, the closed political system, and unfavorable economic conditions. Industrials, artisans, and workers did take part in the drama of the 13 de marzo, as the Union, Mutual Aid, and Philanthropic Societies joined in some of the mobilizations of that day, although the Union Society later denied any involvement.[28]

If the exact participation of workers in the 13 de marzo remains nebulous, the behavior of the self-styled industrials and workers in the political events of the months and years that followed is much more evident. A significant number of the men who would emerge as labor activists in the coming years were connected to the Unión Republicana, a political conglomeration of moderate Liberals and Historical Conservatives that seized the opportunity made available by Reyes's fall from power. The Republican Union was formally organized in April by Carlos E. Restrepo, Guillermo Quintero Calderón, Nicolás Esguerra, and others. Leading industrials were involved in the Union from its inception. Its principles included bipartisan politics, open elections, and religious tolerance.[29]

Much to the country's surprise, Reyes left for England in June after delegating power to Jorge Holguín. The newly elected congress then appointed General Ramón González Valencia as president until August 1910, at which time his successor would assume office. In November 1909, elections were held throughout the country for municipal councils, who in turn selected delegates to a National Assembly that met the following April. That assembly enacted major constitutional reforms, including the reduction of the presidential term of office to four years, the establishment of direct popular presidential elections, and guaranteed minority party representation (one-third of all seats in congress). The assembly also selected Carlos E. Restrepo as the country's president for a four-year term.

## The National Union of Industrials and Workers

Unprecedented steps to politically organize the working class of Bogotá were made while these events unfolded. In August 1909, Emilio Murillo proposed forming a Unión Obrera (Workers' Union) to further the interests of that class.[30] The call was successful, and the *Unión Industrial* began publication on August 15 as the association's mouthpiece. The paper, which was apparently published for only one month, announced that it was dedicated to protection of the nation's industry.[31] The Workers' Union lent its backing to some Republican candidates in the November municipal council elections, a contest that returned a strong Republican victory. Support by Murillo's group was seemingly an advantage, as the candidates with the largest vote totals were those backed by both Republicans and the Union.[32]

The initiatives of the latter half of 1909 led to the formation of the Unión Nacional de Industriales y Obreros (National Union of Workers and Industrials—UNIO) in February 1910. The UNIO was, according to Alberto Navarro B., first and foremost an attempt to unify workers for their common well-being, for protection of their trades, and to help their families. Its intent was to avoid partisan political alignments, he continued, although temporary dealings with traditional parties were not to be dismissed. While the UNIO's organizers recognized that its members were Catholics, and thus vowed not to attack their religion, they pledged not to abandon the group's basic interests in conflicts with the official line of the church. Other objectives of the UNIO included free obligatory education, trade schools for industrial education, adult schools, and the formation of a savings bank. Finally, Navarro noted that "the group . . . will work in all elections by common accord, and its candidates will be those citizens who fulfill the indispensable conditions to be genuine representatives of the people who elect them."[33]

At first glance, the organizational efforts undertaken by workers in 1909 seem to have led directly to the establishment of the UNIO in 1910. This is true insofar as the fall of Reyes created the opportunity for such ventures, but as time revealed, two distinct political tendencies were present among workers. Members of the Workers' Union of 1909 tended to align themselves with the Republican movement until it weakened later in the decade. By contrast, most of those associated with the UNIO were more clearly affiliated with the Liberalism of Rafael Uribe Uribe, a circumstance that would hamper efforts to unite non-Conservative workers' groups until after his assassination in 1914. Nonetheless, in the early months of the UNIO's existence, this polarization was not visible; workers of both tendencies took part in its formation.

The UNIO quietly pursued its goals of building a unified organization throughout 1910. Its newspaper, La Razón del Obrero, publicized the Union's principles and addressed issues relating to workers, including education, tariff protection, living conditions, and the developing workers' movement. UNIO's April elections resulted in Domingo E. Alvarez's becoming its president; Alejandro Torres Amaya, vice-president; Juan N. Paniagua, secretary; and Andrés Luna E., treasurer.[34] Although the National Assembly met from May until November 1910, the UNIO refrained from commenting on most of its deliberations. In its one direct observation, it expressed support for free and obligatory primary education. Other workers, however, reminded the assembly of their protectionist needs.[35] When the assembly deliberated on candidates for the country's next president, the UNIO made no official endorsement, although many of its members signed statements backing Guillermo Quintero Calderón.[36] Since both he and Carlos E. Restrepo, the assembly's choice, were active in the Republican Union, it is unlikely that many politically expressive workers were upset with the incoming president.

The UNIO represented itself as the Workers' party in the elections of 1911 as the nation returned to normalized political activity.[37] The UNIO's Central Workers Election Directory, which oversaw the effort of the Workers' party, called upon shop owners, industrials, and workers to form committees in each barrio to work with the central body. The Directory also urged the formation of similar groups throughout the nation. By December, it had received favorable replies from Popayán, Cali, Ibagué, Zipaquirá, and numerous other towns. On November 26, the Proteccionista (the Directory's mouthpiece) reported 1,500 subscribers in the capital alone, while the Directory included representatives from all of the city's barrios.[38] The Directory's political objectives focused upon tariff protection, which it coupled with reductions in duties on items for internal consumption and elimination of export duties on coffee, measures it felt would benefit the nation as a whole. Protection was hardly a new demand, but the Directory insisted that, to be effective, it had to come about as the result of political pressures by workers, not as a gift from the state.

The elections of 1911 offer dramatic insights into the power of workers' political organizations throughout the decade. Four groups—Conservatives, Liberals, Republicans, and Workers—exerted significant electoral strength. Liberals and Workers joined forces for the February elections for positions in the departmental assembly, tallying 5,124 votes; the Conservatives received 3,593, and the Republicans, 1,907.[39] Republicans joined the Worker/Liberal *liga* (alliance) for the May selection of national congressmen, out-polling the Conservative party 7,083 to 4,936 votes.[40] Two incidents of urban disorder involving the UNIO—one in May and the other in July—shattered the liga, especially when the UNIO demanded its own slate for the October elections.[41] As a result, ten lists faced voters for the city council elections.[42] The Conservative list finished first with 2,750 votes; the Liberal list received 2,050 votes; the Workers' party was third with 1,850; Republicans tallied 1,350; and other groups shared 500 votes. The secretary of the Workers' party, Rafael Reyes Daza, charged that at the last moment Liberals had usurped the names from the UNIO slate, causing numerous voters to erroneously think that a pact had indeed been arranged. Even so, he expressed a degree of satisfaction because those three candidates had received the most votes of any on the Liberal slate. Despite the loss by his own party, Reyes Daza concluded that the stance assumed by the organization would enhance the real power of the Workers' party, and that the 1,850 votes it collected held promise of future victories.[43]

In this frantic set of elections, only the Conservative party demonstrated the capacity to achieve electoral victory without alliances. Alliances or pacts between the other parties could achieve victory. As a consequence, the votes held by workers and their political societies were crucial to the Republican and Liberal parties, a point not ignored by either group. On the other hand, the UNIO was not strong enough to win elections by itself, and faced the dilemma of victory through cooperation and possible betrayal of its raison d'être.

After the hectic pace of 1911, the various political parties used the subsequent non-election year as a time of reassessment and reorganization. Church officials began their own efforts to counter political initiatives undertaken by workers, moves that the Conservatives undoubtedly supported. Conservative Laureano Gómez, for example, rightly observed that industrial members of the UNIO had won representation in the year's elections, but that they hardly represented workers whose interests were quite distinct from their own. Workers' needs, he continued, were largely social in nature and could be best met by the church, not by political action.[44] Spokesmen for the UNIO objected to Gómez's allegations, noting that while no dogmatic differences separated the UNIO and the Catholic church, political disagreements did exist, and for that reason the UNIO could not support the Conservative party (as did the church hierarchy). Juan N. Paniagua alleged that the Union was being denounced from the pulpits of the city as a consequence of that political decision.[45]

As early as 1908, during the first formal conference of the nation's bishops, the church had spoken in favor of actions to benefit Colombia's workers. The bishops followed the directives of Pope Leo XIII, whose 1891 papal encyclical, *Rerum Novarum*, had urged the faithful to prevent the spread of socialist doctrines by addressing the needs of Europe's laboring classes.[46] Father José María Campoamor established a Círculo de Obreros (Workers' Circle) in early 1911 to defuse "nontraditional" (leftist) workers' activities by raising living standards and inspiring workers' commitment to church principles. The Workers' Circle created a savings bank, restaurant, school, and various other social services for its members. The church's endeavors met with government approval, receiving four-thousand pesos annually from 1913 until 1927.[47] These limited activities, as might be expected, did little to defuse workers' partisan political activities even though they undoubtedly provided real material assistance. Not until 1946 did the church-sponsored Union of Colombian Workers compete with secular union efforts.

Rafael Uribe Uribe began his effort to bring workers into the Liberal camp in 1911. In a speech to the UNIO, he claimed a long identification with workers' issues, dating, he said, to his 1904 speech in favor of state socialism. At that time Uribe Uribe had proclaimed his belief in "socialism from above," not below; a socialism that would expand the role of the state in economic development, the protection of workers, the establishment of savings banks, and the protection of national industries.[48] Now, the Liberal chieftain forwarded four ideas to improve the condition of the country's workers: electoral reform, better public education, improved public hygiene, and "rational protection" of the nation's industries.[49] Officials of the UNIO protested the press coverage of the meeting, which they claimed was worded to convey the impression that the UNIO and Uribe Uribe were cooperating politically. That, they insisted, was not true.[50] Other Liberals also courted workers and the UNIO in an attempt to convince them that the Liberal party was the appropriate forum for expression of workers' needs.[51]

Republicans, too, moved to retain the relationship they had developed with workers after the fall of Reyes. In a May 1912 reorganization of the party, several new planks seem to have been shaped to achieve that result. These included declarations in favor of expanded public education, development of the nation's industry with moderate protectionist barriers, and unspecified measures to develop workers "morally and economically."[52] These "proworker" planks were, of course, practically the same as those of Uribe Uribe.

The UNIO faced the task of continuing its momentum toward becoming an economic, political, and social force independent from Liberals and Republicans. Conflicting opinions existed within the UNIO as to the priority of political versus "social" and economic considerations, a dispute obviously won by the pro-political members in 1911. The choice of this strategy suggests that some of the UNIO's membership envisioned it as a primarily political force even while others stressed social issues. The inactivity and disorganization of the UNIO in 1912—a non-election year—further indicates that, without the political struggle, much of the catalyst for the group was lost, in spite of pressing social concerns.

The UNIO appeared incapable of representing workers' needs outside the political arena.[53] Members of the shoemaker's trade, many of whom were also part of the UNIO, bypassed that organization by directly petitioning the Chamber of Representatives to double the existing duty on imported shoes. This, they felt, was necessary to maintain the competitiveness of national shoes.[54] In September 1912, typesetters, also prominent members of the UNIO, were faced with a concerted effort by printing shop owners to drive down their wages. The Typesetters' Society organized in favor of the workers, while the UNIO seemingly ignored the problem.[55]

As part of its initial preparations for the 1913 electoral season, the directory of the UNIO met in October 1912 to determine its political objectives. It agreed to a list of nine goals: to ask departmental authorities to foster industries so as to make importation of foreign goods unnecessary, to make the judicial process more equitable in its treatment of all classes, to request the same of police officials, to lower taxes on articles of primary necessity and to eliminate them altogether on real estate valued at less than five-hundred pesos, to control rents, to sponsor savings banks, to improve expenditures of public service funds, to improve transportation routes in order to bring more foodstuffs into the city, and to increase salaries paid by the department.[56] At the same time, Uribe Uribe met with the UNIO, as did several other Liberal leaders.[57] The results of the Liberal recruitment became clear in December when their forces completely dominated selection of the UNIO's electoral directory, allegedly because the meeting was packed with illiterate street cleaners obligated by patronage ties to Liberal officials. Marco T. Amorocho, who would play an important role as a political activist in the coming years, claimed that the electoral committee did not represent the "artisans and workers who constitute the nerves and strengths of Bogotá." Amorocho insisted that if the "unrepresentativeness" were not corrected, he would pursue a path independent of the UNIO.[58]

The striking fact in these developments is that the pledge of an independent Workers' party was forsaken, almost without comment, in the wake of intense partisan appeals to working-class voters. The February 1913 election saw Republicans emerge victorious with 4,147 votes, closely followed by the Conservative tally of 4,118, while Liberals trailed with 3,128 votes. Republican analysts felt that the returns demonstrated the futility of a Workers'/Liberal union and the advantage of the Workers' association with themselves.[59] A more accurate assessment of the entire electoral process would note the enormous difficulties facing individuals wishing to forge an independent workers' party and the lack of influence on the part of those workers dedicated to socioeconomic issues. It was evident that the Republican and Liberal parties were more concerned with defeating the Conservatives than with making workers an integral part of their operations. Once again they formed an alliance for the congressional elections in May and soundly defeated the Conservative opposition. Not surprisingly, no workers were included on any electoral slate.[60]

## The Unión Obrera Colombiana

The Unión Obrera Colombiana (UOC—Colombian Workers' Union), founded in May 1913, represented a marked departure from the policies of the UNIO. The founders of the UOC proposed a social, economic, and political agenda that would satisfy the needs of workers, not the industrials that they viewed as dominant within the UNIO. The group announced that it was dedicated to the establishment of an independent union of workers that would pursue an end to illiteracy, a program of public education, an increase in salaries and protection of national industries, protection of workers of both sexes against exploitation by capitalists, savings banks, mutual aid, and political autonomy. The new organization stressed the need for workers' unity in support of a "militant" program, the first such agenda in Bogotá to be couched in terms of socialist analysis. The UOC adopted the organizational principles and many of the same socioeconomic objectives of the UNIO.[61] In order to insure a more homogenous membership, only those who practiced a trade or who worked for a salary could join the UOC. Groups of thirty or more workers constituted the primary organizational unit of the UOC, with each group supplying two representatives to a board of directors. By August 1913, some fifteen groups were said to be in existence, with a membership claimed to be almost three-thousand.[62]

The UOC's public statements were in keeping with its avowed support of socioeconomic concerns. It proposed and established an Oficina del Trabajo (Work Office) to act as a clearinghouse where workers could solicit employment and owners could find employees. The Work Office was not limited to members of the UOC, and by August it was claimed that the office was functioning smoothly with over four-thousand people registered. In another instance, the UOC praised the efforts of a few representatives who had spoken in favor of workers' legislation in the new congress. The Union used the pages of its newspaper to put pressure upon local authorities to improve basic services to areas of the city inhabited by workers and urged groups in other towns to do the same.[63]

The UOC called attention to the economic and social needs of workers from a socialist perspective. The Union denied that it wished to "juxtapose" capital and labor, but few of its public analyses avoided doing just that. In an article entitled "The Vampires of the Pueblo," one of the group's members commented on the traditional inability of workers to resist exploitation by capitalists. As a result, workers rented "miserable hovels" at exorbitant prices they could ill afford at their low wages. Given the opposing interests of industrials and workers, the UOC accentuated its departure from stances taken by the UNIO.[64]

The appearance of the Workers' Union did not go unnoticed by the UNIO. The two groups made frequent overtures to each other that culminated in a joint session on June 22, 1913, which a thousand people reportedly attended. The Workers' Union on that occasion refused, however, to recognize the legitimacy of the earlier organization's claim to represent workers; it assumed that right for itself.[65] Thereafter, there seems to have been little official interaction between the two organizations.

As increased numbers of industrial wage laborers entered the city's labor force, governments at both local and national levels grappled with innovative legislative measures. A worker's compensation law (ley de accidentes del trabajo), patterned after Spanish legislation, was introduced within the chamber in August 1911 by a representative from Cundinamarca, Gustavo Gaitán Otálora. The proposed legislation would have reimbursed a worker injured on the job from funds collected for that purpose from owners of industries with over five employees. Even though Gaitán's bill won some support, it died in the second debate, amid accusations that it was socialistic. Attempts to get the legislation through the 1912, 1913, and 1914 congresses also failed. Finally, the 1915 congress approved legislation providing six forms of accident compensation; the maximum award was one year's salary to the family of a worker killed on the job.[66] Critics voiced complaints regarding the shortcomings of the legislation, emphasizing the low levels of compensation and the lack of clauses that would force owners to take preventive measures to protect workers from accidents. These defects were supposed to be resolved by the Council of State, but as late as August 1918, repeated petitions from the UOC had failed to get that body to take any action.[67]

Bogotá's workers also faced a shortage of adequate, inexpensive housing. Calls for some form of government-sponsored housing for workers, first heard in the 1890s, finally elicited a favorable response from the municipal council of Bogotá in 1912. In that year, the González Ponce brothers donated an eighteen-block area in San Victorino to the city to be used as a *barrio obrero*—sufficient land for 597 lots, which could be purchased by workers at reduced prices. The city in turn agreed to provide water, city services, educational assistance, and a monthly stipend of one-hundred pesos (gold) for its management.[68] The neighborhood was officially dedicated on February 22, 1914, and renamed "Antonio Ricaurte." Some seventy houses were then under construction and ten had been completed. The city declared that plans were underway for extension of water lines to the barrio and noted that several "fine" artesian wells kept it fully supplied until pipes were laid. (Two years later, water lines were still not in place.) The barrio's meeting hall quickly became a focal point of worker activity, most notably at celebrations such as May Day.[69]

The assassination of Rafael Uribe Uribe in October 1914 recast the shape of the workers' movement for the remainder of the decade. Without him, the Liberal party lost its dominance over the UNIO, which it had enjoyed since 1911. Numerous workers' groups moved to fill the political opening left by Uribe Uribe's death.[70] Republicans were especially active in trying to mobilize workers for the February 1915 departmental elections; they included Marco T. Amorocho as one of their principal candidates, only to lose to the Conservatives.[71] In the May congressional elections, however, the Conservative party was divided, and a Liberal Union/Republican slate polled the most votes.[72] A reunited Conservative party faced an alliance of Republicans, Liberals, and Workers in the October municipal council election. Amorocho, José Joaquín Munévar, and Antonio Aguirre, who won seats on the body, expected to express themselves autonomously as workers; but according to Amorocho, Liberals and Conservatives had secretly worked out an arrangement so that they could dominate the appointment process to the exclusion of the workers. While workers' representatives on the council disrupted its operations with their complaints for a while, they could not overcome the Liberal/Conservative collusion.[73] This confrontation further undermined the faith of workers' leaders in conventional political activity, and, in so doing, set the stage for the founding of the second Workers' party.

## The Partido Obrero

The Partido Obrero (Workers' party) built upon the experience and activities of other labor organizations that had operated during the 1910s. The eight-hundred workers who issued its organizational manifesto on January 1, 1916, included members from various mutual aid societies, as well as many participants in the UOC. Its leaders rejected partisan politics in favor of social and economic measures that would more directly benefit the Colombian worker. *El Partido Obrero*, the group's newspaper, indicated that the party would seek workers' unity and socioeconomic justice.[74]

The first of these focal points, the rejection of partisan politics, had slowly gained force throughout the decade. Although the UNIO was supposedly interested in social and economic concerns, it became deeply embroiled in the political process and fell under the control of *uribista* Liberals. The UOC, by contrast, had dedicated itself to the socioeconomic concerns of workers and claimed to be their "legitimate" representative. The organizers of the Workers' party saw cooperation with Liberals to be a political quagmire and announced that it was best to abstain from political participation as long as the traditional parties were abusive and the workers unorganized. This attitude did not prevent "legitimate" accords with the established parties on occasion, nor did the party deny that Liberals had helped workers in a limited fashion over the years.[75] Still, the failure of traditional parties to pass compulsory education, give protection to small industries, or establish savings banks allegedly warranted the need for an independent workers' political organization according to the group. Moreover, in the opinion of the party's newspaper editors, private property had spawned the problems that the workers faced, a concept rejected by both Conservatives and Liberals.[76]

The organizational structure of the Workers' party drew upon earlier patterns. Neither the Partido Obrero nor the UOC used the barrio as its unit of organization, a move that ignored the potential political strengths of that subdivision of city politics. The UOC had employed affiliated groups of workers to form a central directory, while the Workers' party proposed organizing each trade in a body that would select two delegates to a Workers' Directory, which in turn would assume control of the party on May 1, 1916. Its leaders thought that such an organizational format would allow the sometimes diverse interests of the various trades to be heard with no single trade's concerns dominating the others.[77]

Clearly, the Workers' party understood the issues of the day from a more socialist perspective than had its predecessors. The editors of *El Partido Obrero* described a society in which class inequities denied the worker equal enjoyment of material possessions or social rewards, suggesting that labor, and not capital, should control production and the distribution of its benefits. Fundamental social changes would be necessary to reach such a goal, they realized, but in the short run, workers' education, improvements in social services, wage increases, and increased cooperation between the trades could be achieved. These demands had all been heard before, but the Workers' party also expressed concern for the particular problems of women laborers, regarded strikes as legitimate tools for the rectification of injustices, and called for a national workers' convention.[78]

The Partido Obrero encountered public opposition as it sought to define its ideology and organizational character. Its spokesmen stressed that the party did not favor an anarchistic socialism that desired elimination of all property, but rather "protectionist socialism," by which the state in cooperation with workers would carry out the task of restructuring society. The party's rationale in determining its label, the editors of *El Partido Obrero* wrote, took account of socialism's negative public image and the fact that the title "Workers' party" conveyed the desired sentiment; a union of "workers that asks for social guarantees, education, work, and just remunerations."[79] More radical socialists criticized the use of the name "Workers' party," suggesting that it implied that the group was dedicated to political action, which was obviously not the case. Moreover, the critics continued, the exclusivism of the workers cut off the group from many of its real allies, who were not manual laborers. Nonetheless, the editors of the socialist newspaper *La Libertad* declared that they would cooperate fully with the party.[80]

Liberals associated with the UNIO and loyal to Uribe Uribe expressed more pointed opposition to the new organization. Ramón Rosales, who would become minister of labor under President Alfonso López Pumarejo in the 1930s, claimed that the group represented a Republican device to confront the Liberal party. If one favored workers' issues, Rosales insisted, then the Liberal party was the only place to find support. Leaders of the UNIO made similar comments.[81] In response, members of the Workers' party charged that Rosales was a political boss whose sole concern was to use the votes of workers and that his allegations were hardly cause for them to cease their labor.[82]

Rosales's comments that Republicans were intimately involved in the foundation of the Workers' party were at least partially accurate. Republicans had been losing cohesion as a party for some time, with some of their adherents returning to the Liberal fold and others striking out in new directions. *La Gaceta Republicana*, the party's mouthpiece since 1909, had changed hands in late 1915, when Juan Ignacio Gálvez become its director. Gálvez, it will be recalled, was active in the 1904 Union of Industrials and Workers; that he promptly invited workers' groups to use the paper for their announcements indicates that Rosales's point had a degree of validity.[83] Nonetheless, antecedents such as the UOC suggest that the Workers' party was less a product of desperate Republicans than part of the emerging working-class labor movement.

The non-partisan stance of the Partido Obrero was evident in the 1917 departmental elections. Liberals and Republicans, who united in a "Liberal Union" for the contest, cautioned workers that their plan to steer free of politics might be well-intended, but that partisan politics remained the only legitimate route to fundamental change.[84] The Liberal Union defeated the two slates presented by Conservatives, but it proved unable to draw the Workers' party into the alliance. Most observers commented that large numbers of workers refused to take part in the election, which, as a consequence, drew the smallest number of voters for any departmental election in the decade.[85] Both Liberal and Republican editorialists condemned this new variant of workers' politics, insisting that they could satisfactorily address workers' needs.[86] Officials of the Workers' party in turn condemned "los dirigentes de la política" (political bosses) who had consistently denied that workers could shape their own future by their own hands. They noted that changing socioeconomic conditions had produced a more aware working class, one that was, through the Workers' party, planting the seeds for its own future.[87]

The movement away from political activities to those more directly concerned with social and economic conditions was visible in the Workers' party's inclusion of strikes as legitimate weapons in the struggle to improve working conditions and wages. Strikes were not unknown in nineteenth-century Bogotá but, given the predominance of artisan production, they were few. As wage labor became more common, the frequency, although not necessarily the duration, of strikes increased. Early strikes in transportation industries, especially on the Railroad of the Sabana by non-unionized workers, often opposed wage reductions or favored wage increases to offset inflation.[88] In the first days of 1918, a wave of strikes, spawned by these grievances, swept the major cities of the northern Colombian coast, stimulating railroad workers in Bogotá also to demand higher wages.[89] When the Cartagena strike turned violent, the government issued a decree that acknowledged the right of native-born workers to strike, but prohibited permanent strike committees or the use of violence by workers. The same decree imposed a state of siege until the situation was brought under governmental control.[90]

The outbreak of strikes in 1918 most likely resulted from the economic pressures created by the First World War; a "modern" response to modern phenomena. At the same time, workers in Bogotá were using modern methods to counter an old problem, that of international competition. The tariff of 1905 had lessened, though not stilled, clamors for protective legislation, but in the 1910s governmental solicitation of bids from foreign producers caused a flurry of protests. In October 1916, for example, cabinetmakers expressed outrage that the Railroad of the Sabana had ordered windows and doors from the United States, calling the move typical of the foreignism (*extranjerismo*) that denied the competence of native producers.[91] Three years later, the government's announced intention to purchase military uniforms abroad spurred workers to stage a massive demonstration on March 16, 1919. During the course of the protest, confrontations broke out between demonstrators and police; armed authorities opened fire, killing at least seven people and wounding an unknown number. In order to understand the size and tenor of the demonstration, and the reaction it precipitated by the government, it must be placed in the context of the meeting of the Asamblea Obrera (Workers' Assembly).

## The Asamblea Obrera

The workers' mobilizations of the 1910s culminated in an assembly of organizations in early 1919. The Sindicato Central de Obreros (Central Workers' Syndicate) and the Confederación de Acción Social (Social Action Confederation) met in late 1918 to determine possible alternatives for the future, the result being a call for the Asamblea Obrera (Workers' Assembly). The latter group, presided by Dr. Eduardo Carvajal, had been formed to help bogotanos cope with the 1918 outbreaks of typhoid and influenza. Members of the Confederation were a varied lot, united only by the fact that they had shown concern for social issues throughout the 1910s. They included labor activists such as Pablo Amaya and Luis Ezpeleta; Liberals such as Alberto Sicard and Bernardino Rangel; and the dissident Conservative Laureano Gómez. The origins of the Central Workers' Syndicate are somewhat more obscure, although it was rooted in the tradition of the UOC and the 1916 Workers' party. Pablo E. Mancera, one of the founders of both the Syndicate and the UOC, related that it was created in 1917 as a group of five people to study the city's socioeconomic misery.[92] In any case, the January 19 opening of the Assembly attracted a broad spectrum of individuals and groups that had been connected with organized workers over the previous fifteen years. Delegates from the Mutual Aid Society, the UOC, the Society of Death Insurance, the Barbers' Society, and at least five other groups were among the estimated five-hundred people in attendance. The delegates announced their commitment to social, moral, and economic unity and their inclusion in the international workers' movement.[93] As the Asamblea continued its deliberations, it invited other groups to organize and become affiliates. That call resulted in the establishment and affiliation of various organizations, ranging from those of tailors and cobblers to cabinetmakers and railroad workers. Within two weeks after its opening, the number of affiliates had doubled from the initial ten. By the time the Assembly declared its work completed in June, it claimed over one-hundred affiliates.[94]

The Assembly's first pronouncement declared itself to be the Socialist party. The Asemblea called for an activist state program to be directed by workers, to combat social injustices such as poor housing, illiteracy, and unequal material conditions. The Assembly included in its platform a clause calling for nationalization of the police, the telegraph, and the teaching trades, which, it presumed, would improve their social conditions. Various components of the platform directly addressed the needs of workers: an eight-hour workday, maternity benefits, protective tariffs, the right to strike, wages determined by workers' committees, a strengthened workers' compensation law, paid May Day holidays, and state-managed retirement funds. The platform did not envision the state to be the primary catalyst for workers' betterment; that improvement, it insisted, would come from education and material progress, which, in turn, would enable the Socialist party to place reformist pressure upon the state. In regard to political action, the Assembly declared itself to be independent, supportive only of those who favored the socioeconomic advancement of the proletariat. The group declared that it would practice abstention when no clear pro-worker candidates were available.[95] The Assembly released plans for the creation of the Central Workers' Syndicate to serve as the basis for future action. Local syndicates would have responsibility for organizing laborers and other pro-socialist sympathizers for the development of programs such as savings banks, mutual aid societies, consumers' cooperatives, and workers' housing. Representatives of local groups would then form the Central Syndicate, which would be charged with direction of political plans, coordination of agencies for improvement of socioeconomic conditions, and communication with international groups. A national workers' congress, scheduled to meet on August 7, 1919, was to formalize the Central Syndicate.[96]

The increasingly dynamic organization called for a public show of strength on March 16, 1919. It is unclear whether the plan and demonstration was prompted by President Marco Fidel Súarez's decision to purchase the Army's uniforms abroad, or whether it was simply coincident—both seem to have been announced on the same day.[97] There is no doubt, however, that the Assembly promptly linked the two, declaring the demonstration to be in protest of the decree, proclaiming, "Workers, the hour of our justice begins!"[98] An estimated five- to ten-thousand people gathered in the Plaza de Bolívar on Sunday, March 16, to protest the government's decision. The crowd peacefully listened to the Assembly's president, Marco T. Amorocho, and others criticize the plan. Súarez himself stepped forward to address the multitude, only to be met with disorder and stones. Isolated shots rang out, then barrages of machine-gun fire, which forced the demonstrators to flee for safety. Gunfire and other disturbances lasted until nightfall, leaving at least seven persons dead and unknown numbers wounded. Numerous leaders of the protest were arrested, including Amorocho, Eduardo Carvajal, and Alberto Manrique Páramo (director of La Gaceta Republicana), and the government imposed a state of siege.[99]

Somewhat unexpectedly, the government did not suspend the Assembly and quickly released those arrested. The Assembly in late April 1919 announced the creation of an Executive Socialist Directory, which was then elected on May Day. The Assembly's final document, approved on May 20, formally renamed the organization the Socialist party. It declared itself both free of established parties and religious groups and exclusively dedicated to measures that would favor the cause of the proletariat. With its work accomplished, the Assembly moved to adjourn, but not before a National Executive Socialist Directory was elected and declarations of solidarity signed by the groups that had been included in the Assembly's deliberations.[100]

The May congressional elections offered the movement an opportunity to display its organizational strength. It had earlier urged its members not to vote in the February departmental elections, which produced the lowest vote total in the decade (4,219), less than half of the turnout for the 1915 elections (9,200), and considerably less than the 5,684 votes two years later—an election also characterized by workers' abstention.[101] The Assembly initially announced that it would support only those individuals with socialist goals in the May contest and that in no case would it assume an active role. It nonetheless gave a list of possible workers' candidates to the committee of Liberals, Republicans, and dissident Conservatives—men with very questionable socialist credentials. Negotiations among the three groups failed to concur on a common slate, so Liberals presented a list separate from the unified slate presented by dissident Conservatives and Republicans; the latter slate included Amorocho as a principal candidate. True to its pledge, the Assembly abstained from active electioneering. The election was won by the Nationalist Conservative slate.[102]

It seemed that the Assembly had resolved the nagging problem faced by all workers' groups in Bogotá during the 1910s—how to balance political and socioeconomic action and not to become a tool for the interests of non-workers. The route to that end was to be the Socialist party, "adapted to the needs and aspirations of the Colombian people," which, by assumption, were those of the workers.[103] In fact, however, the conflict of interests continued. May consultations among members of the Socialist Directory and representatives of the Workers' Directory of Girardot, who were grappling with the same problem, failed to produce an accord. Members of the Bogotá group who were not workers urged the Girardot association to consider the broader implications of the workers' needs, which, in their view, made it necessary to emphasize the political cause before more purely worker issues. Even Amorocho seemed to agree with this, although he cautioned that workers' trade organizations had to serve as the base for any such movement. When the same non-worker members of the Bogotá directory commented on the May election, they insisted that the apathetic attitude displayed by workers in that contest needed to be changed if they were to progress, seemingly suggesting the priority of political action. Finally, it is noteworthy that none of the workers' delegates who signed the closing manifesto of the Asemblea Obrera were selected as members of the National Executive Socialist Directory; workers and non-workers seemed to be following two distinct orientations.[104]

## Conclusion

The first two decades of the twentieth century constituted a transitional era for Bogotá's labor movement, from one that had been dominated by artisans to one that reflected the particular interests of wage laborers. Certain issues were common to both types of workers, foremost among these the demand for effective political participation. However, fundamentally contrasting social and economic realities produced more points of departure than convergence in the platforms expressed by the two classes of laborers. Whereas tariff protection had been central to artisan political statements, this issue was seldom raised after the War of the 1000 Days, and even then more often by industrials than by workers. For the Colombian Workers' Union, the tariff question, which originated from the artisans' desire to protect established professions, took a backseat to socioeconomic priorities such as increased educational opportunities and higher wages. While tradesmen certainly had raised their voices in favor of the former, the question of wages was less relevant to the independent craftsmen than the more general issue of income. Similarly, demands for accident compensation and the right to strike were only pertinent to modern wage laborers.

Both types of laborers issued calls for effective political participation, albeit with different goals. During most of the nineteenth century, men claiming to speak for craftsmen had espoused the virtues of republicanism, an ideology that they felt would properly reward their social and economic contributions with political influence—if it were not subverted by partisan egoism. Artisans, as a middle-sector group, did not desire to rewrite the political rules, only to reform them, which, presumably, they could accomplish. By contrast, the 1910s saw a gradual evolution by certain bogotano workers toward a socialism that would alter the basic economic, social, and political fabric of the Colombian state. The point of departure for workers was the same as it had been for artisans; a bipartisan system seemingly run by and for the elite. Groups such as the UNIO posited that if a united industrial/worker political front could be formed, then it could bring about the reforms necessary to make the system more responsive to their will and needs. Ideally, the UNIO hoped, such a movement would be independent of the established parties, but reality dictated relations with Republicans and Liberals, compromises not dissimilar to those made earlier by artisans. However, the groups of the 1910s did not fall back to earlier positions when their exploitation became obvious. Rather, they came to believe that abstention from traditional parties in favor of socialist politics might be the appropriate way to achieve effective workers' participation. It is not surprising that politically conscious workers, aware of their seeming inability to alter their subordinate position within society, would seek a solution that would create a new system, as opposed to reforming the old one.

It was nonetheless the case that while the needs of Bogotá's workers were articulately expressed, and a socialist solution for the basic problems elaborated, the ever-present question of cooperation with or independence from traditional political parties persisted. At no point during the 1910s did the capital's workers, to say nothing of workers from other areas of the country, obtain sufficient power or unity to impose their wishes upon local, departmental, or national politics. The labor movement entering into the 1920s was more conscious, politically mature, and better organized, yet it had to confront the decision of cooperation (and possible co-optation) with other groups, or an independent route and probable impotence.

# SEVEN

# SOCIOECONOMIC CHANGE, PARTISAN POLITICS, AND ARTISAN ORGANIZATIONS

T HE PACE AND CHARACTER OF THE ARTISAN LABOR MOVEMENT IN Bogotá were shaped by two variables. The generally downward trend in the socioeconomic position of bogotano craftsmen, caused by competition from foreign goods and by the rise of industrial wage laborers in the city and region, spurred artisans to protect themselves by organized activity, much of it political in nature. At the same time, the partisan struggle for power drew craftsmen into the political arena as the parties attempted to broaden their base of support. Taken together, these factors help to explain the pace of artisan political and organizational activity, its objectives, and, to a certain degree, its impact.

Artisans and their handicrafts evolved during the one-hundred years after independence from the single most important productive sector in the Colombian urban economy to one portion of a complex mix of workers utilizing a variety of productive techniques. This was hardly a rapid transformation that might have provoked craftsmen to violently resist threats to their socioeconomic well being. Rather, it was a long process that slowly eroded the importance of artisans within the productive and social hierarchy of the city. Nor did all crafts share a similar experience. Some suffered rapid changes while others underwent a gradual transformation. The responses by different craftsmen to economic change varied; political efforts often depended upon their particular fortunes.[1] Existing information suggests that the trades of tailors and cobblers, which suffered from early competition, were more active in organizations of the liberal reform era. Other craftsmen, those who practiced construction activities, were more vocal in the last third of the century.

Public statements by craftsmen are perhaps the surest route to the examination of issues affecting their socioeconomic condition, especially as the detailed analysis of artisan lifestyles awaits further study. Public declarations do not reflect the full range of craftsmen's concerns, but they do serve as possible barometers of crisis, revealing pressing issues that threatened the way of life held dear by artisans, or at least by their public spokesmen. Repeated references to particular topics indicate either their perceived importance or the intensity of the threat—or both. How the content of those statements varied through time further suggests internal changes in the artisan class and signals when the class began to lose some of its cohesion.[2]

Commonly voiced concerns fall into four interrelated areas: economic, political, social welfare, and the public image of artisans. The most frequently expressed grievances were economic, especially the desire for tariff protection, but included opinions on industrial education, internal trade order, credit, and the economic dislocations caused by war. Political comments centered on the aspirations of craftsmen to gain a legitimate voice in the polity and a general disenchantment with partisan politics. Welfare concerns ranged from the desire for better educational and health facilities to support for agencies that afforded a degree of social protection, such as the church or mutual aid societies. Finally, craftsmen projected their social, economic, and political contributions so as to mold a positive public image they felt was their due. This pride "de ser artesano" served to reinforce the right of craftsmen to express themselves publicly.

Craftsmen reasoned that the tariff structure that insulated their production from foreign competition was critical for their socioeconomic well-being. As the moderately protectionist tariffs of the early national period gave way to liberal tariff reductions, craftsmen from Bogotá and other areas of the country repeatedly petitioned for the restoration of a protective tariff policy.[3] When tariff rates were raised in the 1880s, craftsmen praised the Regeneration government and certain trades seemed to benefit from the decrease in foreign competition.[4] However, neither the tariffs of Núñez nor those of Reyes were necessarily intended to foster a resurgence of artisanal production, but to foster development of manufacturing industries within the country. While certain artisans may have enjoyed short-term benefits from these tariffs, the long-term effect was increased competition for artisanal producers from native or foreign manufactures.

Craftsmen thought that governmental measures in addition to the maintenance of tariff barriers could help their industries. Demands that primary products and machines used by native craftsmen in their trades should be allowed to enter the country with a minimum of duties and restrictions were presented first in the 1846 petition and were included in almost every other petition thereafter, including that of the Colombian Workers' Union of the 1910s.[5] As early as the 1840s, craftsmen sought exposure to the techniques of foreign artisans, even if they were critical of those foreigners in Bogotá who refused to associate with their native counterparts.[6] Artisans often requested that the government organize workshops to disseminate new skills and that it try to attract foreign craftsmen willing to train natives, or send Colombians abroad to learn the latest skills.[7] Craftsmen claimed to need additional sources of credit, and thus supported the Caja de Ahorros and repeatedly tried to start their own savings institutions. Every mutual aid society included at least plans for a bank, as did political associations such as the Unión Nacional de Industriales y Obreros in the 1910s.[8]

Conceivably, artisan political pressure had the potential to force the Colombian government to protect their industries, to begin programs of industrial education, and to establish credit institutions. Political pressure had less ability to affect the cost of transportation, a buffering factor in the price of foreign goods in Bogotá. The importance of high transportation costs as a protector of interior craftsmen was apparently not appreciated by artisans, even though they probably equalled tariff duties in adding costs to the consumers of foreign products. Permanent steamboat navigation on the Magdalena River lowered transportation costs by perhaps one-third and aggravated the onslaught of foreign goods by the 1860s.[9] Rail links to the river, established in the first years of the twentieth century, undoubtedly amplified the amount of imported merchandize available in the Colombian capital.

The civil wars that accompanied the ever-present partisan strife disrupted the local and national economies and caused serious dislocations among craftsmen.[10] Artisans lost many orders during the wars and saw credit, which was expensive and in short supply in the best of times, rise in price and be diverted to fund military adventures. Moreover, artisans were frequently called to service as members of the militia, an obligation that kept them from working and sometimes led to injury and death.[11] Since partisan machinations caused practically every conflict, artisans urged that parties alternate in control or share power—anything to reduce the level of strife. This undoubtedly accounted for the popularity of Núñez and perhaps contributed to the appeal of Mosquera and Reyes, all men who seemed dedicated to the notion of political stability, even at the expense of constitutional guidelines or competitive elections. Craftsmen thought that partisan abuses denied them a political voice, which in turn provoked demands for more effective representation in politics. On numerous occasions this sentiment was expressed by the complaint, "we were used as a ladder for Liberal [or Conservative] ambitions, only to be thrown away when we were no longer needed."[12]

The artisans' economic and political interests shared the characteristic that they could be furthered primarily by power or influence within the realm of political activity. This was generally not true of their immediate social welfare concerns, which artisans more frequently tried to resolve on their own. Although limited in its actual delivery of services, the church offered artisans and their children educational programs and health care until the reform era, when clerical authorities were stripped of many temporal functions and resources, a move artisans condemned in several public statements.[13] The Society of Artisans, the Popular Society, and the Union Society all attempted to answer the need for adult education by conducting their own classes. After the 1860s craftsmen appealed to the government to expand its educational programs. Social welfare needs were met in a similar fashion, with general mobilizations such as the Union Society attempting to look after the needs of its membership. The mutual aid societies (that were developed after 1872) responded directly to these concerns, even if their membership was limited to the artisan elite. At least some of the support for the Regeneration can be attributed to the restitution of the church as a formal agent in the maintenance of Colombian society.

Why did artisans think that their complaints should be recognized and addressed by the nation's "natural" elite? A reading of craftsmen's public manifestations suggests that artisans thought their contributions to the nation valuable enough to earn a political voice and policy influence. Craftsmen's consciousness seems to have been based upon the belief that the labor of producing the nation's consumer goods, while not always rewarding financially, was both honorable and necessary. The 1858 article "The Artisan of Bogotá" stressed that while the rich and social luminaries refused to abandon the colonial attitude that "the arts dishonor," artisans maintained that "it is worth more to be an honorable poor man than a rich man and a thief."[14] José Leocadio Camacho, writing in the 1860s for *La Alianza*, argued that production itself contributed to society by its creative function and justified the resultant feelings of self-respect, personal worth, and economic value.[15]

The trades that craftsmen practiced afforded them a feeling of economic independence and a middling social rank that set them apart from the masses. This status was a source of pride and self-respect. The work of an artisan might not produce wealth, but it did avoid vagabondage. By contrast, artisans often juxtaposed the value of their production with the "social evil" of *empleomanía*. The employee who consumed the scarce taxes of the nation and produced nothing tangible was anathema to many craftsmen. Craftsmen viewed themselves as positive political forces: they paid taxes to support local, state, and national governments, acted as night watchmen in their barrios, served in the militia, defended the constitutional order, and, in general, acted as good republican citizens.[16]

The aims that craftsmen tried to satisfy, either through organizational pressure or by individual initiative, originated in their socioeconomic status as independent producers and from their political rights as citizens. The transformation of Bogotá and Colombia's economy threatened the ability of many artisans to preserve their traditional social position and caused most of the pressures that craftsmen tried to alleviate by political action. The persistence of demands such as tariff protection and industrial education throughout the nineteenth century indicates the ongoing threat to the artisans' socioeconomic status. The appearance of new demands in the 1910s, for laws pertaining to work accidents and for basic education, evidences the emergence of the wage laborer as an important component of Bogotá's working population and, by implication, the eclipsed status of artisans as the leaders of the labor movement. Similarly, artisan demands for effective political participation within a republican system gave way to workers' calls for a vaguely defined socialist state. Craftsmen had a strong stake in Bogotá's social, economic, and political life; they wanted not to abolish it, but to shape it more to their advantage. The same was not necessarily true of the wage laborers, many of whom backed socialist calls for a transformed state.

## The Partisan Struggle for Power

The conjuncture of the republican ideal and the partisan struggle for power shaped the initial stages of artisan political participation in early national Colombia. The leaders of the Colombian movement for independence and those who shaped the country's constitutional structure not only rejected Spanish domination but also the rule of absolute monarchs, whom they felt fostered tyranny and lessened the opportunities for social, economic, or moral progress. Those who compared the fortunes of Spain with that of the United States reached the conclusion that republican government fostered economic prosperity, social progress, and political stability; it was therefore the ideal form of government for the emerging nation. The republican model implied popular participation in the election of representatives to govern the nation (to the relief of many, it had been demonstrated in the United States that a responsible citizenry could avoid the popular anarchy of revolutionary France and usually selected the "natural" elite as its rulers). Throughout the nineteenth century, with only a few exceptions, constitutions granted citizenship to "respectable" individuals, as determined by property holdings, income, occupational status, or literacy.[17] Artisans constituted a significant portion of the urban population deemed worthy of participation in the republican political system. The extension of this right surely evoked a favorable response from craftsmen who reasoned that as honorable citizens, as defenders of the legitimate order, and in recognition of their productive functions, they deserved such a privilege.

The reality of nineteenth-century Colombian politics, however, was far removed from the republican ideal. An intense struggle for power and frustrated efforts to form a stable governmental structure lasted until after the disastrous War of the 1000 Days.[18] Regional forces fought for political power and control of the state through the guises of the Conservative and Liberal parties and their multiple factions. Fundamental programmatic differences separated these groups only on social and church-related issues; control of the nation's purse strings and appointative powers were the central bones of contention. Since no single group could monopolize power, broadened bases of electoral and popular support quickly became necessary. In rural areas, traditional patronage ties simplified the matter; the power of landlords, clerics, or others readily translated into votes. Some of the same patronage relations, notably those of the church, influenced urban politics, but the presence of relatively autonomous individuals such as artisans made the cities, especially Bogotá, distinct political environments.

The necessity of partisan groups to recruit clients and the ideal of popular participation in a republican government resulted in the appeal for the political allegiance of urban craftsmen. The 1838 struggle between factions of the developing Conservative and Liberal parties led directly to the recruitment of artisans into the Catholic Society and the Democratic-Republican Society of Progressive Artisans and Laborers. Both Societies solicited votes and attempted to instill in their members a particular ideology. There is, however, little evidence to indicate either that a rigid alignment between politically active artisans and parties emerged, or that craftsmen accepted without question partisan ideological stances, either in the 1830s or beyond, although during some periods more craftsmen tended to work for the endeavors of one or the other party. More often than not, the most visible political associations linked artisans to the leaders of dissident or third-party movements such as the draconianos (1850s), Manuel María Madiedo (1860s), the Independent Liberals (1870s), Núñez (1880 and beyond), and the Republicans (1910s).

Various reasons explain craftsmen's associations with third parties, or with groups that did not fit neatly into the Conservative or Liberal camps. In the early 1850s, I suspect that much of the Democratic Societies' relationship with the draconianos stemmed from their loyalty to Obando and many members of the military, whose social status was akin to that of the craftsmen. Artisans shared the draconiano common interest in slowing down, if not halting altogether, several aspects of the reform agenda, and from the necessity of joining forces to enhance their potential strength in opposition to groups favoring the reform process. These three factors—loyalty to particular leaders, ideological similarities, and the mutual advantages of concerted action by "outsiders"—account for the majority of the artisan/third-party associations, with the desire to advance each other vis-à-vis the dominant parties probably the single most important factor. This is evident in the relationship that workers developed with the Republicans of the 1910s, a group that finally was eclipsed by the two traditional parties.

The relationship between artisans and the mainstream Conservative and Liberal parties was considerably less complex. During periods of intense political rivalry, parties regularly recruited artisan support. The records of the two Societies of 1838, of the Democratic and Popular Societies of the reform era, and of the electoral organizations thereafter illustrate this tendency. Significantly, the frequency of such appeals dropped off sharply in the 1870s almost to disappear between 1880 and 1910. The fragmentation of the artisan class that occurred after the 1860s, along with the development of party infrastructures, accounts for this tendency.[19] By the 1870s, after years of propaganda and efforts to inculcate party loyalty into the voting populace, it seems that people spontaneously identified themselves as Conservatives or Liberals in most elections. This lessened the need to use artisan-based ad hoc electoral groups and diminished the importance of artisan associations. The revival of open recruitment in the 1910s can be attributed to the damage done to party loyalties by the National party of Núñez in the 1880s, by the Reyes government in the years after 1904, and by the need to rebuild the party system. Importantly, the dominant parties in the twentieth century eventually became patrons to labor unions, much to the disadvantage of non-aligned labor organizations.

The initial opening whereby artisans could participate politically thus came not from their own pressures, but rather from above, as a result of the partisan struggle for power. Partisan patrons recruited political clients, who in the urban setting were drawn from the ranks of the artisan sector. In return for their votes, craftsmen expected that their special interests would be heard and that the ideal republic would function in fact. That it did not is hardly surprising. Nevertheless, the expression of goals and objectives particular to the artisan population and the collective activity undertaken to satisfy those desires, despite repeated failures, left a record that deserves careful examination.

## Craftsmen's Organizations and Periodization

Numerous problems plague the periodization of artisan activity and the construction of a typology of organizations in which they participated. General Latin American labor histories typically describe the nineteenth century as either a "formative period" or as a period of "workers movement without a working class,"[20] without attempting to subdivide the period of "artisan hegemony" or to determine reasons for variations in artisan organizational activity.[21]

Bogotano craftsmen articulated their particular interests through four types of organized expression: temporary electoral groups, broad-based mobilizations, mutual aid societies, and direct action. The functions of these organizations were not mutually exclusive, but were sufficiently distinct to require separate analysis. The periods of organizational activity visible in this study are, 1832–46, 1846–68, 1868–1904, and 1904–19. Partisan "top-down" recruitment by leaders of the emerging Conservative and Liberal parties characterized the fourteen years after 1832. The party-dominated Catholic Society and the Democratic-Republican Society of Progressive Artisans and Laborers attempted to instill in craftsmen and others the particular beliefs of the two parties.[22] The most intense artisan political activity of the nineteenth century took place in the 1846–68 period, when general mobilizations of artisans exercised a marked influence upon bogotano and Colombian politics. However, before 1855, these organizations tended to be more oriented toward the Liberal party, while after the defeat of Melo in 1854 they were more oriented toward the Conservative party.

The Society of Artisans represents the first formal effort by laborers to autonomously influence the workings of the Colombian state. Craftsmen mobilized to protect their trades and livelihoods from the dangers they saw in the 1847 tariff law—which they sought to repeal—but they also attempted to enhance their intellectual "awareness" and to work for their mutual aid. The Society's involvement in the 1848 presidential election brought it under the influence of non-artisans associated with the Liberal party, an alliance that was cemented in the 7 de marzo. That election spurred Conservatives to form the Popular Society, a group that articulated the interests of both the Conservative party and those craftsmen who had favored the candidacy of Joaquín Gori in 1848. Partisan confrontations between the Democratic and Popular Societies resulted in the suppression of the latter group, while the former successfully advanced the reform objectives of its gólgota patrons. Gólgotas used artisans as political instruments, just as Progressives had used craftsmen in the Democratic-Republican Society. However, in contrast to the 1830s, by the early 1850s, artisans manifested a clear recognition of their own class concerns and their notions of how Colombia should properly be structured. Many craftsmen perceived that reformers would not favor their demands for a protective tariff and came to view the redefinition of the role of the church in Colombian society as detrimental to social morality and welfare. In time, many Democratic craftsmen joined with draconiano Liberals and disgruntled elements of the military to stage the ill-fated 17 de abril insurrection against the reform package.[23]

The movement away from reformers evident in the 17 de abril accelerated in the 1855–68 period. The most important similarity between this and the earlier period was the continued appeal to, and use of, tradesmen by political parties. The opportunistic nature of the recruitment process generated feelings of political exploitation among craftsmen, who perceived that only their votes or service as cannon fodder mattered to the political elite. President Mosquera's anti-church decrees, which threatened what many craftsmen saw as the source of a "moral" life, further alienated tradesmen. The depression that affected Bogotá after the 1859–62 civil war brought economic misery to all social levels, especially the artisan sector. In the face of economic hardship, wartime abuses, and political disillusionment, the Union Society rejected the system that used tradesmen as partisan tools. It tried instead to assert both the value and potential political power of united artisans. Like the Society of Artisans, the Union Society was a general organization established by artisans to defend their special interests, which, by 1866, were conceptualized in a more conscious and ideologically mature fashion than had been the case in 1847. The

Union Society focused its concerns on the tariff, the need for industrial education, the shortage of agencies to which craftsmen could turn for social welfare assistance, and a powerful rejection of partisan manipulation of artisans as political puppets. The Union Society earnestly attempted to shape an organization that could meet the needs of mutual protection and thereby alleviate some of the economic pressures upon its members in particular and the artisan class in general. It assumed an essentially non-partisan stance, but tended to side with dissident Conservatives such as Madiedo. Partisan political action was rejected outright by almost all craftsmen, but the 1867 coup attempt by Mosquera and subsequent political turmoil splintered the Union Society, leading to its collapse in November 1868.

No broad-based organization of artisans appeared during the last three decades of the nineteenth century. Temporary political groups periodically appeared around elections. The divergent courses of action taken by "elite" and "mass" artisans during this period supports the notion that the shared experiences of the Liberal Reform era that had shaped the artisan class consciousness of the Union Society had changed, which in turn led to distinct socioeconomic experiences. Associations such as the Mutual Aid or Philanthropic Societies reflected the efforts of artisans who had maintained their productive integrity to look after their own social welfare concerns, as did trade organizations. These craftsmen maintained their relationship with the partisan camps, especially with the Nationalists, who most closely approximated their ideologies. With members of the artisan elite seeking to protect themselves, and in the absence of general mobilizations, the mass of less-successful artisans and other popular sectors were left without the means to express their socioeconomic grievances. This may help to explain why the only major incidents of direct action that occurred during the whole of the years under investigation took place during the 1869–1904 period. Since no institutional vehicle was available to alleviate the very real needs of the rank-and-file craftsmen and urban poor, the bread riot of 1875 and the police riot of 1893 attempted to rectify perceived injustices.

The organizations that dominated the final years of this study illustrate the halting cooperation between the artisan, industrial, and wage laborer.[24] Mutual aid societies persisted, but their visibility tended to be eclipsed by organizations such as the National

Union of Industrials and Workers (UNIO). The National Union reflected the complex nature of Bogotá's laboring population, which now consisted of artisans, small industrials, and wage laborers. The group attempted to form a coalition of these sectors, but the contrasting concerns of industrials and workers doomed the venture. Organizations such as the Colombian Workers' Union (UOC), representing increasingly articulate wage laborers, replaced the National Union. Craftsmen probably identified themselves intellectually and socially with industrials, but their socioeconomic situation was undoubtedly more akin to that of workers. Partisan efforts to use labor organizations intensified after the collapse of the Reyes quinquenio in 1909. Liberal followers of Rafael Uribe Uribe appealed to the industrials of the UNIO, while the Republicans favored fledgling socialist groups. However, just as had happened with the Union Society in the 1860s, the parties' manipulation of workers' organizations brought about a powerful backlash, which contributed to development of a socialist ideology and the rejection of partisan politics. These trends appeared in the 1919 Workers' Assembly and saw more forceful expression in the Socialist congresses of the 1920s. The Conservatives also made efforts to mobilize workers on their behalf, especially in the clerical-dominated Workers' Circle that tried to counter the influence of "foreign" ideologies. This organization did little more than previous informal mobilizations of workers by Catholics, but it demonstrated that Conservative forces would not abandon workers to Liberals and others without contention.

The organization of craftsmen of Bogotá between 1832 and the 1920s took place within a dynamic political system that enabled artisans to seek goals relevant to their social sector. In rejecting an analysis that would treat artisans as singularly responsible for their own organizational destiny, I do not mean to suggest that the special socioeconomic conditions of artisans did not affect their political activity, only that they did not serve as the initial precipitant for those efforts. In reaction to top-down pressures from partisan groups, artisans took advantage of the political opening to pursue numerous objectives originating in their particular social and economic positions, which, with only a few exceptions, differed from those presented by the political parties. The pre-1870s period was characterized by a more homogeneous artisan experience, as well as by threats to many trades in the form of foreign competition, and partisan appeals to the artisans to serve the limited interests of the parties. During this period, craftsmen's collective interests were voiced through broad-based organizations. When the artisan class fragmented after the 1860s, collective activity tended to reflect the interests of the divisions of the artisanal population and not of the entire craft sector. Mutual aid societies and direct actions characterized these years. As a new wage-labor population emerged in the early years of this century, and as petty industrials replaced craftsmen as the most prominent producers, artisans who had retained their independent status fluctuated in aligning themselves politically with workers or industrials in coalition groups. Craftsmen initially sided with industrials, men who often came from the artisan ranks. Over time, however, craftsmen developed strong associations with wage laborers, insofar as they both shared less promising futures. This was especially the case when industrials fell victim to traditional partisan tactics and as socialism emerged as an alternative to "politics as usual."

Especially in the last third of the nineteenth century, the middling status of artisans within bogotano society was clearly exposed. A constant class experience, subjected to partisan and socioeconomic pressures, sustained the popularization of politics in the mid-nineteenth century. As elites recoiled from the specter of armed melistas challenging their authority, the Conservative and Liberal parties recruited craftsmen only timidly. As the artisan class lost its cohesion, it could only undertake diluted and uncoordinated action. Not until the early years of the present century did craftsmen again participate in large-scale organizations that attempted to forge class alliances.

Artisan leaders such as José Leocadio Camacho, José Antonio Saavedra, or Emeterio Heredia were central characters in the relationship between the political parties and artisan organizations. They acted as middlemen: their persistence as leaders depended upon their capacity to negotiate for the interests of the two sides. The parties sought loyal followers; as potential patrons they had to offer some form of return to artisans in payment for craftsmen's clientage. For craftsmen, attention to their specific socioeconomic interests was the price parties were expected to pay in exchange for their support. Many of the grievances that artisans expressed came from the failure of politicians to fulfill their election pledges to craftsmen. It was the function of artisan leaders to seek objectives consistent with the needs of the broader artisan sector and to turn out voters on election days. Leaders such as Camacho—who maintained his preeminent stature for almost fifty years—consistently voiced concerns held by the rank-and-file artisans. By contrast, the fall of Heredia from his leadership role in the Democratic Societies after the 1850s probably lay in his inability to recognize the more conservative tendencies among his fellow craftsmen and from his ardent commitment to partisan politics even after the Melo coup. Although he lived through the 1880s, after 1857 he was unable to mobilize large numbers of craftsmen. Leaders, then, were men who satisfied the interests of political patrons by turning out the vote, but who also satisfied the interests of artisan clients by representing their needs to the parties. The success of a leader seems not to have been in the satisfaction of artisan needs, but leaders had to defend such interests in their dealings with the parties.

## A Comparative Perspective

The political activity of artisans in nineteenth-century Bogotá was bound up in the struggle between parties for political domination and the socioeconomic pressures upon artisans. Urban craftsmen throughout Latin America struggled to maintain their status as independent producers against threats originating in the abandonment of colonial economic policies, increased competition from foreign goods, and the emergence of native industrial production. The definition of national political cultures provided varied opportunities for artisans to express their social, economic, and political interests. I suspect that craftsmen's voices were most audible during the political openings created by competition for power by individuals, parties, or regions. When competition for power was heated, as it often was in Mexico City, Santiago, or Lima, artisans offered elite political associations an additional weapon to be employed in their struggle for political domination. Autonomous political activity seems to have been most frequent around the Liberal Reform period. Toward the end of the period under study, craftsmen were bound up with the early stages of modern labor organizations, even though their voices were sometimes lost to more ideologically outspoken individuals.

Geography and the pace of structural economic change shaped the lives of artisans in distinct fashions. The physical isolation of the Colombian capital buffered bogotano craftsmen from direct and immediate competition with goods produced in the industrializing nations of the North Atlantic region. High transportation costs protected artisans in Bogotá, Quito, Córdoba, La Paz, and countless other cities from less expensive industrial manufactures long after liberals had lowered tariff rates. Craftsmen who lived in coastal areas easily reached by foreign manufactures, such as Buenos Aires or Rio de Janeiro, suffered more abrupt competition than those living in the less accessible interior.[25] The steamboat and the railroad paralleled the factory as threats to artisanal production in Latin America. As these technologies lowered transportation costs, the buffers of geographic isolation were reduced. Indeed, I suspect that the profile of the urban laboring population was as profoundly affected by reduced transportation costs as by lowered tariff schedules, although considerable research is required to verify the hypothesis.

Those areas of Latin America that were earlier and more completely integrated into the world market have been the object of considerably more scholarly attention than countries such as Colombia, Guatemala, or Peru, whose nineteenth-century economic histories probably reflect the more common Latin American experience. A slower pace of economic development or the lack of demand for export commodities correlated to less rapid changes in urban and rural social structures. Conversely, a city such as Buenos Aires, with a strong economy, extensive industrial concerns, reliable transportation connections to Europe and the United States, and an expanding population, had a markedly distinct occupational profile at the end of the nineteenth century than it had had at the beginning. The social structure of Quito, more typical of 1900 urban Latin America, changed less over the course of the century than did its Argentine counterpart.

Craftsmen who had been part of the colonial guild structure entered the nineteenth century with a heritage distinct from that of artisans who had labored in the absence of guilds. In Mexico City and Lima, where guilds seem to have been the strongest, conflicts between masters and journeymen hindered the expression of a cohesive artisan voice.[26] In these cities, skilled craftsmen served a clientele enriched by mines, landholdings, administrative coffers, and commercial activities. Guild craftsmen had strained relations with their less wealthy counterparts. In Mexico City, according to one account, property-holding craftsmen "constructed an ideological wall" to maintain the separation between themselves and the propertyless poor.[27] In the national period, artisans in such cities were trapped in a paradoxical situation as the abolition of guilds enabled journeymen to establish their own shops and to take advantage of new economic opportunities but, at the same time, undermined guild protective mechanisms at a time of increased economic competition. Cohesive economic agents were reduced and divisive influences increased for some urban craftsmen in the early national period.[28]

In geographically remote urban centers where guilds had been weak, such as Bogotá, the likelihood of cohesive behavior in the face of economic threats seems to have been greater. By contrast, in the port of Buenos Aires, whose economic structure had developed in cadence with an export economy, many craftsmen in trades that benefited from the international trading system were therefore less vocal protectionists. Spanish efforts to establish a strong guild structure fell victim to internal trade dissension and to competition between those well positioned to take advantage of the Atlantic economy and those who preferred economic protection.[29] Thus, when Spanish authorities opened the port of Buenos Aires to free trade in 1809, the artisan reaction was relatively muted.[30]

The economic liberalization of the mid-nineteenth century engendered widespread political activity by Latin America's artisans. In Lima, artisans who had earlier been divided because of guild-based economic differences cooperated to win passage of the 1849 Ley de Artesanos, which raised a short-lived tariff barrier around the country, reinforced the dwindling economic power of the guilds, and enhanced the political capacity of craft organizations.[31] Artisans in Bolivia echoed President Manuel Isidor Belzu's call for higher tariff rates in support of "nationalist" economic policies.[32] In Buenos Aires, where economic liberalism became standard policy early in the national period, *porteño* craftsmen, by contrast, raised fewer voices in favor of protective tariffs, although their counterparts from interior cities labored fruitlessly for such measures.[33] These efforts seldom reached the intensity of the struggle by artisans of the Democratic Society of Bogotá, but they certainly represented a common response by craftsmen to similar economic programs.

Quite significantly, the era of Liberal Reform frequently brought artisans into the political arena as either pawns or allies of elite political forces. Chilean liberals who had been inspired by the events of 1848 in Europe recruited craftsmen into the Sociedad de Igualidad (Society of Equality), a group that collapsed within three years.[34] Paul Gootenberg and Jorge Basadre trace a dynamic recruitment process in Peru, one which, however, ended in the abandonment of craftsmen by the end of the 1850s and the exclusion of artisans from the polity until the end of the century.[35] Somewhat surprisingly, Mexican artisans appear to have been quiescent during the reform era, perhaps because the Mexican polity had been at least partially closed to non-elite voices in the beginning of the 1830s, although it certainly expanded somewhat during the reform process. Or perhaps for some, other interests, such as anarchism, diverted their attention from events in the political arena. Numerous accounts attest to the political role of craftsmen in the years before the revolution. In any case, further research is needed on the nineteenth-century Mexican craftsman,[36] a statement true of other countries as well.

Craftsmen throughout the Western world assumed a major role in the transition from artisanal to wage-labor-based labor movements. Michael Hanagan's *Logic of Solidarity* suggests that labor militancy (as measured by strike activity) in late nineteenth-century France was greatest in settings where either artisans were threatened by technological change or where artisans and industrial workers forged coalitions for joint action. Settings dominated by only industrial workers were less prone to militancy.[37] The associational tradition of craftsmen, coupled with a defense of threatened livelihoods, which resulted in artisan/worker coalitions, is also visible in United States labor history.

Yet, while European and United States labor history almost takes this as a given, recent studies of the transitionary period from artisanal to proletariat labor movements in Latin America tend to ignore these insights. Peter Blanchard, for example, recognizes the contributions of artisan mutual aid societies to the Peruvian labor movement, but allows that anarchist ideology, not craft-based organizations, spurred its early militancy. Blanchard gives the Sociedad de Artesanos de la Unión Universal credit for the momentum for the reincorporation of craftsmen into the polity in the 1890s and suggests the importance of political openings for the expression of artisan class interests, but he fails to fully incorporate craftsmen into his account of the Peruvian labor movement.[38] Peter DeShazo gives craftsmen even less importance in the early Chilean labor movement, even though the conditions he describes produced artisan political activity in many other countries.[39] Argentine craftsmen, both native and immigrant, were instrumental in the formation of labor organizations in late nineteenth-century Buenos Aires, although the pace of that city's industrialization rapidly diminished their influence.

Several recent studies of Colombian labor history suggest that artisans played a more important role in the twentieth century than has been recognized heretofore. Mauricio Archila's studies of the 1910–30 period emphasize the artisanal presence in the urban workforce and in the labor organizations of Bogotá, Cali, and Medellín. Archila suggests that artisan mentalities shaped the labor movements through the 1920s, although Gary Long contends that this influence continued until the late 1940s. Long, especially, following the analysis of Herbert Braun, suggests that Jorge Eliécer Gaitán's ideology of small producers appealed most systematically to urban craftsmen, who constituted a significant proportion of his following. Gaitán's ideological cornerstone that "no individual ought to work for another" coincided perfectly with the premise of nineteenth-century artisan republicanism and with the ideology of artisans of twentieth-century France.[40]

The recognition of the continued role of the artisan within Latin America's twentieth-century workforce and in the range of organized activities undertaken by those workers demands a reconsideration of the modern labor movement. The emphasis upon the industrial worker that shaped early labor historiography contained a European/United States bias. Scholars in those areas of the world that experienced early and full industrialization rightfully focused upon the complex surrounding the industrial worker as a means of understanding the economic, political, and social consequences of industrialization. In Latin America, studies of the industrial workforce became both a measure of "modernization," that is, how much the area had "progressed," and a means whereby Marxist critics could condemn the structural dynamic for that "progress." Analysts from the dependency school, notably Bergquist, have partially corrected this interpretive bias by directing attention at the export worker, a clear recognition of the labor structure that was defined by Latin America's place in the world economy.[41] A linkage of these two schools of thought, focusing upon both export and industrial workers, as Reid Andrews has suggested, offers a more complete understanding of twentieth-century Latin American labor history.[42] So, too, does the increased recognition of the significance of household and informal laborers in Latin America's working population.[43] The outlines of a labor history that incorporates the public activities, private lives, and working conditions of export workers, industrial proletariat, household workers, and informal laborers are now visible.

That study is not complete without the artisan however. Most areas of Latin America were not wholly transformed either by industrialization or by the impact of dependent economic relations. Artisans continue to be important members of urban and rural society. Small producers are visible in every city of the region, making a substantial contribution to the urban economy. Craftsmen's heritage of independent thought has important political connotations, although it seldom receives the attention it deserves. In short, artisans persist as important, though not as numerous, elements of Latin America society. Their lives and organized activities have both historical and contemporary importance.

# NOTES

## Abbreviations

| | |
|---|---|
| AC | Archivo del Congresso |
| ACC | Archivo del Cauca |
| ACH | Academia Colombiana de Historia |
| AHN | Archivo Histórico Nacional |
| CN | República de Colombia, *Codificación nacional de todas las leyes de Colombia desde el año de 1821, hecha conforme a la ley 13 de 1912*, 34 vols. (Bogotá: Imprenta Nacional, 1924–), vol. 12 |
| DD | Diplomatic Dispatches |
| HAHR | *Hispanic American Historical Review* |
| ILWCH | *International Labor and Working Class History* |
| JLAS | *Journal of Latin American Studies* |
| LARR | *Latin American Research Review* |

## Preface

1. Archivo del Congreso, Senado, Proyectos negados, 1846, V, folios 118–26 (hereafter AC); Agustín Rodríguez, Vicente Vega, Juan Dederlé, et al., *HH. Senadores* (Bogotá: Imprenta de Nicolás Gómez, May 5, 1846).

2. Colombia underwent several name changes during the nineteenth century: Colombia (along with the territory that is now Ecuador, Panama, and Venezuela), from 1819 until 1830; La República de la Nueva Granada, from 1830 until 1857; La Confederación Granadina, from 1857 until 1863;

Los Estados Unidos de Colombia, from 1863 until 1886; and, finally, La República de Colombia, from 1886 to the present.

3. Exceptions include the series of articles by Humberto Triana y Antorveza: "El aprendizaje en los gremios neogranadinos," *Boletín Cultural y Bibliográfico*, 8:5 (1965), 735–42; "El aspecto religioso en los gremios neogranadinos," *Boletín Cultural y Bibliográfico*, 9:2 (1966), 269–81; "Examenes, licencias, fianzas y elecciones artesanales," *Boletín Cultural y Bibliográfico*, 9:2 (1966), 65–73; "Extranjeros y grupos étnicos en los gremios neogranadinos," *Boletín Cultural y Bibliográfico*, 8:1 (1965), 24–32; and "La libertad laboral y la supresión de los gremios neogranadinos," *Boletín Cultural y Bibliográfico*, 8:7 (1965), 1015–24.

4. The list of scholars drawn to examination of the Democratic Societies is extensive. Aside from those of Urrutia, representative studies include: Gustavo Vargas Martínez, *Colombia 1854: Melo, los artesanos y el socialismo (La dictadura artesanal de 1854, expresión del socialismo utópico en Colombia)* (Bogotá: Editorial la Oveja Negra, 1973); Enrique Gaviria Liévano, "Las Sociedades Democráticas o de artesanos en Colombia," *Correo de los Andes*, No. 24 (January–February 1984), 67–76; Germán R. Mejía Pavony, "Las Sociedades Democráticas (1848–1854): Problemas historiográficos," *Universitas Humanística*, 11:17 (March 1982), 145–76; Antaloli Shulgovski, "La 'Comuna de Bogotá' y el socialismo utópico," *América Latina* (August 1985), 45–56; and Carmen Escobar Rodríguez, *La revolución liberal y la protesta del artesanado* (Bogotá: Editorial Suramérica, 1990).

5. Miguel Urrutia, *The Development of the Colombian Labor Movement* (New Haven, CT: Yale University Press, 1969).

6. Edgar Caicedo, *Historia de las luchas sindicales en Colombia* (Bogotá: Ediciones CEIS, 1982), 57.

7. For discussion of historiographical tendencies, see Kenneth Paul Erickson, Patrick V. Peppe, and Hobart Spalding, Jr., "Research on the Urban Working Class and Organized Labor in Argentina, Brazil, and Chile: What Is Left to Be Done?" *LARR*, 9:2 (Summer 1974), 115–42; Charles Bergquist, "What Is Being Done? Some Recent Studies on the Urban Working Class and Organized Labor in Latin America," *LARR*, 16:1 (1981), 203–23.

8. Judith Evans, "Results and Prospects: Some Observations on Latin American Labor Studies," *ILWCH*, No. 16 (Fall 1979), 29–30.

9. Julio Godio, *El movimiento obrero de América Latina, 1850–1918* (Bogotá: Ediciones Tercer Mundo, 1978), 15–16.

10. Hobart Spalding, Jr., *Organized Labor in Latin America: Historical Case Studies of Workers in Dependent Societies* (New York: Harper & Row, 1977).

11. Charles W. Bergquist, *Labor in Latin America: Comparative Es-*

*says on Chile, Argentina, Venezuela, and Colombia* (Stanford, CA: Stanford University Press, 1986), 1–14.

12. Bergquist, *Labor in Latin America*, 376–78.

13. George Reid Andrews, "Review Essay: Latin American Workers," *Journal of Social History*, 21:2 (Winter 1987), 312. The wealth of studies can be glimpsed by various calls for studies or research reviews of the past fifteen years. See, for example, Emilia Viotti da Costa, "Experience versus Structure: New Tendencies in the History of Labor and the Working Class in Latin America—What Do We Gain? What Do We Lose?" *ILWCH*, No. 36 (Fall 1989), 3–24; Erickson, Peppe, and Spalding, "Research on the Urban Working Class"; Daniel James, "Dependency and Organized Labor in Latin America," *Radical History Review*, 18 (Fall 1978), 155–60; Evans, "Results and Prospects"; Bergquist, "What Is Being Done?"; J. Samuel Valenzuela, "Movimientos obreros y sistemas políticos: Un análisis conceptual y tipológico," *Desarrollo Económico*, 23:91 (October–December 1983), 339–68; Ronaldo Munck, "Labor Studies Renewal," *Latin American Perspectives*, 13:2 (Spring 1986), 108-14; Ian Roxborough, "Issues in Labor Historiography," *LARR*, 21:2 (1986), 178–88; and Peter DeShazo, "Workers, Labor Unions, and Industrial Relations in Latin America," *LARR*, 23:2 (1988), 145–56.

14. E. P. Thompson, *The Making of the English Working Class* (New York: Vintage Books, 1963); Joan Wallach Scott, *The Glassworkers of Carmaux: French Craftsmen and Political Action in a Nineteenth-Century City* (Cambridge, MA: Harvard University Press, 1974); William H. Sewell, Jr., *Work & Revolution in France: The Language of Labor from the Old Regime to 1848* (Cambridge, MA: Harvard University Press, 1980); Sean Wilentz, *Chants Democratic: New York City and the Rise of the American Working Class, 1788–1850* (New York: Oxford University Press, 1984).

15. Lyman L. Johnson, "The Racial Limits of Guild Solidarity: An Example from Colonial Buenos Aires," *Revista de Historia de América*, No. 99 (January–June 1985), 7–26; Lyman L. Johnson, "The Silversmiths of Buenos Aires: A Case Study in the Failure of Corporate Social Organization," *JLAS*, 8:2 (November 1976), 181–213; Lyman L. Johnson, "The Role of Apprenticeship in Colonial Buenos Aires," *Revista de Historia de América*, No. 103 (January–June 1987), 7–30; Lyman L. Johnson, "Artisans," in *Cities and Society in Colonial Latin America*, ed. by Louisa Schell Hoberman and Susan Migden Socolow (Albuquerque: University of New Mexico Press, 1986), 227–50; Mauricio Archila, "La clase obrera colombiana (1886–1930)," in *Nueva historia de Colombia*, III, *Relaciones internacionales, movimientos sociales* (Bogotá: Planeta, 1989), 219–44; Mauricio Archila, "La memoria de los trabajadores de Medellín y Bogotá, 1910–1945," draft in author's possession; Gary Long, "Communists, Radical Artisans,

and Workers in Colombia, 1925–1950," draft in author's possession; Frederick J. Shaw, "The Artisan in Mexico City (1824–1853)," in *El trabajo y los trabajadores en la historia de México*, ed. by Elsa Cecilia Frost, Michael C. Meyer, and Josephina Zoraida Vásquez (Mexico City: El Colegio de México, 1979), 399–418. Carlos Luis Fallas Monge, *El movimiento obrero de Costa Rica, 1830–1902* (San José: Editorial Universidad Estatal a Distancia, 1983); Mario Oliva Medina, *Artesanos y obreros costaricenses, 1880–1914* (San José: Editorial Costa Rica, 1985); Paul Gootenberg, "The Social Origins of Protectionism and Free Trade in Nineteenth-Century Lima," *JLAS*, 14:2 (November 1982), 329–58; Peter Blanchard, *The Origins of the Peruvian Labor Movement, 1883–1919* (Pittsburgh: University of Pittsburgh Press, 1982); Manuel Pérez Vila, *El artesanado: La formación de una clase media propriamente americana (1500–1800)* (Caracas: Academia de la Historia, 1986).

## Chapter One

1. Gabriel García Márquez, *One Hundred Years of Solitude*, trans. by Gregory Rabassa (New York: Avon Books, 1970), 195.
2. "Santa Fé de Bogotá," *Harper's New Monthly Magazine*, Vol. 71 (June–November 1885), 47–58; "Up and Down Among the Andes," *Harper's New Monthly Magazine* (1857), 739–51; J. A. Bennet, "My First Trip up the Magdalena, and Life in the Heart of the Andes," *Journal of the American Geographical Society of New York*, Vol. 9 (1879), 126–41.
3. Luis H. Aristizabal, "Las tres tazas: De Santafe a Bogotá, a través del cuadro de costumbres," *Boletín Cultural y Bibliográfico*, 25:16 (1988), 61–79.
4. Robert L. Gilmore and John P. Harrison, "Juan Bernardo Elbers and the Introduction of Steam Navigation on the Magdalena River," *HAHR*, 28:3 (November 1948), 335–59; Frank Safford, "Commerce and Enterprise in Central Colombia, 1821–1870," Ph.D. dissertation, Columbia University, 1965. 313–15; Luis Ospina Vásquez, *Industria y protección en Colombia, 1810 a 1930* (Bogotá: Editorial Santafé, 1955), 216.
5. Gaspar Theodore Mollien, *Viaje por la República de Colombia en 1823* (Bogotá: Banco de la República, 1944), 197; Miguel Cané, *En viaje, 1881–1882* (París: Garnier Hermanos, 1883), 139; John Steuart, *Bogotá in 1836–7. Being a Narrative of an expedition to the Capital of New-Granada and a residence there of eleven months* (New York: Harper & Brothers, 1838), 48; William Lindsay Scruggs, *The Colombian and Venezuelan Republics*, 2d ed. (Boston: Little, Brown, 1910), 64; Alfred Hettner, *La cordillera de Bogotá: resultados de viajes y estudios*, trans. by Ernesto Guhl (Bogotá: Banco de la República, 1956), 68; Clímaco Calderón and Edward E. Britton, *Colombia, 1893* (New York: Robert Sneider, 1894), 49.

6. Hettner, *La cordillera de Bogotá*, 67–68, 81, 92; Scruggs, *The Colombian and Venezuelan Republics*, 68; Ernst Röthlisberger, *El Dorado: Estampas de viaje y cultura de la Colombia suramericana* (Bogotá: Banco de la República, 1963), 66–67.

7. Peter Amato, "An Analysis of the Changing Patterns of Elite Residential Locations in Bogotá, Colombia" Ph.D. dissertation, Cornell University, 1968; Peter Amato, "Environmental Quality and Locational Behavior in a Latin American City," *Urban Affairs Quarterly*, 5:1 (September 1969), 83–101. Bogotá's spatial distribution of social classes conforms to patterns common to most Latin American cities of the day. See Alejandro Portes and John Walton, *Urban Latin America: The Political Condition from Above and Below* (Austin: University of Texas Press, 1976), 22–23; David J. Robinson, ed., *Social Fabric and Spatial Structure in Colonial Latin America* (Syracuse, NY: Department of Geography, Syracuse University, 1979).

8. Juan Friedel and Michael Jiménez, "Colombia," in *The Urban Development of Latin America, 1750–1920*, ed. by Richard M. Morse (Stanford, CA: Center for Latin American Studies, Stanford University, 1971), 61–76; William Duane, *A Visit to Colombia, in the Years 1822 & 1823* (Philadelphia: Thomas H. Palmer, 1826), 464–65.

9. Richard E. Boyer and Keith A. Davies, *Urbanization in 19th Century Latin America: Statistics and Sources* (Los Angeles: Latin American Center, 1973), 7, 9–10, 37–39, 59–61; Rodney D. Anderson, "Race and Social Stratification: A Comparison of Working-Class Spaniards, Indians, and Castas in Guadalajara, Mexico in 1821," *HAHR*, 68:2 (May 1988), 215.

10. Douglas Butterworth and John K. Chance, *Latin American Urbanization* (New York: Cambridge University Press, 1981), 109–10; Emilio Willems, "Social Differentiation in Colonial Brazil," *Comparative Studies in Society and History*, 12:1 (January 1970), 31–49; Ruben E. Reina, *Paraná: Social Boundaries in an Argentine City* (Austin: University of Texas Press, 1973), 48–53; Andrew Hunter Whiteford, *An Andean City at Mid-Century: A Traditional Urban Society* (East Lansing: Michigan State University, 1977), 100–243; Charles Wagley and Marvin Harris, "A Typology of Latin American Subcultures," in *The Latin American Tradition: Essays on Unity and Diversity of Latin American Culture* (New York: Columbia University Press, 1968), 81–117.

11. R. S. Neale's classes include: "(1) *Upper class*, aristocratic, landholding, authoritarian, exclusive. (2) *Middle class*, industrial and commercial property-owners, senior military and professional men, aspiring to acceptance by the upper class. Deferential towards the upper class because of this and because of concern for property and achieved positions, but individuated or privatized. (3) *Middling class*, petit bourgeois, aspiring professional men, other literates, and artisans. Individuated or privatized like the

middle class, but collectively less deferential and more concerned to re-move the privileges and authority of the upper class in which, without radical changes, they cannot hope to realistically share. (4) *Working class A*, industrial proletariat in factory areas, workers in domestic industries, collectivist and non-deferential and wanting government intervention to protect rather than liberate them. (5) *Working class B*, agricultural work-ers, other low-paid non-factory urban labourers, domestic servants, urban poor, most working-class women whether from working-class A or B households, deferential and dependent" (R. S. Neale, *Class and Ideology in the Nineteenth Century* [London: R.K.P., 1972], 30–33).

12. Anthony P. Maingot, "Social Structure, Social Status, and Civil-Military Conflict in Urban Colombia, 1810–1858," in *Nineteenth-Century Cities: Essays in the New Urban History*, ed. by Stephan Thernstrom and Richard Sennett (New Haven, CT: Yale University Press, 1969), 297–355. See also, Torcuato S. Di Tella, "The Dangerous Classes in Early Nine-teenth Century Mexico," *JLAS*, 5:1 (May 1973), 79–105.

13. Neale, *Class and Ideology*, 19–20.

14. José Escorcia, *Sociedad y economía en el Valle del Cauca*. Tomo III. *Desarrollo político, social y económico, 1800–1854* (Bogotá: Biblioteca Banco Popular, 1983), 45–75; José Escorcia, "La sociedad caleña en la pri-mera mitad del siglo XIX," in *Santiago de Cali—450 años de historia* (Cali: Alcaldía de Santiago de Cali, 1981), 101–25.

15. Of the various nineteenth-century censuses of the city, only the manuscript sheets for the barrio of Las Nieves collected during the 1851 census have escaped either loss or destruction. No nineteenth-century census of the department of Cundinamarca is available due to the 1948 destruction of these documents during the 9 de abril. The various data collected by the municipal government were lost to fire in 1903; only some death records published in a newspaper in the late 1880s remain to the investigator. Aggregate information is available for the twentieth-cen-tury censuses, but often without full descriptions of the categories of infor-mation.

Analysis of every third household of Las Nieves barrio provides the basis for the 1851 data. Deaths recorded by the mayor's office (*alcaldía*) and announced in a newspaper supplied the 1888 information. Approxi-mately 70 percent of the deaths for a fifteen-month period were analyzed. The 1893 data are drawn from a commercial directory graciously provided by Dr. J. León Helguera. It clearly overcounts commercial and professional occupations, while underrepresenting informal and low-skill activities. I used the same skill and functional categorization scheme to determine occupational strata for all data, modified by certain judgment calls. For example, I included midwives as professionals. Perhaps arbitrarily, the wide range of sewing activities by women were classified as unskilled. The classification codes are available from the author.

16. The male artisan sector of San José and Cartago, Costa Rica, ranged from 25.8 to 30.3 percent, respectively, in the 1840s. Lowell Gudmundson, *Costa Rica Before Coffee: Society and Economy on the Eve of the Export Boom* (Baton Rouge: Louisiana State University Press, 1986), 37. In 1849 Mexico City, the figure was 38 percent. Frederick J. Shaw, "The Artisan in Mexico City (1824–1853)," in *El trabajo y los trabajadores en la historia de México*, ed. by Elsa Cecilia Frost, Michael C. Meyer, and Josefina Zoraida Vásquez (Mexico City: El Colegio de México, 1979), 400. See also James R. Scobie, *Secondary Cities of Argentina: The Social History of Corrientes, Salta, and Mendoza, 1850–1910*, completed and edited by Samuel L. Baily (Stanford, CA: Stanford University Press, 1988), 187; Fernando H. Cardoso and José Luis Reyna, "Industrialization, Occupational Structure, and Social Stratification in Latin America," in *Constructive Change in Latin America*, ed. by Cole Blasier (Pittsburgh: University of Pittsburgh Press, 1968), 24; Alan Middleton, "Division and Cohesion in the Working Class: Artisans and Wage Labourers in Ecuador," *JLAS*, 14:1 (May 1982), 171–94; and Donald B. Keesing, "Structural Change Early in Development: Mexico's Changing Industrial and Occupational Structure from 1895 to 1950," *Journal of Economic History*, 29:4 (December 1969), 726–30.

17. Steuart, *Bogotá in 1836–7*, 154–57. Scobie insists that Argentine interior towns displayed only two social classes, the *gente decente* and the *gente del pueblo*, who were divided by family background. Scobie, *Secondary Cities of Argentina*, 140.

18. Röthlisberger, *El Dorado*, 93–96, 103; Hettner, *La cordillera de Bogotá*, 72–77, 91.

19. Francisco Silvestre, *Descripción del Reyno de Santa Fé de Bogotá escrita en 1789 por D. Francisco Silvestre, secretario que fué de virreinata y antiguo governador de la provincia de Antioquia* (Bogotá: Universidad Nacional de Colombia, 1968), 33.

20. Cané, *En viaje*, 158; Hettner, *La cordillera de Bogotá*, 72–74, 77; Isaac F. Holton, *New Granada: Twenty Months in the Andes* (New York: Harper & Brothers, Publishers, 1857), 162–63; Scruggs, *The Colombian and Venezuela Republics*, 66, 109.

21. República de Colombia, *Censo de población de la República de Colombia levantado el 14 de octubre de 1918 y aprobado el 19 de septiembre de 1921 por la ley No. 8 del mismo año* (Bogotá: Imprenta Nacional, 1921), 251.

22. *Diccionario de la lengua Castellano* (Madrid: Imprenta Francisco del Hierro, 1726), 424.

23. *The Oxford English Dictionary*, 13 vols. (Oxford: Oxford, Clarendon Press, 1978), I, 475.

24. *El Núcleo*, 1858.

25. Karl Marx, *The Communist Manifesto of Karl Marx and Frederick Engels* (New York: Russell and Russell, 1963), 122; Michael Hanagan, "Artisan and Skilled Worker: The Problem of Definition," *ILWCH*, No. 12 (November 1977), 28.

26. Eric Hobsbawm, *Workers: Worlds of Labor* (New York: Pantheon Books, 1984); Eric Hobsbawm, "Artisans or Labour Aristocrats?" *Economic History Review*, 2d series, 37:3 (August 1984), 355–72.

27. For a discussion of such a skill ranking for Argentina, see Mark D. Szuchman and Eugene F. Sofer, "The State of Occupational Stratification Studies in Argentina: A Classificatory Scheme," *LARR*, 11:1 (1976), 159–71. The genesis of this model is Michael B. Katz, *The People of Hamilton, Canada West: Family and Class in a Mid-Nineteenth-Century City* (Cambridge, MA: Harvard University Press, 1975), esp. 343–48. For the United States, see David Montgomery, *Workers' Control in America* (New York: Cambridge University Press, 1979), and *The Fall of the House of Labor: The Workplace, the State, and American Labor Activism, 1865–1925* (New York: Cambridge University Press, 1987).

28. Howard B. Rock, *Artisans of the New Republic: The Tradesmen of New York City in the Age of Jefferson* (New York: New York University Press, 1979), 9.

29. E. P. Thompson, *The Making of the English Working Class* (New York: Vintage Books, 1963), 9–10.

30. *La Alianza*, October 20, 1866; January 23, February 3, 1868.

31. Francisco Robledo, "Ynstrucción de gremios en gral.Pa todos oficios aprobada pr el Exmo Sor. Virrey del Rno. Siguense a ella quantos papeles y providens se han creado en el asunto," *Revista del Archivo Nacional*, Nos. 10–11 (October–November 1936), 13–37.

32. David Bushnell, *The Santander Regime in Gran Colombia* (Newark: University of Delaware), 130.

33. *El Núcleo*, 1858. The issues of the paper were not dated.

34. *La Bandera Tricolor*, July 16, 1826.

35. *El Tiempo*, May 13, 1858.

36. *El Núcleo*, 1858; *La Alianza*, December 10, 1866.

37. *El Concurso Nacional*, October 12, 1908.

38. Felipe Pérez, *Geografía general física y política de los Estados Unidos de Colombia y geografía particular de la ciudad de Bogotá* (Bogotá: Imprenta de Echeverría Hermanos, 1883), 400–404, 416–20.

39. *Los Hechos*, June 18, 1904.

40. *El Tiempo*, March 27, 1914.

41. Sean Wilentz, *Chants Democratic: New York City and the Rise of*

*the American Working Class* (New York: Oxford University Press, 1984), 107–42.

42. *Diario de Cundinamarca,* July 28, 1874.

43. *El Tiempo,* March 27, 1914.

44. *La Alianza,* June 14, 1867.

45. *La Alianza,* August 1, 1867; *El Pueblo,* July 13, 1867.

46. *El Artesano,* June 13, 1897.

47. *El Correo Nacional,* July 8, 1904. On the attempt to instill Taylorism into the Colombian mentality, see Alberto Mayor Mora, *Etica, trabajo y productividad en Antioquia: Una interpretación sociológica sobre la influencia de la Escuela Nacional de Minas de la vida, costumbres e industrialización regionales,* 2d ed. (Bogotá: Editorial Tercer Mundo, 1985).

48. *La República,* October 9, 1867.

49. *El Faro,* January 26, 1906.

50. Thompson, *The Making of the English Working Class,* 9–10; Peter Winn, *Weavers of Revolution: The Yarur Workers and Chile's Road to Socialism* (New York: Oxford University Press, 1986), 85.

51. *La Alianza,* December 10, 1866. Master craftsmen, who in early national Guadalajara, Mexico, were addressed by the honorific "Don," might well have occupied a similar social status, although the weak colonial guild system in Colombia suggests that such distinctions may have been less important in Bogotá. See Anderson, "Race and Social Stratification: A Comparison of Working-Class Spaniards, Indians, and Castas in Guadalajara, Mexico, in 1821," *HAHR,* 68:20 (May 1988), 233–44.

52. Stanley J. Stein and Barbara H. Stein, *The Colonial Heritage of Latin America* (New York: Oxford University Press, 1970); D.C.M. Platt, "Dependency in Nineteenth Century Latin America: An Historian Objects," *LARR,* 15:1 (1980), 113–30; Stanley J. Stein and Barbara H. Stein, "Comment," *LARR,* 15:1 (1980), 131–46; D.C.M. Platt, "Reply," *LARR,* 15:1 (1980), 147–50; Joseph L. Love, "The Origins of Dependency Analysis," *JLAS,* 22:1 (1990), 143–68.

53. José Antonio Ocampo, *Colombia y la economía mundial, 1830–1910* (Bogotá: Siglo Veintiuno Editores, 1984); Bushnell, *The Santander Regime,* 78–81; William Paul McGreevey, *An Economic History of Colombia, 1845–1930* (Cambridge: Cambridge University Press, 1971), 39; Ospina Vásquez, *Industria y protección,* 127; Luis Eduardo Nieto Arteta, *Economía y cultura en la historia de Colombia* (Bogotá: Editorial Viento del Pueblo, 1975), passim; Anthony McFarlane, "The Transition from Colonialism in Colombia, 1819–1875," in *Latin America, Economic Imperialism and the State: The Political Economy of the External Connection from Independence to the Present,* ed. by Christopher Abel and Colin M. Lewis (London: Athlone Press, 1985), 101–24.

54. McGreevey (*An Economic History of Colombia,* 1–5) in particular

favors this term to suggest the essential continuity of Spanish economic patterns established by the Bourbon reformers into the Republican period.

55. Bushnell, *The Santander Regime*, 78–81; McGreevey, *An Economic History of Colombia*, 39; Ospina Vásquez, *Industria y protección*, 88–102, 127; Nieto Arteta, *Economía y cultura*, passim.

56. The degree to which these tariffs actually protected native crafts is disputed. Ospina Vásquez suggests that tariff rates effectively buffered native artisan production from foreign competition. Safford, however, insists that craftsmen, especially those who produced consumer goods (shoes, clothing, etc.) suffered from the impact of foreign production even under the moderate protectionist rates in the years prior to 1847. Neither scholar bases his claim on much more than informed opinion, so that resolution of this question must await more substantial data. One should note, however, that artisans expressed few complaints about tariff policies during the years prior to passage of the 1847 tariff law. Thereafter, craftsmen often reflected upon the Neo-Bourbon tariff structure with nostalgia, suggesting that they had at least felt protected. Ospina Vásquez, *Industria y protección*, 172; Safford, "Commerce and Enterprise," 77, 150–51.

57. McGreevey, *An Economic History of Colombia*, 33.

58. Ospina Vásquez, *Industria y protección*, 76–78.

59. José Manuel Restrepo, *Diario político y militar*, 4 vols. (Bogotá: Imprenta Nacional, 1954), II, 275.

60. Ospina Vásquez, *Industria y protección*, 152–53, 164; Nieto Arteta, *Economía y cultura*, 198; Malcolm Deas, "The Fiscal Problems of Nineteenth-Century Colombia," *JLAS*, 14:2 (November 1982), 288.

61. Safford, "Commerce and Enterprise," 17–18.

62. Ospina Vásquez, *Industria y protección*, 91–92.

63. Safford, "Commerce and Enterprise," 9–10, 102–5; Frank Safford, *The Ideal of the Practical: Colombia's Struggle to Form a Technical Elite* (Austin: University of Texas Press, 1976), 26.

64. Steuart, *Bogotá in 1836–7*, 145; Duane, *A Visit to Colombia*, 476.

65. Mario Arango Jaramillo, *Judás Tadeo Landínez y la primera bancarrota colombiana (1842)* (Medellín: Ediciones Hombre Nuevo, 1981); Safford, "Commerce and Enterprise," 68–80; Safford, *The Ideal of the Practical*, 71–77; Ospina Vásquez, *Industria y protección*, 145; José Manuel Restrepo, *Diario político y militar. Memorias sobre los sucesos importantes de la época para servir a la historia de la Revolución de Colombia y la Nueva Granada, desde 1819 para Adelante*, 4 vols. (Bogotá: Editorial El Catolicísmo, 1963), II, 283–84.

66. Jorge Orlando Melo, "La economía neogranadina en la cuarta década del siglo XIX," *Universidad Nacional de Colombia. Medellín*, 2:3 (May–December 1976), 52–63.

67. Ospina Vásquez, *Industria y protección*, 161–84; Safford, "Commerce and Enterprise," 157–72.

68. Ospina Vásquez, *Industria y protección*, 17; Safford, "Commerce and Enterprise," 157–66; Victoria Peralta de Ferreira, "Historia del fracaso de la ferrería de Samacá," *Universitas Humanística*, No. 24 (July–December 1985), 12.

69. Safford, "Commerce and Enterprise," 164–72; Ospina Vásquez, *Industria y protección*, 167–68, 176, 182.

70. Ospina Vásquez, *Industria y protección*, 180–84; Safford, "Commerce and Enterprise," 179; Safford, *The Ideal of the Practical*, 43; Arango Jamarillo, *Primera bancarrota*, 188–90.

71. AC, Cámara, Informes de comisiones, 1836, VIII, 156–59r; Frank Safford, "The Emergence of Economic Liberalism in Colombia, 1821–1870," in *Guiding the Invisible Hand: Economic Liberalism and the State in Latin American History*, ed. by Joseph L. Love and Nils Jacobsen (New York: Praeger, 1988), 45.

72. The confusion of multiple currencies, for example, was addressed by the abandonment of the old eight-real peso in favor of a decimal-based silver real and a peso fuerte composed of ten reals, a system that went into effect in 1853.

73. Ospina Vásquez, *Industria y protección*, 211.

74. David Bushnell, "Two Stages of Colombian Tariff Policy: The Radical Era and Return to Protection (1861–1885)," *Inter–American Economic Affairs*, 9:4 (Spring 1956), 5–7.

75. *Memoria de hacienda*, 1859, as cited in McGreevey, *An Economic History of Colombia*, 86.

76. Safford, "Commerce and Enterprise," 255.

77. Miguel Samper, *La miseria en Bogotá y otros escritos* (Bogotá: Biblioteca Universitaria de Cultura Colombiana, 1969), passim; Ospina Vásquez, *Industria y protección*, 228; *El Neo-Granadino*, April 9, 1857.

78. *La Opinión*, October 14, 1863, October 12, 1864, January 4, 1865.

79. Samper, *La miseria en Bogotá*, 9, 11.

80. *La República*, October 9, 1867.

81. On numerous occasions, the slogan "Abajo las ajiotistas" was associated with artisans. *Agiotistas* were money lenders who purchased government bonds issued to individuals in repayment for forced loans during wartime or as compensation for other debts. In the absence of other sources of credit, the speculator played an important role in the local economy. See Deas, "Fiscal Problems," 318–20; Safford, "Commerce and Enterprise," 56–57.

82. David Sowell, "*La Caja de Ahorros de Bogotá*, 1845–65: Credit, Development, and Savings in Early National Colombia," unpublished paper.

83. *Diario de Cundinamarca,* June 21, 1877.

84. Also founded in the 1870s were the Chaves Chocolate plant, a quinine laboratory, and small industries to produce candles, soap, and perfume. *La América,* April 9, 1874; Ospina Vásquez, *Industria y protección,* 264–69.

85. The women earned from two to seven pesos a week, depending on their output. Ospina Vásquez, *Industria y protección,* 310, 314; *El Criterio,* June 4, 1883; *La Crónica,* September 21, 1898, August 12, 1899; *El Diario Nacional,* July 27, 1918; *Las Noticias,* September 23, 1889.

86. José Antonio Ocampo, "Comerciantes, artesanos y política económica en Colombia, 1830–1880," *Boletín Cultural y Bibliográfico,* 27:22 (1990), 21–45.

87. Ospina Vásquez, *Industria y protección,* 278–323; Darío Bustamante Roldán, "Efectos económicos del papel moneda durante la regeneración," *Cuadernos Colombianos,* 1:4 (1974), 561–660.

88. Salomón Kalmanovitz, "Los orígenes de la industrialización en Colombia (1890–1929)," *Cuadernos de Economía,* 2d epoch, 5 (1983), 87.

89. Ospina Vásquez, *Industria y protección,* 300–307, 334–44.

90. Ospina Vásquez, *Industria y protección,* 313; *La Patria,* June 22, 1894; *El Correo Nacional,* July 8, October 17, 1904; *El Yunque,* May 6, 1906.

91. Ospina Vásquez, *Industria y protección,* 303–4; *El Yunque,* May 6, 1906; *El Telegrama,* February 14, 1895.

## Chapter Two

1. Eduardo Santa, *Sociología política de Colombia* (Bogotá: Ediciones Tercer Mundo, 1964), 37.

2. Charles W. Bergquist, "On Paradigms and the Pursuit of the Practical," *LARR,* 13:2 (1978), 247–51; Frank Safford, "On Paradigms and the Pursuit of the Practical: A Response," *LARR,* 13:2 (1978), 252–60. Helen Delpar, "The Liberal Record and Colombian Historiography: An Indictment in Need of Revision," *Revista Interamericana de Bibliografía,* 31:4 (1981), 524–37; Frank Safford, "Acerca de las interpretaciones socioeconómicos de la política en la Colombia del siglo XIX: Variaciones sobre un tema," *Anuario Colombiano de Historia Social y de la Cultura,* No. 13–14 (1985–86), 91–151.

3. Indalecio Liévano Aguirre, *Rafael Núñez* (Bogotá: Cromos, 1944); Gerardo Molina, *Las ideas liberales en Colombia, 1849–1914,* 6th ed. (Bogotá: Ediciones Tercer Mundo, 1979); Germán Colmenares, *Partidos políticos y clases sociales en Colombia* (Bogotá: Universidad de Los Andes, 1968).

4. Luis Eduardo Nieto Arteta, *Economía y cultura en la historia de Colombia* (Bogotá: Editorial Viento del Pueblo, 1975), 13, 117, 122.

5. Charles W. Bergquist, "The Political Economy of the Colombian Presidential Election of 1897," *HAHR*, 56:1 (February 1976), 1–30; Charles W. Bergquist, *Coffee and Conflict in Colombia, 1886–1910* (Durham, NC: Duke University Press, 1978), 7; Charles W. Bergquist, *Labor in Latin America: Comparative Essays on Chile, Argentina, Venezuela, and Colombia* (Stanford, CA: Stanford University Press, 1986), 281, 286–94.

6. Helen Delpar, *Red Against Blue: The Liberal Party in Colombian Politics, 1863–1899* (University: University of Alabama Press, 1981); James William Park, *Rafael Núñez and the Politics of Colombian Regionalism, 1863–1886* (Baton Rouge: Louisiana State University Press, 1985); Robert Louis Gilmore, "Federalism in Colombia, 1810–1858," Ph.D. dissertation, University of California, 1949, present the strongest evidence of regionalism's primacy in Colombian politics.

7. Frank Safford, "Bases of Political Alignment in Early Republican Spanish America," in *New Approaches to Latin American History*, ed. by Richard Graham and Peter Smith (Austin: University of Texas Press, 1974), 102–3.

8. Emilia Viotti da Costa, *The Brazilian Empire: Myths and Histories* (Chicago: University of Chicago Press, 1985), 72.

9. Jay Robert Grusin, "The Colombian Revolution of 1848," Ph.D. dissertation, University of New Mexico, 1978, passim.

10. Jaime Jaramillo Uribe, *El pensamiento colombiano en el siglo XIX* (Bogotá: Editorial Temis Librería, 1982), 95–97; John L. Young, "University Reform in New Granada, 1820–1850," Ph.D. dissertation, Columbia University, 1970; David Bushnell, *The Santander Regime in Gran Colombia* (Newark: University of Delaware Press, 1954), 183–94.

11. It might be possible to make the case for the influence of "ideas" in nineteenth-century politics using these arguments, save that these issues paralleled life chances as well. See Charles A. Hale, "The Reconstruction of Nineteenth Century Politics in Spanish America: A Case for the History of Ideas," *LARR*, 8:2 (1973), 53–73.

12. José María Samper, *Ensayo sobre las revoluciones políticas y la condición social de las repúblicas colombianas (Hispano-Americanos)* (Bogotá: Biblioteca Popular de Cultura Colombiana, n.d.), 231.

13. Jaramillo Uribe, *El Pensamiento colombiano*, 30–33.

14. José María Samper relates that the term *gólgota* came from a newspaper commentary on his correlation of socialism with the ideals of the "Martyr of Golgotha." Thereafter, *gólgota* identified the more radical reformers. José María Samper, *Historia de una alma, 1834 a 1881*, 2 vols. (Bogotá: Biblioteca de Cultura Colombiana, 1948), I, 268–69.

15. The classic account of this process is Samper's *Historia de una alma*. For Núñez, see Helen Delpar, "Renegade or Regenerator? Rafael Núñez as Seen by Colombian Historians," *Revista Interamericana de Bibliografía*, 35:1 (1985), 25–39.

16. Daniel Pécaut, *Orden y violencia: Colombia, 1930–1954*, 2 vols. (Bogotá: Siglo Veintiuno Editores, 1987), I, 20; Bergquist, *Coffee and Conflict*, 95–99.

17. Suffrage rights were granted by the constitution of 1832 to males over the age of twenty-one (or younger, if married) who did not earn their subsistence as unskilled manual laborers or domestic servants. Criminals and the mentally insane were also barred from voting, as were those individuals who were in default on debts to the nation. William Marion Gibson, *The Constitutions of Colombia* (Durham, NC: Duke University Press, 1948), 120; *La Crónica Semanal*, April 13, 1832.

18. Ambrosio López, *El desengaño o confidencias de Ambrosio López, primer director de la Sociedad de Artesanos de Bogotá, denominada hoi "Sociedad Democrática" escrito para conocimiento de sus consocios* (Bogotá: Imprenta de Espinosa, por Isidoro García Ramírez, 1851), 11–13; Hugo Latorre Cabal, *Mi novela: Apuntes autobiográficos de Alfonso López* (Bogotá: Ediciones Mito, 1961), passim; J. León Helguera and Robert H. Davis, eds., *Archivo epistolar del General Mosquera: Correspondencia con el General Ramón Espina, 1835–1866* (Bogotá: Editorial Kelly, 1966), 263.

19. See Sean Wilentz, *Chants Democratic: New York City and The Rise of the American Working Class, 1788–1850* (New York: Oxford University Press, 1984); Foster Rhea Dulles and Melvyn Dubofsky, *Labor in America: A History*, 4th ed. (Arlington Heights, IL: Harlan Davidson, 1986), 21–69.

20. Bushnell, *The Santander Regime*; David Bushnell, "The Last Dictatorship: Betrayal or Consummation?" *HAHR*, 63:1 (February 1983), 65–105.

21. Gibson, *The Constitutions of Colombia*, 35–66, 109–51; Gilmore, "Federalism in Colombia," 139–41.

22. Thomas F. McGann, "The Assassination of Sucre and Its Significance in Colombian History, 1828–1848," *HAHR*, 30:3 (August 1950), 269–89.

23. José Manuel Restrepo, *Diario político y militar. Memorias sobre los sucesos importantes de la época para servir la historia de la Revolución de Colombia y de la Nueva Granada, desde 1819 para Adelante*, 4 vols. (Bogotá: Emprenta Nacional, 1954), II, 228; Gilmore, "Federalism in Colombia," 138–39. Nieto Arteta sees in these camps the "conservative liberalism" of Santander as opposed to the "doctrinaire liberalism" of Azuero that would in the 1850s divide draconiano Liberals, including Lo-

renzo María Lleras, and gólgota Liberals such as Manuel Murillo Toro. See his *Economía y cultura*, 83, 180.

24. Ignacio Morales served as the Society's director, sharing seats on its Executive Council with representatives from the Archbishopric, four religious orders, Pedro Herrera Espada, Juan Madiedo, and José Felix Merizalde, and Vice-Director Antonio Herrán. Ignacio Morales, Antonio Herrán, Felipe Bernal, et al., *Invitación que hace la Sociedad Católica de Bogotá a los fieles de la América* (Bogotá, May 10, 1838).

25. *El Investigador Católico*, March 25, 1838.

26. *El Investigador Católico*, August 1, October 15, 1838; Morales, *Invitación*; José Restrepo Posada, "La Sociedad Católica de Bogotá—1838," *Boletín de Historia y Antiqüedades*, 43:499/500 (May–June 1956), 310–21.

27. *El Investigador Católico*, October 15, 1838.

28. *La Bandera Nacional*, May 27, 1838. For their part, the editors of *El Investigador Católico* claimed that the Catholic Societies represented a genuine outpouring of support for the church; progressives countered that members of the organization had been forced into membership by clerical pressures. *El Investigador Católico*, October 15, 1838.

29. *La Bandera Nacional*, June 3, 17, 1838.

30. *El Argos*, June 24, 1838.

31. *El Argos*, July 1, 1838.

32. *El Labrador i Artesano*, September 16, 1838, p. 2.

33. *El Labrador i Artesano*, September 16, 1838. Membership lists are found in *El Labrador i Artesano*, October 7, 14, 1838, and January 20, 1839. Progressives urged their counterparts in other regions to form organizations modeled after that of Bogotá. Lleras wrote that "instruction of the masses is the most essential guarantee of popular governments." Lleras insisted that the creation of like-minded societies would raise the level of the inferior classes and would help make social classes more equal. Progressives founded similar groups in Villa de Leiva, Tunja, Gachetá, Santa Marta, Cucutá, Soatá, La Mesa, and Santa Rosa de Viterbo.

34. *El Labrador i Artesano*, November 4, 1838.

35. *El Labrador i Artesano*, December 8, 1838.

36. *El Labrador i Artesano*, October 14, 21, 28, November 4, 18, 25, December 8, 16, 1838.

37. *El Labrador i Artesano*, September 23, October 28, December 16, 23, 1838; January 13, 1839.

38. *El Amigo del Pueblo*, September 16, 1838.

39. AC, Senado, peticiones, 1839, XI, folios 79–86r; Bonifacio Quijano, Ramón Torres, Gaspar Jiménez, et al., *H. H. senadores i representantes* (Bogotá: Impreso por J. A. Cualla, April 16, 1839).

40. Gilmore observes that santanderistas began to employ federalist

rhetoric precisely when they lost control of the administration in 1837. See his "Federalism in Colombia," 166–67.

41. Gibson, *The Constitutions of Colombia*, 145; *Constitucional de Cundinamarca*, June 10, 1832; *El Día*, July 17, 1842.

42. *El Boletín Liberal*, October 13, 1840; Un Albañil, *Artesanos laboriosos de Bogotá* (Bogotá: Imp. por Juan Vanegas, 1840).

43. Joseph León Helguera, "The First Mosquera Administration in New Granada," Ph.D. dissertation, University of North Carolina, 1958, 54–72.

44. Young, "University Reform," 37–38, 78, 106–11; Gilmore, "Federalism in Colombia," 187–88.

45. Helguera, "The First Mosquera Administration," 34.

46. Ibid., 37–38; David Bushnell, "Elecciones presidenciales colombianas, 1825–1856," in *Compendio de estadísticas históricas de Colombia*, ed. by Miguel Urrutia Montoya and Mario Arrubla (Bogotá: Universidad Nacional de Colombia, 1970), 249–57.

47. Helguera, "The First Mosquera Administration," 247–48; Frank Safford, "Commerce and Enterprise in Central Colombia, 1821–1870," Ph.D. dissertation, Columbia University, 1965, 115.

48. Helguera, "The First Mosquera Administration," 326; Aníbal Galindo, *Historia económica i estadística de la hacienda nacional desde la colonia hasta nuestros días* (Bogotá: Imprenta de Nicolás Pontón i Compañía, 1874), 56–60.

49. Manuel María Madiedo, *Ideas fundamentales de los partidos políticos de la Nueva Granada*, 3d ed. (Bogotá: Editorial Incunables, 1985), 31–32.

50. AC, Senado, Proyectos Negados, 1846, V, folios 118–26. The petition was also published as a handout. See Agustín Rodríguez, Vicente Vega, Juan Dederlé, et al., *HH. senadores* (Bogotá: Imprenta de Nicolás Gómez, May 5, 1846); AC, Cámara, Informes de Comisiones, 1847, X, folios 229–241r.

51. Signers who had, or would, play a role in artisan politics include: Agustín Rodríguez, José María Vega (cobbler), Francisco Londoño, Hilario Novoa, Narcisco Garai, and Rafael Tapias (carpenter). Many signers had been members of the Democratic-Republican Society of Artisans and Laborers or had signed the "books" petition of 1839. David Sowell, "'La teoría i la realidad': The Democratic Society of Artisans of Bogotá, 1847–1854," *HAHR*, 67:4 (November 1987), 616.

52. Galindo, *Historia económica*, 60–61; *CN*, XII, 214–62; Luis Ospina Vásquez, *Industria i protección en Colombia, 1810 a 1930* (Bogotá: Editorial Santafé, 1955), 208–14.

53. The Society selected Rodríguez as its first director in early November; Cayetano Leiva was named vice-director and Martín Plata was ap-

pointed secretary. Agustín Rodríguez, *Al director i miembros de la Sociedad Democrática* (Bogotá: n.p., 1849), 1, 2; Sociedad de Artesanos, *Reglamento para su réjimen interior i económico* (Bogotá: Imprenta de Nicolás Gómez, 1847), 16; Salvador Camacho Roldán, *Memorias*, 2 vols. (Bogotá: Biblioteca Popular de Cultura Colombiana, 1946), I, 106–7; Latorre, *Mi novela*, 26. Members of the board included José María Solano, Francisco Torres Hinestrosa, Francisco Londoño, Pedro Aguilar, Rafael Lasso, Ambrosio López, Bartolemé Andrade, Antonio Chaves, Camilo Cárdenas, Dr. Evanjelista Durán, José Benito Mirando, José María Vega, Francisco Garzón, Gregorio Lugo, Hilario Novoa, Francisco Vásquez Guevara (tailor), and Rudesino Zuñer (tailor).

54. Sociedad de Artesanos, *Reglamento*, 1.

55. *Reglamento de la Sociedad de Artesanos, Bogotá, 1848*, as cited by Jaime Jaramillo Uribe, "Las Sociedades Democráticas de Artesanos y la coyuntura política y social colombiana de 1848," in *La personalidad histórica de Colombia y otros ensayos* (Bogotá: Editorial Andes, 1977), 205.

56. Sociedad de Artesanos, *Reglamento*.

57. *El Clamor de la Verdad*, November 14, 1847.

58. *El Día*, December 11, 1847.

59. *El Clamor de la Verdad*, December 26, 1847.

60. Ibid.

61. Rodríquez, *Al director*, 3; *El Aviso*, October 8, 1848.

62. Grusin, "Revolution of 1848," 43–49.

63. Gilmore, "Federalism in Colombia," 179.

64. Ibid., 182.

65. Ambrosio López issued many of the invitations. López, *El desengaño*, 1–5.

66. For example, see Jaramillo Uribe, "La influencia de los románticos franceses y de la revolución de 1848 en el pensamiento político colombiano del siglo XIX," in *La personalidad histórica de Colombia y otros ensayos* (Bogotá: Editorial Andes, 1977), 181–201.

67. Gilmore, "Federalism in Colombia," 213; Robert Louis Gilmore, "Nueva Granada's Socialist Mirage," *HAHR*, 36:2 (May 1956), 190–210. The language of the times has plagued an accurate reading of the society.

68. Latorre, *Mi novela*, 72.

69. *La América*, June 4, 1848.

70. Ibid.

71. *El Aviso*, June 18, 1848. A list of presidential electors favored by the organization included the names of the leading liberals of the capital, as well as numerous artisans. Artisans proposed from the barrio of Catedral included Martín Plata, José María Vergara Tenorio, Evanjelista Durán, and Rudecindo Zuñer; from San Victorino, Carlos Martín, Francisco Lon-

doño, Ambrosio López, and Francisco Torres Hinestrosa; and from the barrio of Las Nieves, Pedro A. Castillo and Ramón Groot.

72. *El Día*, April 8, 22, 29, May 6, 13, 24, June 7, 1848.

73. *A los artesanos de Bogotá* (Bogotá: n.p., n.d.).

74. *El Día*, May 28, 1848.

75. *La América*, June 18, 25, 1848.

76. *El Nacional*, June 11, 1848.

77. Bushnell, "Elecciones presidenciales colombianas," 258–59, 265; *El Nacional*, June 11, 1848; *El Día*, June 28, July 1, and July 19, 1848. Twenty-nine of Gori's votes came from electors in the parochial districts of Catedral, San Victorino, and Santa Barbara, while it appears that López won the nine votes from Las Nieves. A curious change in the first and final electoral counts merits mention. In the first announcement, Agustín Rodríguez, on the conservative list, and Jenaro Ruiz, a progressive elector, both artisans, were named as winning electors. Their names were absent from the final list; this happened to only one other of the thirty-one electors from Bogotá. See *El Día*, June 28, July 29, 1848.

78. The Society also participated in local politics. In the December 1848 election for a new *cabildo*, 69 progressives were selected out of a total of 166 municipal electors. Five members of the Society were chosen: Ambrosio López, Cayetano Leiva, Juan Evanjelista Durán, Francisco Torres Hinestrosa, and Francisco Vásquez. Conservatives assessed these elections, which were quite heated, as proof of the progressives' unpopularity among the citizens, as they were unable to obtain a majority. See *El Nacional*, December 25, 1849.

79. Ibid.

80. *El Aviso*, January 11, 1849.

81. *El Patriota Imparcial*, March 1, 1850. It is difficult to determine who led the preparations for the elections. Both Ambrosio López and Emeterio Heredia later claimed responsibility; others, however, contend that the locksmith Miguel León directed the Society's plans; still others believe that young Liberals were in charge of its maneuvers. López, *El desengaño*, 23; Ambrosio López, *El triunfo sobre la serpiente roja, cuyo asunto es del dominio de la nación* (Bogotá: Editorial Espinosa, 1851), 10; Emeterio Heredia, *Contestación al cuaderno titulado "El desengaño o confidencias de Ambrosio López etc." por El Presidente que fue de la Sociedad de Artesanos El 7 de Marzo de 1849* (Bogotá: Imprenta de Núcleo Liberal, 1851), 41–45; José Manuel Restrepo, *Historia de la Nueva Granada*, 2 vols. (Bogotá: Editorial El Catolicismo, 1963), II, 102; Angel Cuervo and Rufino José Cuervo, *Vida de Rufino Cuervo y noticias de su época*, 2 vols. (Bogotá: Biblioteca Popular de Cultura Colombiana, Prensas de la Biblioteca Nacional, 1946), II, 126–28; *La Civilización*, December 27, 1849.

82. *La Civilización*, January 10, 1850; Restrepo, *Historia de la Nueva Granada*, II, 102.

83. Cuervo and Cuervo, *Vida de Rufino Cuervo*, 127.

84. Latorre, *Mi novela*, 24; Isaac F. Holton, *New Granada: Twenty Months in the Andes* (New York: Harper & Brothers, 1857), 521.

85. José María Cordovez Moure, *Reminiscencias de Santa Fé de Bogotá*, 9 vols. (Bogotá: Imprenta de la Cruz, 1910), III, 343–46.

86. *La Gaceta Oficial*, May 17, 1849; *El Neo-Granadino*, March 10, 1849; Restrepo, *Historia de la Nueva Granada*, II, 103–6; Jaime Duarte French, *Florentino González: Razón y sinrazón de una lucha política* (Bogotá: Banco de la República, 1971), 425.

87. *El Aviso*, March 8, 1849.

88. *La Sociedad de Artesanos de Bogotá a la nación* (Bogotá: Imp. de Sanchez y Compañía, March 8, 1849). The Society's meager treasury had been drained by the election efforts. Fortunately, as an expression of gratitude for the artisans, several wealthy "patriots" decided to sponsor a civic dinner in honor of López to replenish its coffers. It was held on March 25, 1849, the day of López's return to the capital, and earned 650 pesos. A letter circulated to various liberals requesting support netted another 89 pesos. These monies, after expenses were paid, left the Society with a treasury balance of 805 pesos (Rodríguez, *Al director*, 4, 5).

89. Neither political orientation was sufficiently cohesive or precise in its ideology to warrant the title of party until 1849. After the election of that year, both groups clarified their platforms and mutual antagonisms so as to justify the label of parties. Therefore, both *Liberals* and *Conservatives* will be capitalized when referring to individuals aligned with one or the other group, and lowercased in reference to the non-partisan use of the word.

90. Correspondence from the Societies published in *La Gaceta Oficial* was directed to, and responded to by, Zaldúa, although the precise nature of the relationship has yet to be determined. Between August 1849 and February 1850, the Society was referred to as both the Society of Artisans and the Democratic Society of Artisans. It is not clear when the name change occurred, or at whose initiative. After February 1850, the name *Democratic Society* predominated.

91. *El Sentimiento Democrático*, May 3, June 14, 1849; *Reseña histórica de los principales acontecimientos políticos de la ciudad de Cali, desde el año de 1848 hasta el de 1855 inclusivo* (Bogotá: Imprenta de Echeverría Hermanos, 1856), 14, 27.

92. José Escorcia, *Sociedad y economía en el Valle del Cauca*, Vol. III. *Desarrolla político, social y económico, 1800–1854* (Bogotá Biblioteca Banco Popular, 1983), 61, 121; J. León Helguera, "Antecedentes sociales de

la revolución de 1851 en el sur de Colombia, 1848–1849," *Anuario Colombiano de Historia Social y de la Cultura*, No. 5 (1970), 62.

93. *El Sentimiento Democrático*, May 3, June 14, 1849; *Reseña histórica*, 14, 27–28; Helguera, "Antecedentes sociales," 62; Escorcia, *Desarrollo político*, 121.

94. *Reseña histórica*, 27–30; Gustavo Arboleda, *Historia contemporánea de Colombia desde la disolución de la antigua república de ese nombre hasta la época presente*, 6 vols. (Bogotá: Casa Editorial de Arboleda y Valencia, 1918–35), III, 282.

95. *Reseña histórica*, 28–32; *El Sentimiento Democrático*, December 20, 1849; Helguera, "Antecedentes sociales," 59; Escorcia, *Desarrollo político*, 107. The rancor between the two organizations can be followed in the pages of *El Ariete* and *El Sentimiento Democrático* during the latter half of 1849 and the first months of 1850.

96. *El Sur-Americano*, January 19, 1850.

97. *El Porvenir*, September 15, 1849.

98. Some confusion exists as to the precise date of the Popular Society's foundation. Its newspaper, *El Amigo de los Artesanos*, cited its first meeting as having taken place on December 10, a second on December 18 (with four-hundred present), and a third on December 21 (seven-hundred present). Other sources suggest that its first meetings had taken place in 1848, and that it was reinstalled on December 17, 1849. *El Amigo de los Artesanos*, December 21, 28, 1849; *El Día*, December 26, 1849.

99. *El Día*, June 26, 1845; *Reglamento de la Sociedad de Artistas* (Bogotá, 1891); José Joaquín Borda, *Historia de la Compañía de Jesús en la Nueva Granada*, 2 vols. (Poissy: Imprenta de S. Lejay et Çe., 1872), II, 171–72, 195–99.

100. Camacho Roldán, *Memorias*, 107–9.

101. *El Día*, December 26, 1849.

102. *El Amigo de los Artesanos*, December 28, 1849.

103. *El Día*, December 26, 1848; *Reglamento orgánico de la Sociedad Popular de instrucción mútua i fraternidad Cristiana* (Bogotá: Imprenta de El Día, 1849), 1–4.

104. *El Día*, December 26, 1849, p. 1.

105. *El Día*, March 23, 1850.

106. *La Civilización*, January 17, 1850; *El Día*, January 19, 1850; *El 7 de Marzo*, January 20, 1850; Restrepo, *Historia de la Nueva Granada*, 137.

107. *El 7 de Marzo*, January 20, 1850; *El Cañón*, January 17, 1850.

108. *El Día*, January 19, 1850.

109. *El Día*, January 19, 1850; *El 7 de Marzo*, January 20, 1850; *El Cañón*, January 17, 1850; *La Civilización*, January 17, 1850; Arboleda, *Historia contemporánea*, III, 39; Restrepo, *Historia de la Nueva Granada*, II, 136. Francisco Londoño headed the commission, which also included

Agustín Rodríguez, Dr. Carlos Martín, Miguel León, José María Samper, Enrique Parra, Carlos Sáenz, Bartolomé Ibarra, Raimundo Russi, Francisco Vázquez, and Germán G. Piñares. *La Civilización* said that the group also asked for the breakup of the Popular Society. *El 7 de Marzo*, December 23, 1849, favors that idea.

110. Restrepo, *Historia de la Nueva Granada*, II, 136.

111. Arboleda, *Historia contemporánea*, 97; *El Neo-Granadino*, January 25, 1850. Somewhat later, a moderate paper reminded all artisans that they were brothers and noted that the political fighting only created dissension within the artisan class. *El Patriota Imparcial*, March 15, 1850.

112. *El Día*, April 17, 1850.

113. *El Día*, February 13, 16, 1850; *La Civilización*, May 24, 27, 1850; Simón José Cárdenas, *El juicio de imprenta celebrado el día 13 de mayo de 1850 promovido por Camilo Rodríguez contra el infrascrito* (Bogotá: Imprenta del "El día" por J. Azarza, May 14, 1850).

114. *El Cernícalo*, June 10, 1850.

115. *La Gaceta Oficial*, March 13, 1851; *El Neo-Granadino*, March 14, 1851.

116. *El Neo-Granadino*, May 15, 1851; *La Civilización*, May 15, 1851.

117. Some of the tensions caused by the war are visible in Miguel León, *Señor jefe político Doctor Eustaquio Alvárez* (Bogotá, August 31, 1851); *La Reforma*, September 7, 1851.

118. *Reseña histórica*, 31, 32, 36–39.

119. *La Gaceta Oficial*, May 2, 1850.

120. *El Baile*, November 24, 1850; *El Día*, December 21, 1850; *La Reforma*, August 24, 1851; *El Neo-Granadino*, December 12, 1851.

## Chapter Three

1. *El Núcleo*, 1858.

2. David Bushnell and Neill Macaulay, *The Emergence of Latin America in the Nineteenth Century* (New York: Oxford University Press, 1988), 209–20; Frank Safford, "The Emergence of Economic Liberalism in Colombia," in *Guiding the Invisible Hand: Economic Liberalism and the State in Latin American History*, ed. by Joseph L. Love and Nils Jacobsen (New York: Praeger, 1988), 35–61; Malcolm Deas, "Venezuela, Colombia and Ecuador: The First Half-Century of Independence," in *The Cambridge History of Latin America*, Vol. III. *From Independence to c. 1870*, ed. by Leslie Bethell (New York: Cambridge University Press, 1985), 507–38; Luis Eduardo Nieto Arteta, *Economía y cultura en la historia de Colombia* (Bogotá: Editorial Viento del Pueblo, 1975), passim; Germán Colme-

nares, *Partidos políticos y clases sociales en Colombia* (Bogotá: Universidad de los Andes, 1968).

3. Bushnell and Macaulay, *The Emergence of Latin America*, 33–37; Leopoldo Zea, *The Latin American Mind*, trans. by James H. Abbot and Lowell Dunham (Norman: University of Oklahoma Press, 1963), 51–52; E. Bradford Burns, *The Poverty of Progress: Latin America in the Nineteenth Century* (Berkeley: University of California Press, 1980), 8; Charles A. Hale, *Mexican Liberalism in the Age of Mora, 1821–1853* (New Haven: Yale University Press, 1968).

4. Emilia Viotti da Costa, *The Brazilian Empire: Myths and Histories* (Chicago: University of Chicago Press, 1985), 53–55; Frank Safford, "Social Aspects of Politics in Nineteenth-Century Spanish America: New Granada, 1825–1850," *Journal of Social History*, 5:2 (Spring 1972), 344–70; Frank Safford, "Bases of Political Alignment in Early Republican Spanish America," in *New Approaches to Latin American History*, ed. by Richard Graham and Peter Smith (Austin: University of Texas Press, 1974), 71–109; Frank Safford, "Politics, Ideology and Society in Post-Independence Spanish America," in *The Cambridge History of Latin America*, Vol. III. *From Independence to c. 1870*, ed. by Leslie Bethell (New York: Cambridge University Press, 1985), 350; Alan Knight, *The Mexican Revolution*, Vol. I. *Porfirians, Liberals, and Peasants* (New York: Cambridge University Press, 1986), 68–69.

5. Anthony McFarlane, "The Transition from Colonialism in Colombia, 1819–1875," in *Latin America, Economic Imperialism and the State: The Political Economy of the External Connection from Independence to the Present*, ed. by Christopher Abel and Colin M. Lewis (London: Athlone Press, 1985), 107; Robert Louis Gilmore, "Federalism in Colombia, 1810–1858," Ph.D. dissertation, University of California, 1949, 104–10, 116, 121, 182, 225. Whether the period of Liberal Reform began with Mosquera causes some debate. Nieto Arteta, *Economía y cultura*, and Jay Robert Grusin, "The Colombian Revolution of 1848," Ph.D. dissertation, University of New Mexico, 1978, both contend that it began with the Generation of 1849, after the election of José Hilario López. Both insist that the period was revolutionary, one that was little influenced by foreign events or ideas. Bushnell's recent survey of the reform period accepts this traditional date, even while his discussion of reforms begins with the Mosquera presidency. See Bushnell and Macaulay, *The Emergence of Latin America*, 209. J. León Helguera argues for the innovative nature of Mosquera's presidency in "The First Mosquera Administration in New Granada," Ph.D. dissertation, University of North Carolina, 1958.

6. William Marion Gibson, *The Constitutions of Colombia* (Durham, NC: Duke University Press), 191–214; Antonio Pombo and José Joaquín Guerra, *Constituciones de Colombia: Recopiliadas y precedidas de una*

*breve reseña histórica*, 4 vols. (Bogotá: Prensas del Ministerio de Educación Nacional, 1951), IV, 5–27; Alirio Gómez Picón, *El golpe militar del 17 de abril de 1854: La dictadura de José María Melo, el enigma de Obando, los secretos de la historia* (Bogotá: Editorial Kelly, 1972), 115–18; *La Discusión*, May 21, 1853; Gilmore, "Federalism in Colombia," 208–213.

7. Gilmore, "Federalism in Colombia," 212.

8. Gilmore, "Federalism in Colombia," 325–31. The other states were Bolívar, Boyacá, Cauca, Cundinamarca, Magdalena, and Santander.

9. Gilmore, "Federalism in Colombia," provides an outstanding examination of this process, with 400–401 describing the constitution itself.

10. Antonio Pérez Aguirre, *25 años de historia colombiana: 1853 a 1878; del centralismo a la federación* (Bogotá: Editorial Sucre, 1959), 150–59; Jorge Villegas, *Colombia: Enfrentamiento iglesia-estado, 1819–1887* (Bogotá: La Carreta, 1981), 57; Fernando Díaz Díaz, "Estado, iglesia, y desamortización," in *Manual de historia de Colombia*, 3 vols., 2d ed. (Bogotá: Instituto Colombiano de Cultura, 1982), II, 413–66. See the *Boletín del Credito Nacional* for reports of the commission charged with sale of church lands.

11. Tolima was separated from Cundinamarca to form the ninth state.

12. Helen Delpar, "Colombian Liberalism and the Roman Catholic Church, 1863–1886," *Journal of Church and State*, 22:2 (Spring 1980), 274–76.

13. Helen Delpar, *Red Against Blue: The Liberal Party in Colombian Politics* (University: University of Alabama Press, 1981), 11–13; Gibson, *The Constitutions of Colombia*, 264–71; Pérez Aguirre, *25 años*, 188–92, 205–26; Salvador Camacho Roldán, *Memorias*, 2 vols. (Bogotá: Biblioteca Popular de Cultura Colombiana, 1946), I, 283–84.

14. Safford, "Economic Liberalism," 45.

15. AC, Cámara, Informes de comisiones, 1836, VIII, 156–59r.

16. *El Día*, July 17, 1843. The same set of complaints were voiced in the 1831 petition. See Safford, "Economic Liberalism," 45.

17. *El Día*, July 17, 1842.

18. *La Alianza*, April 13, 1867; *La Nación*, December 17, 1886, January 11, 1887; *Diario de Cundinamarca*, June 9, 1875.

19. AC, Cámara, proyectos de leyes negados, 1850, X, folios 28–31.

20. Saturnino González, Antonio Cárdenas V., José L. Camacho, et al., *Representación al Congreso Nacional* (Bogotá: Impreso por Manuel J. Barrera, 1868); *El Bien Público*, December 5, 1870; *Diario de Cundinamarca*, March 15, 25, 1872; Frank Safford, *The Ideal of the Practical: Colombia's Struggle to Form a Technical Elite* (Austin: University of Texas Press, 1976), 203–4.

21. AC, Senado, Proyectos Negados, 1846, V, folios 118–26.

22. Agustin Rodríguez, Vicente Vega, Juan Dederlé, et al. *H.H. senadores* (Bogotá: Imprenta de Nicolás Gómez, May 5, 1846), 4.

23. Thirty-four artisans from Cartagena petitioned the 1849 congress in vain to increase tariffs on imported articles that were produced domestically, to establish schools to train artisans, and to examine the competence of shop owners so that internal quality could be improved. A similar petition was sent to the 1850 congress from about 180 Cartagena artisans. This request further asked for the free importation of machinery so that production methods could be improved. AC, Cámara, Proyectos de leyes negados, 1850, X, folios 43–44r, 45–49r.

24. Ibid., 28–31.

25. *Diario de Debates*, June 5, 15, 19, 20, 26, 1850.

26. *Diario de Debates*, June 5, 1850; AC, Cámara, Proyecto de leyes negados, 1850, X, folios 32–40.

27. AC, Cámara, Informes de Comisiones, 1851, VI, folios 464–73r.

28. José María Samper's attempts to influence the Society are seen in the pages of *El Demócrata* in mid-1850.

29. *El Demócrata*, May 15, 19, 26, June 2, 9, 16, 1850 (quote is from June 9, p. 2); *El Estandarte del Pueblo*, July 7, 14, 1850. Murillo denied that he favored González, despite their apparent ideological harmony. *El Neo-Granadino*, July 12, 1850.

30. *El Estandarte del Pueblo*, July 14, 1850.

31. At the meeting in which the tariff petition was prepared, Samper attempted to convince the craftsmen of the "unscientific" character of the appeal. Samper was shouted down, and left the organization, never to return. José María Samper, *Historia de una alma, 1834 a 1881*, 2 vols. (Bogotá: Biblioteca de Cultura Colombiana, 1969), I, 249–51.

32. *El Día*, October 10, 1850. Orlando Fals Borda described these student members of the elite as trying to disassociate themselves from their elders of the established order. The socialist label was thus adopted as a gesture of protest; very few of the measures that Bogotá's "socialists" favored can be seen as socialist in any strict sense. See Orlando Fals Borda, *Subversion and Social Change in Colombia*, trans. by Jacqueline D. Skiles (New York: Columbia University Press, 1969), 83.

33. Jaime Duarte French, *Florentino González: Razon y sinrazón de una lucha política* (Bogotá: Banco de la República, 1971), 454.

34. *El Día*, September 7, 1850. See also *La Civilización*, May 1, 1850.

35. Ambrosio López, *El desengaño o confidencias de Ambrosio López, primer director de la Sociedad de Artesanos de Bogotá, denominada hoi "Sociedad Democrática" escrito para conocimiento de sus consocios* (Bogotá: Imprenta de Espinosa, por Isodoro García Ramírez, 1851), 1–5, 17, 20, 40–41.

36. Ibid., 19, 30–35, 41, 84.

37. Ibid., 42.

38. *La Gaceta Oficial*, June 7, 1851.

39. Emeterio Heredia, *Contestación al cuaderno titulado "El desengaño o confiencias de Ambrosio López etc." por El Presidente que fue de la Sociedad El 7 de Marzo 1849* (Bogotá: Imprenta de Núcleo Liberal, 1851), 9, 10, 13, 16, 54.

40. Ambrosio López, *El triunfo sobre la serpiente roja, cujo asunto es el dominio de la nación* (Bogotá: Editorial Espinosa, 1851), 8, 14–16, 19–21.

41. Readmitted to Colombia in 1843 after a seventy-six-year absence, the Jesuits were central to the struggle for control of social policies. Conservatives such as Ospina regarded them as a positive force in the creation of a moral society, whereas Liberals and many moderate Conservatives thought that the Jesuits were antithetical to a republic and demanded their expulsion. This had nearly been accomplished by the 1846 congress. Grusin, "The Colombian Revolution of 1848," 199.

42. *El Día*, May 1, 1850. See *Diálogo entre un artesano i un campesino sobre los Jesuítas* (Bogotá: n.p., 1850), for an example of the Liberal propaganda on the Jesuit question.

43. Humberto Triana y Antorveza, "El aspecto religioso en los gremios neogranadinos," *Boletín Cultural y Bibliográfico*, 8:5 (1965), 277. Praise for this Liberal victory came from Democratic Societies and others throughout the country. See, for example, *La Gaceta Oficial*, July 4, 11, 1850. Conservatives, on the other hand, lamented it as further evidence of the decay of society since the 7 de marzo. *El Día* and *La Civilización* were closed for one month by López in order to calm Conservative emotions; he also armed Democrats in case that move did not prove successful. Moderate opinions, expressed in *El Patriota Imparcial*, which claimed to be neither friend nor foe of the Jesuits, appealed for calm, claiming that the Jesuit question had been manipulated for partisan objectives, with a terribly divisive effect upon the country. In reality the proper role of the Jesuits was a social one, and not the political problem as claimed by Liberals or a question of religion as claimed by Conservatives according to the paper's editors. *El Patriota Imparcial*, June 15, 1850; José Manuel Restrepo, *Historia de la Nueva Granada*, 2 vols. (Bogotá: Editorial El Catolicismo, 1963), II, 152; Angel Cuervo and José Rufino Cuervo, *Vida de Rufino Cuervo y noticias de su época*, 2 vols. (Bogotá: Biblioteca Popular de Cultura Colombiana, Prensas de la Biblioteca Nacional, 1946), II, 152.

44. Cruz Ballesteros, *La teoría i la realidad* (Bogotá: Echeverría Hermanos, December 17, 1851).

45. *El Pasatiempo*, January 24, 1852; Miguel León, *Satisfacción, que*

*da el que escribe, al Sr. M. Murillo Secretario de Hacienda* (Bogotá: n.p., January 19, 1852).

46. Restrepo, *Historia de la Nueva Granada*, 180–82. See also *Los Principios*, an Obandista newspaper.

47. The Democratic Society worked hard for Obando's election, helping him to win 28 of the capital's 39 electors. Emeterio Heredia was not only an Obando elector, but also served as president of the asemblea electoral. In the nation, Obando received 1,548 electoral votes to Herrera's 329; 131 votes went to other candidates or were blank. *El Pasatiempo*, June 9, 1852; *Los Principios*, June 30, 1852; *El Neo-Granadino*, August 5, 1852; David Bushnell, "Elecciones presidenciales colombianas, 1825–1856," in *Compendio de estatísticas históricas de Colombia*, ed. by Miguel Urrutia Montoya and Mario Arrubla (Bogotá: Universidad Nacional de Colombia, 1970), 227.

48. Gilmore, "Federalism in Colombia," 117–18.

49. Anthony P. Maingot, "Social Structure, Social Status, and Civil-Military Conflict in Urban Colombia, 1810–1858," in *Nineteenth-Century Cities: Essays in the New Urban History*, ed. by Stephen Thernstrom and Richard Sennett (New Haven, CT: Yale University Press, 1969), 332–36.

50. Gómez Picón, *El golpe militar*, 70.

51. *La Discusión*, December 11, 1852.

52. *El Neo-Granadino*, March 11, 1853; *El Orden*, March 20, 1853.

53. Obando's cabinet appointments were mainly from his own wing of the party: Patrocinio Cuéllar was selected as his Secretary of Government; José María Plata, Minister of Finance; Lorenzo María Lleras was Secretary of Foreign Relations; and, as a conciliatory gesture, Tomás Herrera was named Secretary of War. Gómez Picón, *El golpe militar*, 109.

54. Richard Preston Hyland, "The Secularization of Credit in the Cauca Valley, Colombia," Ph.D. dissertation, University of California, Berkeley, 1979, 72–73.

55. *El Orden*, May 1, 1853, p. 1.

56. Cuervo and Cuervo, *Vida de Rufino Cuervo*, 255; *La Gaceta Oficial*, May 23, 1853. The reference is to events in Caracas of February 24, 1848.

57. *Democracia. Documentos para la historia de la Nueva Granada* (n.p., n.d.); W., *Breves anotaciones para la historia sobre los sucesos del 19 de mayo último* (Bogotá, May 27, 1853); José María Cordovez Moure, *Reminiscencias de Santa Fé de Bogotá*, 9 vols. (Bogotá: Imprenta de La Cruz, 1910), 371–74; *Alcance a la Gaceta Oficial*, May 20, 1853; Gómez Picón, *El golpe militar*, 112–15; José Manuel Restrepo, *Diario político y militar. Memorias sobre los sucesos importantes de la época para servir a la historia de la Revolución de Colombia y de la Nueva Granada, desde 1819 para adelante*, 4 vols. (Bogotá: Imprenta Nacional, 1954), IV, 288. Follow-

ing the episode, numerous artisans were arrested by the government. On May 25, Emeterio Heredia, Tiburcio Cárdenas, Carlos Navarrete, and others asked that they be released from jail. They claimed that it would be impossible to judge their guilt due to the complexity of the disturbances. AC, Cámara, Proyectos negados, 1854, III, folio 77.

58. As early as 1850 Democrats had worn a long ruana, red on one side and blue on the other, and a straw hat, to demonstrate their association with the Society.

59. *Primera banderilla: A los gólgotas en las Nieves* (Bogotá: n.p., June 1, 1853), AHN, Archivo Histórico Restrepo, Caja 89.

60. "One could not transit the central streets of the city without being exposed to verbal lances provoked by the workers, and from six in the evening onward it was dangerous to be caught outside of one's house" (Cordovez Moure, *Reminiscencias*, 383).

61. Ibid., 377.

62. Mil ciudadanos, *El 8 de junio* (Bogotá: n.p., June 9, 1853); Mas de mil artesanos, *El 8 de junio* (Bogotá: n.p., June 9, 1853).

63. Un amigo de los artesanos, *El valor de los artesanos* (Bogotá: n.p., June 9, 1853).

64. José María Plata, *El gobernador de Bogotá a los habitantes de la capital* (Bogotá: Imprenta del Neo-Granadino, June 13, 1853).

65. Blas López, Miguel León, Anselmo Flórez, et al., *Protesta de los artesanos Blas López, Miguel León, Anselmo Flórez y otros* (Bogotá: Imprenta de Nicolás Gómez, June 17, 1853).

66. *El Constitucional*, July 8, 1853; *La Gaceta Oficial*, August 2, 1853; Cordovez Moure, *Reminiscencias*, 384–93.

67. Miguel León, *¡Artesanos ¡desangaños!* (Bogotá: n.p., August 6, 1853).

68. *CN*, 1853, 661–68; Cuervo and Cuervo, *Vida de Rufino Cuervo*, 258.

69. *El Termómetro*, September 4, 11, 18, 1853.

70. In the Province of Bogotá, Conservative Pedro Fernández Madrid won the senate seat sought by Heredia and Miguel León by polling 8,121 votes. Heredia garnered 2,112 votes and León 1,974—respectable totals, but far from enough. Pastor Ospina won the provincial governorship by a three-to-one margin, denying the office to draconiano Rafael E. Santander.

71. Gilmore, "Federalism in Colombia," 293; Venancio Ortiz, *Historia de la revolución del 17 de abril de 1854* (Bogotá: Biblioteca Banco Popular, 1972), 44; *El Catolicismo*, July 16, 1853; *El Constitucional*, October 18, 1853.

72. *El Neo-Granadino*, October 20, 1853.

73. Gilmore, "Federalism in Colombia," 301–4.

74. *Reseña histórica de los principales acontecimientos políticos de la*

*ciudad de Cali, desde el año de 1848 hasta el de 1855 inclusivo* (Bogotá: Imprenta de Echeverría Hermanos, 1856), 14, 27, 64; Ortiz, *El 17 de abril*, 45–50.

75. Samuel S. Green to William L. Marcy, January 4, 1854, United States Department of State, General Records, DD.

76. Gómez Picón, *El golpe militar*, 138–62.

77. Ortiz, *El 17 de abril*, 60; Gómez Picón, *El golpe militar*, 155, 168.

78. Gómez Picón, *El golpe militar*, 155; Ortiz, *El 17 de abril*, 70–71; *Causa de responsibilidad contra el ciudadano presidente de la República i los señores secretarios del despacho* (Bogotá: Imprenta del Neo-Granadino, 1855), 95.

79. *El Neo-Granadino*, January 12, 1854; *Causa*, 72; Ortiz, *El 17 de abril*, 59. Andrés Soriano Lleras, *Lorenzo María Lleras* (Bogotá: Editorial Sucre, 1958), 78. The junta consisted of: Patrocinio Cuéllar, Alejandro Gaitán, José María Melo, Ramón Mercado, Lorenzo María Lleras, Rafael Eliseo Santander, Ramón Ardila, Lisandro Cuenca, José María Gaitán, Erazo Madiedo, Nicolás Madiedo, Rufino Azuero, Ambrosio González, José Maldonado Neira, Emeterio Heredia, Miguel León, Ramón Gómez, Francisco Antonio Obregón, Tomás Lombana, Miguel Vargas, Juan Nepomuceno Conto, Melitón Escobar, Camilo Carrizosa, Juan de Dios Gómez, José Carazo, and Alejandro MacDowell.

80. Some public apprehension surrounded the new group. The leading gólgotan newspaper publicly questioned Lleras's intentions. Apparently the Governor of Bogotá had much the same fears, as he called Heredia and the shoemaker José Antonio Saavedra into his office for questioning about the group's activities. See *El Pasatiempo*, January 11, 1854; *El Liberal*, January 24, 1854.

81. Other proposals that were suggested but not approved included a call for establishment of a national bank to reduce interest rates on loans and formation of a Muzu emerald lottery to help reduce the national debt. AC, Cámara, Informes de comisiones, 1854, folios 296–300; *Causa*, 179, 341–44; *El Neo-Granadino*, March 20, 30, 1854.

82. Obando, Obaldía, and numerous members of the administration spoke at the Society's meeting in honor of Independence. The next day a country excursion and picnic was enjoyed by over 1,300 Democrats, including General López. *El Neo-Granadino*, March 16, 1854.

83. *La Gaceta Oficial*, March 11, 1854.

84. *El Neo-Granadino*, March 20, 30, 1854; *Causa*, 179, 341–44, 371–72.

| Dilemas i su contestación | Dilemmas and their answers |
|---|---|
| Pan o tumba | Bread or riot |
| trabajo o matanza | Work or massacre |

| | |
|---|---|
| libertad o muerte | Liberty or death |
| oro o asesinato | Gold or assassination |
| Melo o lanza | Melo or the lance |
| Lleras o Democrática | Lleras or the Democrats |
| reforma o batalla | Reform or battle |
| trabajad i dormid | Work and sleep |

This poem from *El Espía*, April 11, 1854, indicates the social language of the pre-coup days.

85. Miguel Urrutia, *The Development of the Colombian Labor Movement* (New Haven, CT: Yale University Press, 1969), 41.

86. *La Gaceta Oficial*, March 29, April 6, 1854; *CN*, 1854, 23.

87. *La Gaceta Oficial*, April 4, 1854.

88. *Causa*, 341–44; *Causa de responsibilidad contra el ciudadano presidente de la República, Jeneral José María Obando, i los ex-secretarios de Gobierno in de Guerra, señores Antonio del Real i Valerio Francisco Barriga* (Bogotá: Imprenta de Echeverría Hermanos, 1855), 33–35; Restrepo, *Diario político y militar*, 361.

89. On April 15, 1854, news of a melista uprising in Popayán reached the capital, adding to the general alarm. Some six-hundred soldiers had revolted in that southern city on April 8 in response to a false report of a gólgotan rebellion in Bogotá. The movement did not last long, as the governor was able to convince the men to lay down their arms. See Tomás Cipriano de Mosquera, *Resumén histórico de los acontecimientos que han tenido lugar en la República, extracado de los diarios y noticias que ha podido obtener el General Jefe del Estado Mayor, T. C. de Mosquera* (Bogotá: Imprenta del Neo-Granadino, 1855), 12.

90. Juan Francisco Ortiz, *Reminiscencias de D. Juan Francisco Ortiz (1808–1861)* (Bogotá: Librería Americana, 1914), 300–321.

91. Ortiz, *El 17 de abril*, 80; Gustavo Vargas Martínez, *Colombia 1854: Melo, los artesanos y el socialismo (La dictatura artesanal de 1854, expresión del socialismo utópico en Colombia)* (Bogotá: Editorial la Oveja Negra, 1973), 74–75; Gómez Picón, *El golpe militar*, 260. Melo selected Obregón as his Secretary General; Pedro Mártir Consuegra, Secretary of Interior; José María Gaitán, Secretary of War and Navy; and Ramón Ardila, Minister of Finance.

92. Andres Soriano Lleras, *Lorenzo María Lleras* (Bogotá: Editorial Sucre, 1958), 67–69. Lleras was the most eminent political member of the Society, with a close relationship to Obando. But by the beginning of April, as Lleras began to distance himself from the plan, the influence of Francisco Antonio Obregón rose. All evidence suggests that Lleras and Obregón were in fact the primary planners of the 17 de abril. But, when Obando refused to head the movement, Lleras abandoned the effort. *Diario*

*político y militar*, 361; *El Neo-Granadino*, April 27, 1854; *La Gaceta Oficial*, April 24, 1854.

93. Restrepo, *Diario político y militar*, II, 363–64. Restrepo noted that "others attributed his trip to revolutionary intentions."

94. *El Neo-Granadino*, April 27, 1854; *El 17 de abril*, May 14, 1854; *La Gaceta Oficial*, April 24, 1854; Gilmore, "Federalism in Colombia," 313.

95. Germán Colmenares, "Formas de la conciencia de clase en la Nueva Granada," *Boletín Cultural y Bibliográfico*, 9:12 (1966), 2,412.

96. *Causa*, 346–49.

97. Francisco Antonio Obregón to the Secretary of Government, Bogotá, June 12, 1854, ACC, Sala Mosquera, No. 31,177; Francisco Antonio Obregón to the Secretary of Government, Bogotá, June 12, 1854, ACC, Sala Mosquera, No. 31,177; June 14, 1854, No. 31,178; José María Melo to Felipe Roa, ACC, Sala Mosquera, n.d., No. 31,288.

98. See Orlando Fals Borda, *Historia doble de la costa*, Vol. II. *El Presidente Nieto* (Bogotá: Carlos Valencia Editores, 1981), for process of the coup in the north.

99. Ortiz, *El 17 de abril*, 360–63; Gómez Picón, *El golpe militar*, 277–85.

100. Ortiz and Gómez Picón are the traditional sources for information on the rebellion. Extensive primary materials, however, remain unexplored in the Sala Mosquera of the ACC, the Herrán Archivo of the ACH, and the Fondo Militar of the AHN. The Sala Mosquera has much of the correspondence of the Melo regime, while the Archivo Herrán has much of the Constitutionalist records.

101. *La Gaceta Oficial*, December 10, 1854.

102. *El Bogotano Libre*, January 22, 1855; *El Tiempo*, May 13, 1858.

103. *El Repertorio*, December 20, 1854; *La Gaceta Oficial*, January 5, 15, 1855. Although the pardons had not so indicated, the military service of those accepting its terms was also to be served in Panama. Clearly constitutionalist leaders intended to purge the capital of its melista element. More melistas were exiled from Cali, Pasto, Socorro, Popayán, and other cities. See, for example, *La Gaceta Oficial*, January 1, March 13, 1854.

104. *El Panameño*, January 26, February 21, 1855. The three "pardons" were offered to 324 people. Eighteen escaped en route, but authorities in Panama reported the arrival of at least twenty persons not included in the official pardons. AHN, República, Guerra y Marina, Tomo 843, folio 953.

105. Lorenzo María Lleras, *San Bartolomé en 1855* (Bogotá: n.p., 1855), 12.

106. *La Gaceta Oficial*, March 1, June 8, 25, July 11, 18, 1855.

107. Restrepo, *Diario político y militar*, IV, 576.

108. Algunos presos, *Señor procurador general de la nación* (Bogotá: n.p., March 25, 1855), p. 1.

109. *El Tiempo*, January 9, 16, 1855. José María Gaitán introduced a resolution of impeachment based upon Obaldía's alleged overstepping of his constitutional authority. The chamber ruled by a 31 to 14 vote that no grounds existed for the charge. AHN, República, Congreso, Legajo 31, folios 723–37.

110. *El Repertorio*, February 18, March 5, 1855; Lorenzo María Lleras, *Señor Júez del crímen* (Bogotá: n.p., January 27, 1855); Lleras, *San Bartolomé; El Bogotano Libre*, January 28, 1855.

111. David Sowell, "Agentes diplomáticas de los Estados Unidos y el golpe de Melo," *Anuario Colombiano de Historia Social y de la Cultura*, No. 12 (1984), 11.

112. Restrepo, *Diario político y militar*, IV, 586.

113. *El Tiempo*, April 8, 1856.

114. *El Artesano*, May 22, June 16, July 3, 1856.

115. *El Nacional*, April 3, 1856.

116. *El Ciudadano*, May 31, June 26, July 29, 1856; *El Nacional*, May 29, August 7, 1856.

117. *El Porvenir*, September 2, 1856.

118. José María Vega, Santos Castro, José Antonio Saavedra, et al., *Los artesanos de Bogotá a la nación* (Bogotá: Imprenta de Echeverría Hermanos, November 15, 1857); Unos artesanos de 17 de abril, *Contestación preliminar al cauderno titulado "La revolución"* (Bogotá: Imprenta de "El Núcleo Liberal," n.d.).

119. *El Tiempo*, December 1, 1857; Restrepo, *Diario político y militar*, IV, 700, 704–6; El redactor del Porvenir, *Al pueblo* (Bogotá: Imprenta de la Nación, November 10, 1857); Vega, *Los artesanos de Bogotá; La Patria*, December 5, 1856; Tomás Lombana, *Manifestación* (Bogotá: December 10, 1857).

120. Restrepo, *Diario político y militar*, IV, 725; *La revolución: Orijen, fines, i estado actual de la revolución democrática que se prepara en esta ciudad*, 3d ed. (Bogotá: Imprenta de F. T. Amaya, April 1858); Unos artesanos del 17 de abril, *Contestación preliminar al cuaderno titulado "La revolucion."*

121. *El Núcleo*, January 26, 1858, passim.

122. *El Núcleo*, November 30, 1858; *El Comercio*, December 14, 1858.

123. *El Núcleo*, January 5, February 22, 1859; *El Porvenir*, May 13, 1859. Cárdenas had left the country after being jailed in 1850, visiting first Europe and then the United States. On July 4, 1853, while in New York, he commemorated the U.S. independence by the gift of a portrait of Colombia's July 20, 1810, independence to the New York Historical Society. See *La Esperanza*, July 20, 1855.

124. *El Núcleo*, June 28, 1859; *El Porvenir*, June 7, 1859.

125. One law gave the central government control of local and district election councils and the other enhanced its power over local militia groups. Both moves strengthened Conservative influence in Liberal-controlled states. Pérez Aguirre, *25 años*, 94–95.

126. Pérez Aguirre, *25 años*, 108–9; David Church Johnson, *Santander: Siglo XIX—Cambios socioeconómicos* (Bogotá: Carlos Valencia Editores, 1984), 100–114.

127. Un campañero de Rodríguez Leal, *Los derechos del pueblo* (Bogotá: n.p., July 26, 1863).

128. *Al pueblo* (Bogotá: Imprenta de la Nación, July 21, 1863).

129. Ballesteros spent 3,000 pesos on his house and shop; José Antonio Saavedra bought a house for 1,000 pesos; Fuljencio Roa's house cost 720 pesos; and Cruz Sánchez's house and shop cost 4,200 pesos. *Boletín del Credito Nacional*, November 22, 1862, February 7, October 5, 1863.

130. Un artesano, *Al señor Jeneral Santos Gutíerrez* (Bogotá: n.p., June 29, 1863), p. 1.

131. Robert Louis Gilmore, "Nueva Granada's Socialist Mirage," *HAHR*, 36:2 (May 1956), 190–210.

132. Craig Calhoun (*The Question of Class Struggle* [Chicago: University of Illinois Press, 1982]) coined this phrase to describe the reaction of English artisans and townspeople to the advances of industrial capitalism in late eighteenth-century England.

## Chapter Four

1. *A los artesanos de Bogotá* (Bogotá: n.p., n.d.).

2. Ambrosio López, *El desengaño o confidencias de Ambrosio López, primer director de la Sociedad de Artesanos de Bogotá, denominada hoi "Sociedad Democrática" escrito para conocimiento de sus consocios* (Bogotá: Imprenta de Espinosa, por Isidoro García Ramírez, 1851).

3. Cruz Ballesteros, *La teoría i la realidad* (Bogotá: Echeverría Hermanos, December 17, 1851).

4. Miguel León, *¡Artesanos ¡Desengaños!* (Bogotá: n.p., August 6, 1853).

5. José Antonio Ocampo, *Colombia y la economía mundial, 1830–1910* (Bogotá: Siglo Veintiuno Editores, 1984), 110–11; Luis Ospina Vásquez, *Industria y protección en Colombia, 1810 a 1930* (Bogotá: Editorial Santafé, 1955), 263.

6. Miguel Samper, *La miseria en Bogotá y otros escritos* (Bogotá: Biblioteca Universitaria de Cultura Colombiana, 1969), passim, but especially 90–102.

7. *La República*, October 2, 9, 16, 30, 1867. Samper's responses are in *El Republicano*, November 1, 12, 27, 1867. For other views of the crisis, see *La Prensa*, October 7, 1867; *La República*, January 28, 1868. David Sowell, "José Leocadio Camacho: Artisan, Editor, and Political Activist," in *The Human Tradition in Latin America: The Nineteenth Century*, ed. by Judith Ewell and William H. Beezley (Wilmington, DE: Scholarly Resources, 1989), 269–79.

8. *La República*, October 2, 9, 16, 30, 1867.

9. Ibid.

10. *El Simbolo*, June 14, 1864.

11. Lawrence Goodwin, *The Populist Moment: A Short History of the Agrarian Revolt in America* (New York: Oxford University Press, 1978).

12. Francisco Vega et al., *Cosas de artesanos* (Bogotá: Imprenta de Echeverría Hermanos, March 22, 1866); *La Opinión*, January 4, 18, 1866; *La Libertad*, January 18, 1866; *El Bogotano*, March 9, 1866.

13. At the time, many observers thought that collected funds had been mismanaged. See *El Bogotano*, March 9, 1866; Vega et al., *Cosas de artesanos*.

14. *El Nacional*, February 23, 1867.

15. *El Liberal*, July 16, 1863; *La Opinión*, July 1, December 8, 1863; *El Municipal*, December 21, 1863.

16. Agapito Cabrera, *Díos, libertad i trabajo* (Bogotá: n.p., June 18, 1863), p. 1.

17. Antonio Cárdenas, Fruto Castañeda, Gregorio Espinel, et al., *Manifestación* (Bogotá: n.p., October 8, 1863).

18. Ibid.; *La Libertad*, October 29, 1863. The October parade and pronouncement revived memories of the 1854 coup and sparked a heated polemic. See Unos artesanos que no serán simples espectadores de los hechos ulteriores, *El fruto que los artesanos hemos cojido de las revoluciones pasadas* (Bogotá: n.p., October 19, 1863); *La Libertad*, October 18, 20, 1863; *La Opinión*, October 20, 1863.

19. *El Obrero*, July 15, October 6, 18, 1865.

20. Gareth Stedman Jones, *Languages of Class: Studies in English Working Class History, 1832–1982* (New York: Cambridge University Press, 1983), 7–8.

21. *El Obrero*, July 15, August 1, October 6, 7, 18, November 1, 1865.

22. Antonio Cárdenas Vásquez, Saturnino González, Felipe Roa Ramírez, et al., *Varios artesanos de todos los gremios . . .* (Bogotá: n.p., September 15, 1866). Anjel María Gómez, Cruz Sánchez, Camilo Vásquez, Mariano González, Daniel Boada, Rafael Tapias, and José María Pedraza also signed the circular.

23. *La Alianza*, October 1, November 10, 20, 1866.

24. *La Alianza*, December 12, 1866.

25. *La Alianza*, January 20, February 6, 20, 1867.

26. Helen Delpar, *Red Against Blue: The Liberal Party in Colombian Politics, 1863–1899* (University: University of Alabama Press, 1981), 91; Antonio Pérez Aguirre, *25 años de historia colombiana: 1853 a 1878, del centralismo a la federación* (Bogotá: Editorial Sucre, 1959), 261–62.

27. *La Prensa*, March 5, 15, 19, 1867; Pérez Aguirre, *25 años*, 164–66; Delpar, *Red Against Blue*, 61; Gustavo Humberto Rodríguez, *Santos Acosta: Caudillo del radicalismo* (Bogotá: Biblioteca Colombiana de Cultura, 1972), 128–31.

28. *La Alianza*, February 20, 1867; *La Prensa*, March 15, 1867.

29. *El Mensajero*, February 15, 21, 1867; *El Nacional*, February 23, 24, 1867.

30. Anonymous to Tomás Cipriano de Mosquera, June 27, 1866, Bogotá, ACC, Sala Mosquera, No. 49,590.

31. *La Alianza*, March 4, 1867.

32. *El Nacional*, April 30, 1867; Pérez Aguirre, *25 años*, 267–68; Rodríguez, *Santos Acosta*, 128–31; Pablo E. Cárdenas Acosta, *La restauración constitucional de 1867. Historia de un contragolpe de estado* (Tunja: Imprenta Departamental, 1966).

33. *La Alianza*, May 4, 14, 1867. Mosquera was tried by the congress in November on multiple charges and officially removed from the presidency. The general's three-year jail sentence was commuted to exile in Peru, where he resided until 1871. The pro-Mosquera *La Libertad* carried a detailed defense of the ex-president during the last few months of the year, supposedly made by artisans and other supporters. It centered upon Mosquera's lifelong support of the people against anarchistic Radicalism. Artisan signers of the document included Saavedra, Ignacio Beltrán, Bartolomé Paniagua, Ramón Ordóñez Torres, Agustín Garai, and Prájedes Bermúdez, many of whom had fought with Melo and some of whom were Alianza members. *La Libertad*, October 31, November 6, 13, December 4, 11, 25, 1867; January 1, 1868.

34. Indalecio Liévano Aguirre, *El proceso de Mosquera ante el senado: Tres conferencias* (Bogotá: Editorial Revista Colombiana, 1966), 62, 64, 92, 99. Liévano apparently relied upon Cordovez Moure's *Reminiscencias de Santa Fe y Bogotá* for his account of Saavedra's role, an interpretation that Cárdenas Acosta convincingly repudiates. Cárdenas Acosta, *La restauración*, 86–87.

35. *La Libertad*, October 31, November 6, 13, December 4, 11, 25, 1867; January 1, 1868; *La Alianza*, May 29, 1867.

36. Un liberal honrado, *A los artesanos sensatos* (Bogotá: n.p., June 1, 1867); Uno que no vive de empleo sino de su trabajo, *Degollación de los artesanos* (Bogotá, June 11, 1867); Dos artesanos, *A los artesanos* (Bogotá, June 11, 1867); *El Republicano*, July 17, 1867.

37. *La Alianza,* May 29, 1867, p. 1.

38. *La Alianza,* June 14, 1867; *El Diario Oficial,* June 7, 11, 1867; *La República,* August 14, 1867.

39. *El Republicano,* July 17, 1867.

40. *La Alianza,* August 1, p. 2, August 10, September 5, 1867.

41. *La Alianza,* February 13, May 29, June 14, 1867; April 25, 1868.

42. *La Alianza,* May 29, June 14, 1867.

43. *Unión de artesanos* (Bogotá: Impreso por Foción Mantilla, June 19, 1867); *La Prensa,* June 14, 1867.

44. *La Prensa,* June 25, 1867.

45. *La Prensa,* September 4, 1867; *La Patria,* October 4, 1867; *La Libertad,* December 25, 1867.

46. New officers selected to head the board of directors during its next six months included: Juan Cáceres, president; Agustín Díaz, vice president; Mariano González, secretary; and Fuljencio Roa, treasurer. *La Alianza,* December 5, 21, 1867; February 1, 1868.

47. *La Alianza,* February 1, 1868; *La Prensa,* December 13, 1867. The speeches of the meetings are in *La Alianza,* January 4, 18, 25, 1868.

48. *La Prensa,* December 13, 1867. The speeches of the meetings are in *La Alianza,* January 4, 18, 25, 1868. A non-artisan participant, J. Joaquín Borda, told the meeting of a Sunday School program for "children of the pueblo," which began operation in 1868. *La Prensa,* December 13, 1867.

49. *La Alianza,* January 18, February 1, March 7, 28, 1868.

50. Saturnino González, José L. Camacho, Manuel de J. Barrera, et al., *Representación al Congreso Nacional* (Bogotá: Impreso por Manuel de J. Barrera, 1868). Three weeks later the Junta Piadosa, whose president was Ambrosio López, presented a similar request in support of La Alianza's petition. *La Alianza,* March 15, April 13, 1868.

51. *La Alianza,* April 11, 1868. The Conservative *La Prensa* described the petition process in detail, claiming that the true cause of the economic misery was not foreign imports, but the result of party-generated wars which had robbed consumers of their funds. Thus it noted that the people who rejected the petition were the same people who had caused the problems in the first place. The paper warned that political agitators were ready to take advantage of the artisan's disappointments and counciled craftsmen to remain peaceful. *La Prensa,* April 14, 1868; *La Alianza,* April 18, 1868.

52. *La Alianza,* April 4, 11, May 2, 1868.

53. *La Independencia,* March 28, 1868. Saavedra's leadership of the new Democratic Society firmly linked it to the Mosquera wing of the Liberal party, which was attempting to reverse its setbacks of the previous year. The Democratic Societies were revived in the Cauca as a mosquerista tool as well.

54. *La Paz*, June 5, 1868.

55. Calisto Ballesteros, *Protesta de varios miembros (a) de la Junta Directiva de la Sociedad de la Alianza* (Bogotá: n.p., n.d.).

56. *La Paz*, June 5, 19, 23, July 3, 1868.

57. The reference is to Tapias's June 1867 article "El Lunes," in which he criticized worker's celebration of St. Monday as contributing to political conflict, as well as to a waste of time and money. The article elicited a large negative reaction at the time. *La Alianza*, June 14, August 1, 1867.

58. *La Alianza*, May 23, 1868.

59. Madiedo's article "El Cristo y los Ricos," published in April, presented an articulate analysis of the labor theory of value. This piece coincided with the ideological stance revealed by artisan contributors to *La Alianza* although the reasons for the coincidence are difficult to determine. *La Alianza*, April 25, May 9, 30, 1868. The article produced a splendid polemic. See *La Prensa*, June 2, 1868; *La Paz*, May 26, June 2, 9, 16, 1868. On Madiedo's social thought see Jaime Jaramillo Uribe, *El pensamiento colombiano en el siglo XIX* (Bogotá: Editorial Temis Librería, 1982), 187–97.

60. Ramón Jiménez was chosen president; Féliz Izasa was elected vice-president; and Tomás Rodríguez, the son of the Society of Artisans' founder, Agustín Rodríguez, was named secretary.

61. *La Alianza*, August 15, 1868.

62. Saturnino González, *Dos palabras en la cuestión Alianza* (Bogotá: n.p., June 13, 1868); Isodoro Madero, *El señor Cruz Sánchez i "La Alianza" ante el tribunal de la opinión pública* (Bogotá: n.p., September 30, 1868).

63. *La Alianza*, August 15, 25, September 15, 1868.

64. Ramón Jiménez et al., *La situación* (Bogotá: n.p., October 6, 1868); *La Alianza*, October 4, 25, 1868.

65. *El Noticioso de Cundinamarca*, October 8, 1868.

66. *La Alianza*, October 29, November 7 (p. 1), 1868; Pérez Aguirre, *25 años*, 282–90.

67. Jones, *Languages of Class*, 19.

68. Sean Wilentz, *Chants Democratic: New York City and the Rise of the American Working Class, 1788–1850* (New York: Oxford University Press, 1984), 61–63.

69. The ideology detailed below comes from articles published over a two-year period in *La Alianza*, from a variety of different men. When possible, these artisans are identified.

70. Jaramillo, *Pensamiento colombiano*, 95–97, 107.

71. *La Alianza*, January 4, April 11, 1868.

72. *La Alianza*, April 4, 1868, p. 3.

73. *La Alianza*, October 10, 20, 1866; August 10, 1867; January 4, April 4, 1868.

74. *La Alianza*, August 10, September 5, 1867.

75. *La Alianza*, October 10, December 1, 1866; January 10, 20, May 14, 1867.

76. *La Alianza*, December 1, 1866.

77. *La Alianza*, October 10, 1866.

78. *La Alianza*, April 3, 1867.

79. *La Alianza*, October 20, December 1, 1866; April 13, 1867.

80. *La Alianza*, October 20, December 1, 1866; February 13, April 13, 1867; January 4, 1868.

81. *La Alianza*, February 8, 15, 22, 1868.

82. *La Alianza*, October 20, December 1, 1866; January 20, February 6, 13, April 13, 1867.

83. *La Alianza*, January 10, p. 1, February 13, 1867; January 25, 1868.

84. *La Alianza*, October 20, p. 1, December 10, 1866; January 20, February 13, March 4, April 3, May 14, September 5, 1867; January 25, 1868.

85. *La Alianza*, November 10, 1866; February 13, May 4, 14, 1867; March 14, 1868.

86. *La Alianza*, October 10, December 10, 1866; January 3, April 3, 5, September 5, 1867.

87. Emilia Viotti da Costa, "Experience versus Structure: New Tendencies in the History of Labor and the Working Class in Latin America—What Do We Gain? What Do We Lose?" *ILWCH*, No. 36 (Fall 1989), 3–24; Barbara Weinstein, "The New Latin American Labor History: What We Gain," *ILWCH*, No. 36 (Fall 1989), 25–30; Perry Anderson, "The Common and the Particular," *ILWCH*, No. 36 (Fall 1989), 31–36; Hobart A. Spalding, "Somethings Old and Somethings New," *ILWCH*, No. 36 (Fall 1989), 37–44; June Nash, "Gender Issues in Latin American Labor," *ILWCH*, No. 36 (Fall 1989), 44–50.

88. See, for example, A. G. Quintero-Rivera, "Socialist and Cigarmaker: Artisans' Proletarianizaiton in the Making of the Puerto Rican Working Class," *Latin American Perspectives*, 10:23, issues 37/38 (Spring-–Summer, 1983), 19–38.

89. Paul Gootenberg, "Beleaguered Liberals: The Failed First Generation of Free Traders in Peru," in *Guiding the Invisible Hand: Economic Liberalism and the State in Latin American History*, ed. by Joseph L. Love and Nils Jacobsen (New York: Praeger Publishers, 1988), 81; Paul Gootenberg, "The Social Origins of Protectionism and Free Trade in Nineteenth-Century Lima," *JLAS*, 14:2 (November 1982), 329–58; Ricardo Temoche Benites, *Cofradías, gremios, mutuales y sindicatos en el Perú* (Lima: Editorial Escuela Nueva, S.A., 1985), 78–80.

90. Maurice Zeitlin, *The Civil Wars in Chile (or The Bourgeois Revolutions That Never Were)* (Princeton, NJ: Princeton University Press, 1984).

## Chapter Five

1. *El Liberal*, September 27, 1869.

2. The Society attempted to establish a "deposit of national artifacts" to serve as a clearinghouse where a customer could buy a finished product rather than have to commission its production. See *Diario de Cundinamarca*, April 6, December 13, 1871.

3. Helen Delpar, "The Liberal Record and Colombian Historiography: An Indictment in Need of Revision," *Revista Interamericana de Bibliographía*, 31:4 (1981), 528–30. For the antecedents to Núñez's banking policies, see Richard Preston Hyland, "The Secularization of Credit in the Cauca Valley, Colombia," Ph.D. dissertation, University of California, Berkeley, 1979, 207–8.

4. *La Ilustración*, February 26, March 25, 1870.

5. *Diario de Cundinamarca*, April 8, 1870; *La Ilustración*, July 27, 1870.

6. *Diario de Cundinamarca*, June 21, 1871.

7. *El Bien Público*, June 31, 1871. Later that year a chair made by Genaro Martín that had won a prize at the exhibition was presented to Robert Bunch of the British Legation in recognition of Britain's support for Colombia during its war of independence. See *El Bien Público*, October 13, 1871.

8. *El Bien Público*, January 17, 1874; *El Tradicionista*, April 2, 1872; *La América*, November 16, 1872.

9. *La América*, March 15, 1872.

10. *Diario de Cundinamarca*, January 5, 1875.

11. Simón Sanmiguel, Fulgencio Roa, Ignacio López, and Benjamín Amézquita were the others.

12. Frank Safford, *The Ideal of the Practical: Colombia's Struggle to Form a Technical Elite* (Austin: University of Texas Press, 1976), 206; *El Progreso*, March 11, 1897; *Diario de Cundinamarca*, October 12, 1881. The youths selected were Pompilio Beltrán (mechanic), Juan Nepomuceno Rodríguez (casting), Benjamín Herrera (lathe and construction), and Zoilo Cuéllar (foundry).

13. *Diario Oficial*, April 19, 1872; *Diario de Cundinamarca*, April 22, 23, 1872.

14. Helen Delpar, *Red Against Blue: The Liberal Party in Colombian Politics, 1863–1899* (University: University of Alabama Press, 1981), 112–14; Ospina Vásquez, *Industria y protección*, 268–70.

15. *El Tradicionista*, April 23, 1872; *El Bien Público*, April 23, 1872.

16. *Diario de Cundinamarca*, May 2, 1872.

17. Gerald Michael Greenfield and Seldon L. Maram, eds., *Latin American Labor Organizations* (Westport, CT: Greenwood Press, 1987), xi.

18. Charles W. Bergquist, *Labor in Latin America: Comparative Essays on Chile, Argentina, Venezuela, and Colombia* (Stanford, CA: Stanford University Press, 1986), 54, 105–8.

19. Julio Godio, *El movimiento obrero de América Latina 1850–1918* (Bogotá: Ediciones Tercer Mundo, 1978), 19–49.

20. Hobart Spalding, Jr., *Organized Labor in Latin America: Historical Case Studies of Workers in Dependent Societies* (New York: Harper & Row, 1977), 15–17.

21. Characteristic literature includes: Reynaldo Sordo Cedeño, "Las sociedades de socorros mutuos, 1867–1880," *Historia Mexicana*, Vol. 129, 33:1 (1983), 72–96; José Woldenberg K., "Asociaciones artesanas del siglo XIX (Sociedad Socorros Mutuos de Impresores, 1874–1875)," *Revista Mexicana de Ciencias Políticas y Sociales*, 83 (1976), 71–112; Juan Felipe Leal and José Woldenberg, "Origenes y desarrollo del artesanado y del proletariado industrial en México: 1867–1914," *Revista Mexicana de Ciencia Política*, No. 81 (1975), 131–34; Samuel Baily, "Las sociedades de ayuda mutua y el desarrollo de una comunidad italiana en Buenos Aires, 1858–1918," *Desarrollo Económico*, 21:84 (January–March 1982), 485–514.

22. Peter Blanchard, *The Origins of The Peruvian Labor Movement 1883–1919* (Pittsburgh: The University of Pittsburgh Press, 1982), 16.

23. John M. Hart, *Anarchism and the Mexican Working Class, 1860–1931* (Austin: University of Texas Press, 1987), 30–31, passim; Sordo Cedeño, "Las sociedades de socorros mutuos," 94.

24. Sordo Cedeño, "Las sociedades de socorros mutuos," 77.

25. Rodney Anderson, "Mexico," in *Latin American Labor Organizations*, ed. by Gerald Michael Greenfield and Seldon L. Maram (Westport, CT: Greenwood Press, 1987), 516. Sordo Cedeño, "Las sociedades de socorros mutuos," 93–94, suggests that mutual aid societies served as the primary survival mechanism of artisans, who continued as a major segment of the Mexico City work force. See also Alan Middleton, "Division and Cohesion in the Working Class: Artisans and Wage Labourers in Ecuador," *JLAS*, 14:1 (May 1982), 171–94.

26. *Diario de Cundinamarca*, August 5, 1872; Melitón Angulo Heredia, *Informe del secretario de la Sociedad de Socorros Mutuos* (Bogotá: n.p., February 6, 1873). Membership data is taken from *El Tradicionista*, September 8, 1874.

27. See, for example, *Conferencias leídas en la 'Sociedad de Socorros Mutuos'* (Bogotá: Imprenta de "La Luz," 1888); *La Nación*, September 10, 1886; *El Heraldo*, June 18, 1892; *La Crónica*, August 11, 1898.

28. *La América*, May 28, 1873, p. 1.

29. *Las Noticias*, January 22, 1889; *El Telegrama*, January 22, 1889. For a partial membership list, see *El Telegrama*, July 13, 16, 1889.

30. *El Taller*, July 2, 1891; *El Heraldo*, April 9, 1890; *La Patria*, August 3, 1894; *El Republicano*, March 10, 1896.

31. *La Crónica*, September 20, October 1, 5, 14, 1899.

32. For a culinary history that stresses the introduction of non-Colombian dietary habits to Bogotá see Aída Martínez Carreño, *Mesa y cocina en el siglo XIX* (Bogotá: Fondo Cultural Cafetero, 1985).

33. José María Cordovez Moure, *Reminiscencias de Santa Fé de Bogotá*, 9 vols. (Bogotá: Imprenta de La Cruz, 1910), III, 141–44.

34. "Guerra y muerte a los que nos hambean." *La América*, January 27, 1875, p. 1. These students probably identified themselves as "La liga de Astrea," a shadowy organization that released leaflets attempting to incite the popular classes to radical political action. In the wake of the riot several leaflets claiming to represent the city's artisans recalled the French Commune as the inspiration for the upheaval. See *La América*, January 27, 29, 1875.

35. *La América*, January 26, 27, 29, 30, 1875; *La Ilustración*, January 25, 26, 1875; *El Tradicionista*, January 26, 29, 1875; Eugenio Gutiérrez Cely, "Nuevo movimiento popular contra el laissez-faire: Bogotá, 1875," *Universitas Humanística* 11:17 (March 1982), 179–83.

36. *La América*, January 27, 1875.

37. High food prices in the late-1880s created similar demands for government price controls. See, for example, *El Taller*, January 17, 1889; *El Telegrama*, February 13, 1889; *Las Noticias*, March 15, 1889; E. P. Thompson, "The Moral Economy of the English Crowd in the Eighteenth Century," *Past and Present*, No. 50 (1971), 76–136.

38. *La Ilustración*, January 26, 1875, p. 1.

39. David Sowell, "The 1893 *Bogotazo*: Artisans and Public Violence in Late-Nineteenth Century Bogotá," *JLAS*, 21:2 (May 1989), 271–72; *La América*, January 27, 30, 1875.

40. Darío Bustamante Roldán, "Efectos económicos del papel moneda durante la regeneración," *Cuadernos Colombianos*, 1:4 (1974), 561–660.

41. *El Taller*, January 17, June 1, 1889; *La Unión*, June 7, 1881; *Las Noticias*, March 5, 1889; *El Correo Nacional*, September 9, 1890; *El Amigo del Pueblo*, August 3, 1889; *La Capital*, October 10, 1890; *El Heraldo*, September 10, 1890; *El Telegrama*, February 13, 1889; *Diario de Cundinamarca*, August 3, 1889.

42. *Colombia Cristiana*, December 14, 21, 28, 1892; January 4, 1893.

43. AHN, República, Policía Nacional, Tomo 2, ff. 422–521r, Tomo 3, f. 409, 625–26; *Diario Oficial*, February 2, 3, 1893; *El Correo Nacional*, February 1, 1893; *El Orden*, March 4, 1893.

44. Oscar de J. Saldarriaga Vélez, "Bogotá, la Regeneración y la policía 1880–1900," *Revista Universidad de Antioquia*, 37:211 (January–March 1988), 37–55; Alvaro Castaño Castillo, *La policía, su origen y su destino* (Bogotá: Lit y Edit "Cahur," 1947), VIII, 12–18; Robert D. Storch, "The Plague of Blue Locusts: Police Reform and Popular Resistance in Northern England, 1840–57," *International Review of Social History* (1975), 61–90.

45. AHN, República, Gobernaciones varios, Tomo 28, ff. 954–55.

46. *El Artesano*, April 8, 15, June 2, 17, 1893.

47. Those arrested included Genaro Gómez, Pedro Daza, Carlos Maza, Ricardo Castro, Ricardo Mafla D., Bernardino Rangel, Jorge Miguel Alvarez, Aparicio Reyes, Leonidas Hinostrosa, and Genaro Zeno Figueredo. Most of those detained were described as artisans, who were said to have been affiliated with all political groups.

48. *La Ilustración*, February 12, 1870; *Diario de Cundinamarca*, January 31, 1874; *Rejistro Municipal*, November 15, December 16, 1874.

49. *La Ilustración*, January 7, November 5, 1870; *Diario de Cundinamarca*, March 14, 1870.

50. *La Ilustración*, February 6, 15, 1873; *Diario de Cundinamarca*, January 15, 1874; *El Tradicionista*, May 14, June 1, 4, 1872; *El Deber*, December 16, 1879.

51. *La Ilustración*, July 27, 1870.

52. *La Ilustración*, May 10, July 19, 22, 26, August 19, 24, 26, 1870; Los artesanos, *Basta de abusos* (Bogotá: n.p., July 18, 1870); *El Bien Público*, August 2, 1870.

53. *El Tradicionista*, February 28, 1874. Artisan political tempers flared that day as well. Cruz Ballesteros and Saturnino González, both of whom had been key Alianza members, were reportedly involved in a scuffle at the Plaza de Bolívar polling table. *El Tradicionista*, May 2, 5, 1874; *La América*, May 4, 11, 18, 1874.

54. Helen Delpar, "Renegade or Regenerator? Rafael Núñez as Seen by Colombian Historians," *Revista Interamericana de Bibliografía*, 35:1 (1985), 27–29.

55. Helen Delpar, "Colombian Liberalism and the Roman Catholic Church, 1863–1866," *Journal of Church and State*, 22:2 (Spring 1980), 288–89.

56. Delpar, *Red Against Blue*, 110–11, 114–17; Helen Delpar, "Aspects of Liberal Factionalism in Colombia, 1875–1885," *HAHR*, 51:2 (May 1971), 255–65.

57. *Diario de Cundinamarca*, April 24, 29, 30, 1875; *El Tradicionista*, April 20, 1875; *El Combate*, April 24, 1875.

58. Muchos artesanos de la capital, *Artesanos, juicios*, in *El Diario de Cundinamarca*, May 18, 1875.

59. *La Ilustración*, May 18, 1875; *La Época*, May 17, 19, 1875.

60. *Diario de Cundinamarca*, August 2, 4, 1875.

61. Alonso Valencia Llano, *Estado soberano del Cauca: Federalismo y regeneración* (Bogotá: Banco de la República, 1988), 202–38; Manuel Briceño, *La revolución de 1876–77. Recuerdos para la historia* (Bogotá: Imprenta Nueva, 1878); Constacio Franco V., *Apuntamientos para la historia. La guerra de 1876 i 1877* (Bogotá: Imprenta de la Época, 1877).

62. Liberals in the Cauca valley formed numerous Democratic Societies in support of the existing order. See *Diario de Cundinamarca*, March 11, April 25, May 17, 23, 24, 27, 1876.

63. *Diario de Cundinamarca*, August 2, 3, 12, 1876.

64. Their chiefs included Cruz Ballesteros, Democrat Tiburcio Ruiz, Liberal artisan Antonio Sánchez, and moderate craftsman Pablo Bermúdez. *Diario de Cundinamarca*, August 14, 24, 1876.

65. *Diario de Cundinamarca*, March 12, 1879; *El Liberal*, February 8, 15, March 8, 1879; *La Doctrina*, April 23, 1879.

66. *La Doctrina*, May 7, 1879; *Diario de Cundinamarca*, May 6, 7, 10, 13, 1879; *El Deber*, May 9, 13, 27, 1879; *La Reforma*, June 10, 1879.

67. *El Diario Oficial*, April 8, 1880.

68. Muchos artesanos, *La reforma de la tarifa aduana i la cámara de representantes* (Bogotá: n.p., May 12, 1880), p. 1; *La Reforma*, May 26, 1880.

69. Miguel Samper, "La protección," in *La miseria en Bogotá y otros escritos* (Bogotá: Biblioteca Universitaria de Cultura Colombiana, 1969); *Diario de Cundinamarca*, May 12, 1880.

70. David Bushnell, "Two Stages in Colombian Tariff Policy: The Radical Era and the Return to Protection (1861–1885)," *Inter-American Economic Affairs* 9:4 (Spring 1956), 15–16.

71. Luis Ospina Vásquez, *Industria y protección en Colombia, 1810 a 1930* (Bogotá: Editorial Santafé, 1955), 290–91.

72. Bushnell, "Two Stages," 17, passim.

73. Indalecio Liévano Aguirre, *Rafael Núñez* (Bogotá: Cromos, 1944), 183–93.

74. Camacho, Félix Valois Madero, Cruz Sánchez, Genaro Martín, and Rafael Tapias.

75. Liévano Aguirre, *Núñez*, 175.

76. *La Luz*, July 28, 1882; Bushnell, "Two Stages," 20–21. One should not, however, overlook the fact that these trades were also among the most prosperous at a time when the city was experiencing strong growth.

77. Bushnell, "Two Stages," 20–21. When the Chamber dealt with Núñez's 1884 tariff reforms, numerous artisans praised their efforts. See *La Luz*, February 20, 1884.

78. *Diario de Cundinamarca*, January 6, 14, 20, February 1, 3, 10, March 9, 22, April 15, 26, 1882; *La Ilustración*, September 26, 1882; *El*

*Comercio*, August 30, 1882; *El Patriota*, August 27, 1883. The best sources of information on the group are the *Diario de Cundinamarca*, the Society's newspaper, *Salud Pública*, and numerous leaflets it published, many of which are in the Hemeroteca of the Biblioteca Luis Angel Arango.

79. Alvaro Tirado Mejía, *El estado y la política en el siglo XIX* (Bogotá: El Ancora Editores, 1983), 103–4.

80. Delpar, "Núñez," 33.

81. Jaime Jaramillo Uribe, *El pensamiento colombiano en el siglo XIX* (Bogotá: Editorial Temis Librería, 1982), passim.

82. Charles W. Bergquist, *Coffee and Conflict in Colombia, 1886–1910* (Durham, NC: Duke University Press, 1978), 42–44.

83. Delpar, "Núñez," 29–33.

84. Delpar, "Colombian Liberalism," 288–89.

85. Francisco Leal Buitrago, *Estado y política en Colombia* (Bogotá: Siglo Veintiuno Editores, 1984).

86. Daniel Pécaut, *Orden y violencia: Colombia, 1930–1954*, 2 vols. (Bogotá: Siglo Veintiuno Editores, 1987), I, 10.

87. Tirado Mejía, *Estado y política*, 110–19; William Marion Gibson, *The Constitutions of Colombia* (Durham, NC: Duke University Press, 1948), 299–313.

88. See José María Samper's ideas on the party in *La Nación*, March 12, 1888.

89. *El Instituto*, December 8, 1886; January 1, February 23, 1887; *La Nación*, March 16, 1886.

90. *El Orden*, December 15, 1887; *El Renacimiento*, December 4, 1886.

91. *La Nación*, December 17, 1886.

92. *La Nación*, January 11, 1887.

93. *El Taller*, January 8, 22, 1887.

94. *El Taller*, February 2, 1887.

95. *La Capital*, November 7, 1890; *El Progreso*, March 4, 11, 1897; *Los Hechos*, August 1, 31, September 26, 1894; *El Correo Nacional*, July 1, 1891; *El Grito del Pueblo*, June 16, 1897.

96. *El Correo Nacional*, May 6, 1893; *Los Hechos*, December 6, 1894.

97. *Diario de Cundinamarca*, May 5, June 20, 1893; *El Telegrama*, February 15, 1890, May 22, 1895; *La Capital*, October 31, 1890; *El Correo Nacional*, May 11, 1891; May 28, 1892; May 7, 1894; *El Orden*, March 1, 1893; *Colombia Cristiana*, May 13, 1894.

98. *El Taller*, January 17, June 1, 1889; *La Unión*, June 7, 1881; *Las Noticias*, March 5, 1889; *El Correo Nacional*, September 9, 1890; *El Amigo del Pueblo*, August 3, 1889; *La Capital*, October 10, 1890; *El Heraldo*, September 10, 1890; *El Telegrama*, February 13, 1889; *Diario de Cundinamarca*, August 3, 1889.

99. *El Taller*, June 1, 1889; *El Heraldo*, March 30, 1892.

100. *El Taller*, July 27, 30, August 3, 1892.

101. *El Taller*, April 21, 1891. Camacho was vice-president of the electoral board working for Núñez and Caro's victory in Cundinamarca. See his speech for the two in *La Prensa*, November 14, 1891.

102. *El Heraldo*, December 9, 12, 1891.

103. Delpar, *Red Against Blue*, 144–45, 150–57. Law 61 of May 23, 1888 authorized the executive to quell disturbances of public order by "imprisonment, or deprivation of political rights." Bergquist, *Coffee and Conflict*, 37–38. For examples of the applications of these laws, see *El Heraldo*, August 13, 1890, and *El Precursos*, September 12, 1889.

104. Bergquist, *Coffee and Conflict*, 48.

105. Delpar, *Red Against Blue*, 149–57; Bergquist, *Coffee and Conflict*, 49.

106. *El Telegrama*, January 12, 1895; *Los Hechos*, January 23, 1895.

107. Bergquist contends that issues of political economy in large part defined these divisions. See "The Political Economy of the Colombian Presidential Election of 1897," *HAHR*, 56:1 (February 1976), 1–30.

108. *El Republicano*, March 13, April 17, 1896.

109. *La Crónica*, December 21, 22, 23, 1897.

110. *El Nacionalista*, January 5, 1898; Delpar, *Red Against Blue*, 168.

111. Selected as the Industrial Club's president was Pompilio Beltrán and as its general secretary, Alejandro Torres Amaya. See *La Crónica*, December 30, 1898.

112. *La Crónica*, January 3, 19, 26, 1899. The club founded in Barranquilla had more than political interests; on at least two occasions it engaged in strikes to improve worker's conditions. See *El Autonomista*, May 26, 27, 1899.

113. Bergquist, *Coffee and Conflict*, 103–87.

114. Adolfo Meisel R. and Alejandro López M., "Papel moneda, tasas de interés y revaluación durante la Regeneración," in *El Banco de la República: Antecedentes, evolución y estructura* (Bogotá: Banco de la República, 1990), 83–102.

115. Gonzalo Sánchez, "La Violencia in Colombia: New Research, New Questions," *HAHR*, 64:4 (November 1985), 790.

116. Carlos Eduardo Jaramillo, "La guerra de los Mil Días, 1899–1902," in *Historia política, 1886–1946*. Vol. I. *Nueva historia de Colombia* (Bogotá: Planeta, 1989), 89–112; and "La guerra de los mil días: aspectos estructurales de la organización guerrillera," in *Pasado y presente de la violencia en Colombia*, comp. by Gonzalo Sánchez and Ricardo Peñaranda (Bogotá: Fondo Editorial CEREC, 1986), 47–86.

117. Malcolm Deas, "Algunos interrogantes sobre la relación guerras civiles y violencia," *Pasado y presente de la violencia en Colombia*, comp.

by Gonzalo Sánchez and Ricardo Peñaranda (Bogotá: Fondo Editorial CEREC, 1986), 41–46.

118. *La Constitutión*, October 11, November 26, 1902; *La Juventud*, January 18, 1903; *El Impulso*, March 4, 1903.

119. AC, Senado, Memoriales con informes, IV, 24–40r, 49.

## Chapter Six

1. For discussion of this topic in French towns of the same period, see Michael P. Hanagan, *The Logic of Solidarity: Artisans and Industrial Workers in Three French Towns, 1871–1914* (Chicago: University of Chicago Press, 1980); and John Wallach Scott, *The Glassworkers of Carmaux: French Craftsmen and Political Action in a Nineteenth-Century City* (Cambridge, MA: Harvard University Press, 1974).

2. *Los Hechos*, May 20, 1904.

3. *Los Hechos*, May 27, 1904.

4. *Los Hechos*, April 23, May 10, 1904.

5. *Los Hechos*, June 7, 1904.

6. *Los Hechos*, June 11, 1904.

7. *Los Hechos*, June 18, 1904.

8. *Los Hechos*, October 5, 13, 1904.

9. *Diario Noticioso*, January 11, 1905.

10. Luis Ospina Vásquez, *Industria y protección en Colombia, 1810 a 1930* (Bogotá: Editorial Santafé, 1955), 334–44, 358–59.

11. Eduardo Lemaitre, *Rafael Reyes: Biografía de un gran colombiano* (Bogotá: Banco de la República, 1981), 246–55; Charles W. Bergquist, *Coffee and Conflict in Colombia, 1886–1910* (Durham, NC: Duke University Press, 1978), 219–23.

12. Lemaitre, *Rafael Reyes*, 316–24.

13. *El Faro*, February 18, 25, 1906.

14. *El Yunque*, February 16, March 15, April 14, 19, 27, May 17, 24, 26, 1906.

15. *El Correo Nacional*, June 4, 5, 6, 8, 13, 1906.

16. *XYZ*, August 17, 1907. Many members of the carpenters' group had been members of the carpenters' trade organization in the 1880s, which suggests a certain persistence of trade groups. See *XYZ*, May 9, 1907.

17. *La Fusión*, January 17, 1910.

18. *El Correo Nacional*, March 1, 1905; *La Prensa*, August 13, 1907; *XYZ*, January 31, 1907; *El Público*, January 30, 1907.

19. *Estatutos de la Sociedad Filantrópica* (Bogotá: Imprenta Eléctrica, 1906).

20. *El Correo Nacional,* January 18, 1905; *El Artista,* January 26, p. 1, September 29, December 1, 1906; March 21, 1908.

21. Urrutia, *Development of the Colombian Labor Movement,* 53, 60; Mauricio Archila, "De la revolución social a la conciliación? Algunas hipótesis sobre la transformación de la clase obrera colombiana (1919–1935)," *Anuario Colombiano de Historia Social y de la Cultura,* No. 12 (1984), 98–102.

22. *La Constitutión,* October 8, 1902.

23. *El Correo Nacional,* July 8, 1904; *XYZ,* September 21, 1904; *El Nuevo Tiempo,* January 16, 1909.

24. *El Correo Nacional,* March 24, August 20, 1908; *El Nuevo Tiempo,* January 13, June 14, 1909; *La Unidad,* July 22, 1911; *La Gaceta Republicana,* January 12, 1912; and *La Sociedad,* April 27, 1912.

25. *El Republicano,* April 24, 1907, p. 1; *El Artista,* April 8, 1908; *El Correo Nacional,* April 15, September 4, 1908, p. 1.

26. Bergquist, *Coffee and Conflict,* 242–45; Lemaitre, *Rafael Reyes,* 336–39, 345–57.

27. Medófilo Medina, *La protesta urbana en Colombia el siglo XX* (Bogotá: Ediciones Aurora, 1984), 19, 24, passim.

28. *El Concurso Nacional,* April 2, 1909; *Unión Industrial,* August 29, 1909; Medina, *Protesta urbana,* 24; *El Nuevo Tiempo,* March 13, 1909. Many contemporary sources downplayed the role of artisans in the events of the 13th. *El Nuevo Tiempo,* March 16, 17, 18, 26, 1909; *El Correo Nacional,* March 24, 1909; and *XYZ,* March 19, 1909.

29. Christopher Abel, *Conservative Politics in Twentieth-Century Antioquia (1910–1953)* (Oxford: Latin American Centre, St. Antony's College, Occasional Paper III, 1973), 14–15. See also the circular in *El Nuevo Tiempo,* April 5, 1909.

30. Murillo had been an active supporter of the Republican Union since its founding and had been a key figure in the Directorio de Industriales y Obreros associated with that party.

31. *Unión Industrial,* August 15, 21, 29, September 5, 1909.

32. *La Gaceta Republicana,* November 12, 15, 1909.

33. *El Sufragio,* February 19, 1910, p. 2; *La Fusión,* January 17, 24, February 16, 1910.

34. *La Razón del Obrero,* April 16, 1910.

35. *La Razón del Obrero,* July 22, 1910; *La Correspondencia,* June 10, 1910.

36. *El 13 de Marzo,* June 15, 18, 29, July 2, 1910.

37. Elections for departmental assemblies were held in February, for senators and representatives in May, and for municipal councils in October. *El Proteccionista,* November 26, 1910.

38. *El Proteccionista,* October 29, November 5, 12, 19, 26, December 4, 1910.

39. *La Gaceta Republicana,* January 24, 25, 28, February 1, 4, 6, 1911; *La Unidad,* February 7, 1911; *El Tiempo,* February 24, 1911.

40. *El Comercio,* June 1, 1911; *La Gaceta Republicana,* May 29, June 23, 1911. See *El Liberal,* June 24, 1911, for a list of all those elected and their factional affiliation. See *Comentarios,* July 8, 1911, for an interview with Restrepo.

41. The lectures of the Spaniard Pedro González Blanco sparked a series of clashes between pro- and anti-church partisans; many of the latter were identified with the Workers' party. *El Comercio,* May 6, 1911; *La Unidad,* May 4, June 6, 1911; *La Gaceta Republicana,* May 1, 2, 4, 9, 30, 1911; *El Contemporáneo,* June 3, 1911; *El Tiempo,* May 2, 1911. The UNIO later helped to organize the 20 de julio parade. According to all accounts, the march was well prepared and a success, but, unfortunately, the bullfight held later that evening witnessed a violent confrontation between spectators and police. After several hours of disturbances, at least nine people had been killed and scores wounded. Most observers agreed that the UNIO had nothing to do with the violence; nonetheless its image was badly tarnished. See *La Gaceta Republicana,* July 5, 21, 24, 27, 29, 1911; *El Tiempo,* July 22, 25, 1911; *El Día Noticioso,* July 22, 25, 1911; *Colombia,* July 8, 1911; *La Unidad,* July 27, 1911.

42. *El Tiempo,* September 15, 1911; *3 y 2,* September 13, 1911; *Comentarios,* September 28, 1911.

43. *El Liberal,* October 2, 3, 1911; *La Gaceta Republicana,* October 3, 7, 11, 1911; *La Sociedad,* October 3, 1911.

44. *La Unidad,* February 9, 1911.

45. *La Gaceta Republicana,* February 6, 1911.

46. Kenneth N. Medhurst, *The Church and Labour in Colombia* (Manchester, U.K.: Manchester University Press, 1984), 47.

47. Guillermo and Jorge González Quintana, *El Círculo de Obreros: La obra y su espíritu, 1911–1940* (Bogotá: Editorial de la Litografía Colombiana, 1940), 9–21; *Primer congreso eucarístico nacional de Colombia* (Bogotá: Escuela Tipografía Salesiana, 1914). See also Jeffrey L. Klaiber, "The Catholic Lay Movement in Peru: 1867–1959," *The Americas,* 40:2 (October 1983), 152, 158–59.

48. Jorge Orlando Melo, "De Carlos E. Restrepo a Marco Fidel Suárez. Republicanismo y gobiernos conservadores," in *Historia política,* Vol. I. *Historia de Colombia* (Bogotá: Planeta, 1989), 223.

49. *El Liberal,* October 27, 1911; Vincent Baillie Dunlap, "Tragedy of a Colombian Martyr: Rafael Uribe Uribe and the Liberal Party, 1896–1914," Ph.D. dissertation, University of North Carolina, 1979, 221.

50. *La Gaceta Republicana*, October 31, 1911.

51. See, for example, Ramón Rosales's editorial in *El Liberal*, April 25, 1912.

52. *La Gaceta Republicana*, May 14, June 27, 1912.

53. One of the non-political objectives of the UNIO had been to form a Casa del Pueblo as a center for education and public health. Funds to that end had been collected, but the June critics claimed that no monies had been expended. *El Liberal*, April 13, 1912; *El Tiempo*, May 13, June 8, 18, 1912; *Gil Blas*, May 8, 1912.

54. *El Liberal*, August 14, 1911.

55. *La Gaceta Republicana*, May 14, 1912; *El Tiempo*, September 23, 1912; *El Domingo*, September 21, 1912.

56. *El Liberal*, January 30, 1913.

57. *El Domingo*, October 27, December 8, 1912; *El Liberal*, October 24, 1912.

58. *El Domingo*, December 15, 22, 1912; *La Gaceta Republicana*, December 16, 17, 1912; *El Liberal*, December 19, 1912.

59. *El Tiempo*, February 2, 1913.

60. *La Gaceta Republicana*, February 21, April 1, 14, May 4, 1913; *El Liberal*, April 1, 1913.

61. *La Unión Obrera*, July 10, 16, 27, August 2, 1913.

62. *La Unión Obrera*, July 16, 27, August 2, 1913.

63. *La Unión Obrera*, July 16, August 2, 14, 31, 1913; *La Gaceta Republicana*, June 6, 1913.

64. *La Unión Obrera*, July 16, August 19, 1913.

65. *La Unión Obrera*, July 16, 27, 1913; *La Gaceta Republicana*, June 24, July 8, 1913.

66. *El Tiempo*, August 2, September 29, 1911; *La Sociedad*, August 5, 25, 1911; *El Ariete*, August 18, 25, 1912; *El Liberal*, September 17, 1914; July 29, August 6, 31, November 12, 1915.

67. *El Liberal*, May 1, 1916, April 9, July 27, 1917; *La Gaceta Republicana*, September 4, 1918.

68. *La Gaceta Republicana*, September 11, 1913; *La Sociedad*, September 12, 1913; February 19, 1914.

69. *La Gaceta Republicana*, February 19, 24, 1914; *El Partido Obrero*, February 19, 1916.

70. *El Liberal*, October 13, December 1, 1914; *La Gaceta Republicana*, October 19, November 25, 1914.

71. *La Gaceta Republicana*, January 11, 19, February 2, 1915; *El Liberal*, January 18, 26, February 2, 12, 1915.

72. *La Gaceta Republicana*, May 3, 1915; *El Liberal*, April 28, 29, 30, May 1, 1915.

73. *La Gaceta Republicana*, October 8, December 9, 10, 1915.

74. *El Partido Obrero*, January 22, 1916.

75. *El Partido Obrero*, January 22, 29, April 8, 1916; *El Domingo*, January 16, 27, April 16, 1916.

76. *El Partido Obrero*, January 22, 1916.

77. *El Partido Obrero*, April 1, 15, May 1, 1916.

78. *El Partido Obrero*, January 22, February 6, 12, March 11, May 20, 1916.

79. *El Partido Obrero*, January 29, p. 1, February 19, 1916.

80. The editors were Hernán Caster, G. Arturo Camargo, and Samuel A. Ramos. *La Libertad*, March 4, 12, 17, 1916; *El Partido Obrero*, May 20, 1916.

81. *El Liberal*, January 11, 14, March 29, 1916.

82. *El Partido Obrero*, January 23, 1916.

83. *La Gaceta Republicana*, October 8, 1915.

84. *El Domingo*, September 10, 1916.

85. In 1917, 5,684 votes were cast; 9,200 were cast in 1915; 11,398 in 1913; and 10,624 in 1911.

86. *La Gaceta Republicana*, January 29, February 1, 20, March 3, 13, April 10, 1917; *El Tiempo*, February 2, 5, 1917.

87. *El Tiempo*, April 9, 1917. In spite of this attitude, the Party decided to cooperate with Republicans for the May congressional elections, forming a *liga* that defeated the "nationalist" wing of the Conservative party. *El Tiempo*, April 24, May 3, 13, 17, 1917; *El Liberal*, May 13, 1917.

88. *La Gaceta Republicana*, October 25, November 11, 1909; January 24, 27, 1914.

89. Urrutia, *Development of the Colombian Labor Movement*, 57–58; *El Diario Nacional*, January 16, 1918; Archila, "Algunas hipótesis," passim. See *La Gaceta Republicana*, January 1918, for coverage of the strikes.

90. *La Gaceta Republicana*, January 14, 1918.

91. *La Gaceta Republicana*, October 20, 1916; *El Domingo*, October 22, 27, 1916; *La Libertad*, October 18, 1916. When orders were placed with Colombians, they were ofttimes greeted with praise, such as from shoemakers in 1914. See *La Gaceta Republicana*, January 28, 1914. Two years later, however, the same trade, while thanking the government for an army contract, said that the order should have been given to smaller producers instead of a large factory. See *El Domingo*, March 16, 1916.

92. *La Gaceta Republicana*, December 26, 1918; May 2, 1919. See *La Gaceta Republicana*, December 18, 1918, for the program.

93. *La Gaceta Republicana*, January 21, May 6, 1919.

94. *La Gaceta Republicana*, February 5, 7, 10, 15, 18, March 4, 10, 12, May 7, 11, June 6, 1919.

95. *La Gaceta Republicana*, February 15, 1919.

96. *La Gaceta Republicana*, March 8, 12, 1919.

97. Urrutia insists that the entire pretext for the demonstration and resultant loss of life was unnecessary, pointing out that the government annulled the decree on March 15, 1919, the day before the demonstration. See his *Development of the Colombian Labor Movement*, 63. In fact, the government only suspended bids for uniforms. In early April, an order was placed for 30,000 yards of cloth from a U.S. company. See *La Gaceta Republicana*, April 11, 1919.

98. *El Correo Liberal*, March 14 (p. 1), 17, 21, 1919.

99. *La Gaceta Republicana*, March 22, 1919; *El Correo Liberal*, March 17, 18, 1919. Súarez insisted that the victims were part of an armed uprising against the government and that the military's response was totally justified. In April, however, General Pedro Sicard Briceño was subjected to a governmental investigation for his alleged unwarranted shooting of the demonstrator Gabriel Chaves. See *El Correo Liberal*, March 18, 20, 21, 1919; and *La Gaceta Republicana*, March 22, 24, 25, April 1, 2, 1919.

100. *La Gaceta Republicana*, May 2, 6, 7, 14, 20, June 6, 18, 1919.

101. *La Gaceta Republicana*, January 4, 12, February 4, 1919.

102. *La Gaceta Republicana*, April 2, 16, 22, 26, 28, May 8, 13, 1919; *El Correo Liberal*, May 6, 9, 16, 1919.

103. *La Gaceta Republicana*, June 6, 1919.

104. *La Gaceta Republicana*, May 7, 13, June 6, 18, 1919.


## Chapter Seven

1. The relationship between changes in modes of production and political activity in nineteenth-century France is illustrated in William H. Sewell, Jr., "Uneven Development, the Autonomy of Politics, and the Dockworkers of Nineteenth-Century Marseille," *American Historical Review*, 93:3 (June 1988), 604–37.

2. The widespread use of petitions as methods of expressing "popular ideology" in revolutionary period United States is discussed in Ruth Bogin, "Petitioning and the New Moral Economy of Post-Revolutionary America," *William and Mary Quarterly*, 3rd series, 45:3 (July 1988), 391–425.

3. AC, Senado, Proyectos Negados, 1846, V, folios 118–26; Agustín Rodríguez et al., *H. H. senadores* (Bogotá: Imprenta de Nicolás Gómez, May 5, 1846); AC, Informes de Comisiones, 1847, X, folios 229–41r; Saturnino González et al., *Representación al congreso nacional* (Bogotá: Impresa por Manuel de J. Barrera, 1868); AC, Senado, Memoriales con informes, 1903, IV, 24–40r, 49; *Los Hechos*, April 23, May 10, 20, 27, 1904.

4. Muchos artesanos, *La reforma de la tarifa aduana i la cámara de*

*representantes; El Renacimiento*, December 4, 1886; *El Orden*, December 15, 1887.

5. AC, Cámara, Proyectos de leyes negados, 1850, V, 43–49r; AC, Cámara, Proyectos de leyes negados, Informes de comisiones, 1851, VI, 404–73; González, *Representación*.

6. *El Día*, May 26, 1842; July 17, 1843.

7. The taller modelo of the 1890s culminated these efforts. See *Diario de Cundinamarca*, October 12, 1881; and *El Progreso*, March 11, 1897.

8. See, for example, Melitón Angulo Heredia, *Informe del secretario de la Sociedad de Socorros Mutuos* (Bogotá: Imprenta de Gaitán, February 6, 1873).

9. Robert Louis Gilmore and John P. Harrison, "Juan Bernardo Elbers and the Introduction of Steam Navigation on the Magdalena River," *HAHR*, 30:3 (August 1948), 335–59; Luis Ospina Vásquez, *Industria y protección en Colombia, 1810 a 1930* (Bogotá: Editorial Santafé, 1955), 216.

10. Un artesano, *Al señor Jeneral Santos Gutiérrez* (Bogotá: n.p., June 29, 1863); Agapito Cabrera, *Díos, libertad i trabajo* (Bogotá: n.p., June 18, 1863).

11. For example, Ramón Jiménez et al., *La situación* (Bogotá: n.p., October 6, 1868); *Diario de Cundinamarca*, August 2, 3, 1876.

12. *La Alianza*, December 10, 1866, p. 1.

13. Unos artesanos que no serán sino simples espectadores de los hechos ulteriores, *El fruto que los artesanos hemos cojido de las revoluciones pasadas* (Bogotá: n.p., October 19, 1863); Un compañero de Rodríguez Leal, *Los derechos del pueblo* (Bogotá: n.p., July 26, 1863).

14. "El artesano de Bogotá," *El Núcleo*, 1858.

15. Jacques Rancière warns against idealization of work and workers in assessing past social attitudes, suggesting that many artisans glorified work in order to enhance their own self-concept. See his article "The Myth of the Artisan: Critical Reflections on a Category of Social History," *ILWCH*, No. 24 (Fall 1983), 1–16.

16. These thoughts are articulated in numerous artisans' petitions, but most clearly in *La Alianza*.

17. William Marion Gibson, *The Constitutions of Colombia* (Durham, NC: Duke University Press, 1948), 120, 162, 204, 227, 316. In the period from 1853 until 1865, the State of Cundinamarca granted suffrage rights to all males over twenty-one; after 1865 literacy was required of all state voters. See also *Recopilación de leyes y decretos del Estado Soberano de Cundinamarca, 1857–1868* (Bogotá: n.p., 1868), 145–46, 355.

18. All observers of nineteenth-century Colombia agree on this point. Many, however, disagree on the causes of the conflict. For representative interpretations, see Charles W. Bergquist, *Labor in Latin America: Comparative Essays on Chile, Argentina, Venezuela, and Colombia* (Stanford,

CA: Stanford University Press, 1986), 291–94, and Frank Safford, "Bases of Political Alignment in Early Republican Spanish America," in *New Approaches to Latin American History*, ed. by Richard Graham and Peter Smith (Austin: University of Texas Press, 1974), 71–109.

19. Helen Delpar, *Red Against Blue: The Liberal Party in Colombian Politics, 1863–1899* (University: The University of Alabama Press, 1981) 98–109, 126–27.

20. Hobart Spalding, Jr., *Organized Labor in Latin America: Historical Case Studies of Workers in Dependent Societies* (New York: Harper & Row, 1977); Julio Godio, *El movimiento obrero de América Latina, 1850–1918* (Bogotá: Ediciones Tercer Mundo, 1978), 15–16.

21. Juan Felipe Leal and José Woldenberg, "Orígenes y desarrollo del artesanado y del proletariado industrial en México: 1867–1914 (Bibliografía comentada)," *Revista Mexicana de Ciencia Política*, No. 81 (1975), 131–59; Guillermo Baena Paz, Rocío Guadarrama Olivera, Raúl Trejo Delarbre, and José Woldenberg, "Notas sobre la periodización del movimiento obrero (1860–1979)," in *El trabajo y los trabajadores en la historia de México*, ed. by Elsa Cecilia Frost, Michael C. Meyer, and Josefina Zoraida Vásquez (Mexico City: El Colegio de México, 1979), 2–33. Hart's notable works on Mexican labor history pay close attention to the nineteenth-century anarchist groups, but fail to grapple with the intricacies of artisan organizational activity. See John M. Hart, "Los obreros mexicanos y el Estado, 1860–1931," *Nexos*, 4:37 (1981), 21–27; John M. Hart, *Anarchism and the Mexican Working Class, 1860–1931* (Austin: University of Texas Press, 1987).

22. Miguel Urrutia, *The Development of the Colombian Labor Movement* (New Haven, CT: Yale University Press, 1969), 15; Orlando Fals Borda, *Subversion and Social Change in Colombia*, trans. by Jacqueline D. Skiles (New York: Columbia University Press, 1969), 81.

23. David Sowell, "*'La teoría i la realidad'*: The Democratic Society of Artisans of Bogotá, 1847–1854," *HAHR*, 67:4 (November 1987), 611–30.

24. For a comparable process in Ecuador, see Alan Middleton, "Division and Cohesion in the Working Class: Artisans and Wage Labourers in Ecuador," *JLAS*, 14:1 (May 1982), 171–94.

25. Emilia Viotti daCosta, *The Brazilian Empire: Myths and Histories* (Chicago: University of Chicago Press, 1985) 64–69; Roderick J. Barman, *Brazil: The Forging of a Nation, 1798–1857* (Stanford, CA: Stanford University Press, 1988), 167–69.

26. Miguel Carrera Stampa, *Los gremios en México. La organización gremial en Nueva España, 1521–1861* (Mexico City: EDIAPSA, 1954); Dorothy Tanck de Estrada, "La abolición de los gremios," in *El trabajo y los trabajadores en la historia de México/Labor and Laborers Through*

*Mexican History* (Mexico City: El Colégio de México and The University of Arizona Press, 1979), 311–31.

27. Alejandro Moreno Toscano, "Los trabajadores y el projecto de industrialización, 1810–1867," in Enrique Florescano, Isabel González Sánchez, Jorge González Angulo, et al., *La clase obrera en la historia de México. De la colonia al imperio*, 3d ed. (Mexico City: Siglo Veintiuno Editores, 1983), 308.

28. Juan Felipe Leal and José Woldenberg, *La clase obrera en la historia de México. Del estado liberal a los inicios de la dictadura porfirista*, 3d ed. (Mexico City: Siglo Veintiuno Editores, 1983), 124–25.

29. Lyman L. Johnson, "The Silversmiths of Buenos Aires: A Case Study in the Failure of Corporate Social Organization," *JLAS*, 8:2 (November 1976), 181–213.

30. Ricardo Levene, *Investigaciones acerca de la historia económica del virreinato del Plata*, 2 vols. (Buenos Aires: Biblioteca Humanidades, 1928), II, 285–86; Susan Migden Socolow, *The Merchants of Buenos Aires, 1778–1810: Family and Commerce* (New York: Cambridge University Press, 1978), 129–31.

31. Jorge Basadre, *Historia de la República del Peru, 1822–1933*, 17 vols., 6th ed. (Lima: Editorial Universitaria, 1968), III, 183–84; Paul Gootenberg, "The Social Origins of Protectionism and Free Trade in Nineteenth-Century Lima," *JLAS*, 14:2 (November 1982), 329–58.

32. E. Bradford Burns, *The Poverty of Progress*, 106–110; Herbert S. Klein, *Bolivia: The Evolution of a Multi-Ethnic Society* (New York: Oxford University Press, 1982), 128–31, 133–36; Guillermo Lora, *A History of the Bolivian Labour Movement, 1848–1971*, ed. and abridged by Laurence Whitehead, trans. by Christine Whitehead (New York: Cambridge University Press, 1977), 10–29.

33. Tulio Halperín-Donghi, *Politics and Society in Argentina in the Revolutionary Period*, trans. by Richard Southern (New York: Cambridge University Press, 1975), 8–12, 48; Mark D. Szuchman, *Mobility and Integration in Urban Argentina: Córdoba in the Liberal Era* (Austin: The University of Texas Press, 1980), 7; James R. Scobie, *Secondary Cities of Argentina: The Social History of Corrientes, Salta, and Mendoza, 1850–1910*, completed and edited by Samuel L. Baily (Stanford, CA: Stanford University Press, 1988), 4–10; John Lynch, *Argentine Dictator: Juan Manuel de Rosas, 1829–1852* (New York: Oxford University Press, 1981).

34. L. A. Romero, *La Sociedad de la Igualdad: Los artesanos de Santiago de Chile y sus primeras experiencias políticas, 1820–1851* (Buenos Aires: Instituto Torcuato Di Tella, 1978); Maurice Zeitlin, *The Civil Wars in Chile (or The Bourgeois Revolutions That Never Were)*, (Princeton, NJ: Princeton University Press), 33–49.

35. Basadre, *Historia del Peru,* passim; Gootenberg, "Social Origins of Protectionism"; Paul Gootenberg, "Beleaguered Liberals: The Failed First Generation of Free Traders in Peru," in *Guilding the Invisible Hand: Economic Liberalism and the State in Latin American History,* ed. by Joseph L. Love and Nils Jacobsen (New York: Praeger Publishers, 1988), 63–97.

36. Leal and Woldenberg, *Del estado liberal a la dictadura porfirista;* Leal and Woldenberg, "Orígenes y desarrollo del artesanado"; María del Carmen Reyna, "Las condiciones del trabajo en las panaderías de la ciudad de México durante la segunda mitad del siglo XIX," *Historia Mexicana,* 31:3 (January–May, 1982), 431–48; Frederick J. Shaw, "The Artisan in Mexico City (1824–1853)," in *El trabajo y los trabajadores en la historia de México,* ed. by Elsa Cecilia Frost, Michael C. Meyer, and Josefina Zoraida Vásquez (Mexico City: El Colegio de México, 1979), 399–418; John M. Hart, *Anarchism and the Mexican Working Class, 1860–1931* (Austin: University of Texas Press, 1987).

37. Michael P. Hanagan, *The Logic of Solidarity: Artisans and Industrial Workers in Three French Towns, 1871–1914* (Chicago: University of Chicago Press, 1980).

38. Peter Blanchard, *The Origins of the Peruvian Labor Movement, 1883–1919* (Pittsburgh: University of Pittsburgh Press, 1982).

39. Peter DeShazo, *Urban Workers and Labor Unions in Chile, 1902–1907* (Madison: University of Wisconsin Press, 1983).

40. Mauricio Archila, "De la revolución social a la conciliación? Algunas hipótesis sobre la tranformación de la clase obrera colombiana (1919–1935)," *Anuario Colombiano de Historia Social y de la Cultura,* No. 12 (1984), 51–102; Mauricio Archila, "La memoria de los trabajadores de Medellín y Bogotá, 1910–1945," draft in author's possession; Mauricio Archila, "La otra opinión: La prensa obrera en Colombia, 1920–1934," *Anuario Colombiano de Historia Social y de la Cultura,* No. 13–14 (1985–86), 209–37; Herbert Braun, *The Assassination of Gaitán: Public Life and Urban Violence in Colombia* (Madison: University of Wisconsin Press, 1985), 54, passim; Gary Long, "Communists, Radical Artisans, and Workers in Colombia, 1925–1950," draft in author's possession; Steven M. Zdatny, *The Politics of Survival: Artisans in Twentieth-Century France* (New York: Oxford University Press, 1990).

41. Bergquist, *Labor in Latin America,* and "Latin American Labour History in Comparative Perspective: Notes on the Insidiousness of Cultural Imperialism," *Labour/Le travail,* 25 (Spring 1980), 189–98.

42. George Reid Andrews, "Review Essay: Latin American Workers," *Journal of Social History,* 21:2 (Winter 1987), 312.

43. See, for example, Elsa M. Chaney and Mary García Castro, eds., *Muchachas No More: Household Workers in Latin America and the Caribbean* (Philadelphia: Temple University Press, 1989); Scott Cook and

Leigh Binford, *Obliging Need: Rural Petty Industry in Mexican Capitalism* (Austin: University of Texas Press, 1990); Hernando de Soto, *The Other Path: The Invisible Revolution in the Third World* (New York: Harper & Row, 1989), especially 7–129; Manuel Alvaro Ramírez Rojas and Jesús Antonio Suárez Rosales, *El sector informal urbano en Colombia y las políticas de empleo, 1970–1980: Análisis de los planes y programas de desarrollo y la informalidad económica,* 2d ed. (Bogotá: Ediciones Tercer Mundo, 1987).

# GLOSSARY

| | |
|---|---|
| AGUARDIENTE | Anise-flavored liquor made from sugar cane |
| ALCABALA | Sales tax established in colonial period |
| ALCALDE | Mayor or chief magistrate of town |
| ANTIOQUEÑO | Person from the city or region of Antioquia |
| AREPA | Corn-based pancake used in popular diets |
| BARRIO | Neighborhood |
| BOGOTANO | Resident of Bogotá |
| BOLIVARIANO | A supporter of Simón Bolívar |
| CACHACO | Nineteenth-century dandy or fop |
| CAJA DE AHORROS | Savings bank |
| CALEÑO | A resident of Cali |
| CASTA | Colonial label for racial group; racial division of society |
| CAUCANO | Person from the Cauca valley region |
| CAUDILLOS | Nineteenth-century political strongmen |
| COSTEÑO | Inhabitant of Atlantic coast region |
| DEJAD HACER | Laissez-faire, also referred to as dejar hacer |
| DIEZMO | 10 percent tithe on agricultural production |
| DRACONIANO | Member of the moderate wing of the Liberal party in the 1850s |
| DUEÑOS DE TALLER | Shopkeepers, master craftsmen |

| | |
|---|---|
| EJIDITARIOS | Persons who used community lands, or *ejidos* |
| EJIDOS | Community lands |
| EMPLEADO | Employee, usually in government or commercial positions |
| EMPLEOMANÍA | Critical term that describes tendency to seek government employment or to reward political supporters with governmental positions |
| FUEROS | Rights granted to religious, military, or other corporate bodies |
| GENTE DECENTE | "Decent folk"; described upper-middle- to upper-class person |
| GÓLGOTA | Member of the radical wing of Liberal party in the 1850s |
| GUACHES | Derisive term for lower class, early nineteenth century |
| HACENDADO | Owner of large landholding or hacienda |
| INDUSTRIAL | Small industrialist of early twentieth-century Bogotá |
| JEFE POLÍTICO | Political boss, appointed to manage local political affairs |
| LIGA | An alliance between political parties or their factions |
| LUNES DE LOS ZAPATEROS, EL | Cobbler's Monday; St. Monday |
| MANOS MUERTAS | Properties willed to church |
| MESTIZO | Person of mixed indigenous and European descent |
| MINISTERIAL | 1830s political faction that identified with Márquez |
| MULATO | Person of mixed African and European descent |
| 9 DE ABRIL | Riots that followed assassination of Jorge Eliécer Gaitán on April 9, 1948; also called the *bogotazo* |
| PLAZA DE BOLÍVAR | Central plaza in Bogotá; also called Plaza of the Constitution |
| PROGRESISTA | 1830s follower of Santander |

| | |
|---|---|
| PUEBLO | The "people"; used to describe the lower classes |
| QUINA | Cichona bark, used to make quinine |
| QUINQUENIO | Five-year regime of Rafael Reyes (1904–9) |
| RESQUARDOS | Corporate lands held by Indian communities |
| RUANA | Colombian woolen poncho |
| SABANA DE BOGOTÁ | Highland plain surrounding Bogotá |
| SANTANDERISTA | Supporter of Francisco de Paula Santander |
| SAPO, EL | "The Toad," Ramón Gómez, political boss in 1860s Cundinamarca |
| SEMANA SANTA | Holy Week |
| 7 DE MARZO | March 7, 1849, date of the contentious selection of Liberal José Hilario López as president |
| 17 DE ABRIL | 1854 coup led by General José María Melo |
| SOCIEDAD DE ARTESANOS | Society of Artisans, founded 1847 |
| SOCIEDAD DEMOCRÁTICA | Democratic Society, successor to Society of Artisans; Bogotá chapter became model for Liberal political mobilization throughout the country |
| SOCIEDAD POPULAR | Popular Society, 1849–51; Conservative counterpart to the Democratic Society |
| SOCIEDAD UNIÓN DE ARTESANOS | Union Society of Artisans, 1866–68; highly articulate body that capsulized artisan reform period sentiments |
| SOCIEDAD UNIÓN DE INDUSTRIALES Y OBREROS | Union Society of Industrials and Workers |
| TALLER MODELO | Model Shop, established in 1880s under the regime of Rafael Núñez |
| 20 DE JULIO | July 20, Colombian Independence Day |
| VIOLENCIA, LA | The Violence, 1946–1953; period of savage partisan politics |

# BIBLIOGRAPHY

## PRIMARY SOURCES

### Archives

Archivo Central del Cauca (ACC) (Popayán)
  Sala Tomás Cipriano de Mosquera
Archivo de la Academia Colombiana de Historia (AHC) (Bogotá)
  Archivo Pedro Alcantara Herrán
Archivo del Congreso (AC) (Bogotá)
  Cámara, Proyectos de Leyes Negados
  Informes de Comisiones
  Senado, Proyectos Negados
  Memoriales con Informes
Archivo Histórico Nacional (AHN) (Bogotá)
  República, Congreso
  Guerra y Marina
  Policía Nacional

### Other Primary Sources

*Causa de responsabilidad contra el ciudadano presidente de la República
  i los señores secretarios del despacho.* Bogotá: Imprenta del Neo-Granadino, 1855.
*Causa de responsabilidad contra el ciudadano presidente de la República,
  Jeneral José María Obando, i los ex-secretarios de Gobierno i de*

*Guerra, señores Antonio del Real i Valerio Francisco Barriga.* Bogotá: Imprenta de Echeverría Hermanos, 1855.

*Censo general de la República de Colombia levantado el 5 de Marzo de 1912.* Bogotá: Imprenta Nacional, 1912.

República de Colombia. *Censo de población de la República de Colombia levantado el 14 de octubre de 1918 y aprobado el 19 de septiembre de 1921 por la ley No. 8 del mismo año.* Bogotá: Imprenta Nacional, 1921.

República de Colombia. *Codificación nacional de todas las leyes de Colombia desde el año de 1821, hecha conforme a la ley 13 de 1912.* 34 vols. Bogotá: Imprenta Nacional, 1924–

Robledo, Francisco. "Yntrucción de gremios en gral. Pa todos oficios aprobada pr el Exmo Sor. Virrey del Rno. Siguense a ella quantos papeles y providens se han creado en el asunto." *Revista del Archivo Nacional,* 10–11 (October–November 1936), 13–37.

United States Department of State. Diplomatic Despatches. National Archives Microfilm T33.

## Handouts and Pamphlets

*A los artesanos de Bogotá.* Bogotá: n.p., n.d.

*A los artesanos de Bogotá.* Bogotá: Imp. de J. A. Cualla, n.d.

*Al pueblo.* Bogotá: Imprenta de La Nación, July 21, 1863.

Un Albañil. *Artesanos laboriosos de Bogotá.* Bogotá: Imp. por Juan Vanegas, 1840.

Algunos presos. *Señor procurador general de la nación.* Bogotá: Imprenta de Echeverría Hermanos, March 25, 1855.

Un amigo de los artesanos. *El valor de los artesanos.* Bogotá: n.p., June 9, 1853.

Un artesano. *Al señor Jeneral Santos Gutiérrez.* Bogotá: n.p., June 29, 1863.

Los artesanos. *Basta de abusos.* Bogotá: n.p., July 18, 1870.

Unos artesanos del 17 de abril. *Contestación preliminar al cuaderno titulado 'La revolución.'* Bogotá: Imprenta de "El Núcleo Liberal," n.d.

Unos artesanos liberales desengañados. *Unos artesanos a sus compañeros.* Bogotá: n.p., n.d.

Unos artesanos que no serán simples espectadores de los hechos ulteriores. *El fruto que los artesanos hemos cojido de las revoluciones pasadas.* Bogotá: n.p., October 19, 1863.

¡*Artesanos trabajadores propietarios!* Bogotá: n.p., July 16, 1853.

Ballesteros, Calisto. *Protesta de varios miembros (a) de la Junta Directiva de la Sociedad de la Alianza.* Bogotá: Imprenta de Nicolás Gómez, n.d.

Ballesteros, Cruz. *La teoría i la realidad.* Bogotá: Echeverría Hermanos, December 17, 1851.

Ballesteros, Cruz, and Emeterio Heredia. *El 25 i 26 de febrero de 1862.* Bogotá: n.p., February 23, 1863.

Ballesteros, Cruz, i su círculo. *A los artesanos de buen corazón.* Bogotá: Imprenta de Echeverría Hermanos, June 17, 1863.

Cabrera, Agapito. *Díos, libertad i trabajo.* Bogotá: n.p., June 18, 1863.

Cárdenas, Antonio, Fruto Castañeda, Gregorio Espinel, et al. *Manifestación.* Bogotá: n.p., October 8, 1863.

———. *Segunda manifestación de la comisión de los artesanos.* Bogotá: Imprenta de Nicolás Gómez, October 10, 1863.

Cárdenas, Simón José. *El juicio de imprenta celebrada el día 13 de mayo de 1850, promovido por Camilo Rodríguez contra el infrascrito.* Bogotá: Imprenta de "El Día" por J. Azarza, May 14, 1850.

Cárdenas Vásquez, Antonio, Saturnino González, Felipe Roa Ramírez, et al. *Varios artesanos de todos los gremios. . . .* Bogotá: n.p., September 15, 1866.

Unos católicos sin desfraz de artesanos. *No hai peor sordo que el que no quiere oir.* Bogotá: n.p., n.d.

Un compañero de Rodríguez Leal. *Los derechos del pueblo.* Bogotá: n.p., July 26, 1863.

*Conferencias leídas en la "Sociedad de Socorros Mutuos."* Bogotá: Imprenta de "La Luz," 1888.

*Contestación al artículo inserto en el numero 504 del "Día" titulado "Opinión de un artesano."* Bogotá: Impr. por B. Gaitán, 1848.

*Democracia. Documentos para la historia de la Nueva Granada.* n.p., n.d.

Unos desterrados. *Gratitud i justicia.* Bogotá: Imprenta del Neo-Granadino, April 3, 1855.

*Dialogo entre un artesano i un campesino sobre los Jesuítas.* Bogotá: n.p., 1850.

Dos artesanos. *A los artesanos.* Bogotá: Imprenta del Estado, June 11, 1867.

*Estatutos de la Sociedad Filantrópica.* Bogotá: Imprenta Eléctrica, 1906.

Franco, Habacuc, Angel Gómez, José María González, et al. *A los revolucionarios de 17 de abril.* Bogotá: n.p., August 4, 1856.

García, Pablo. *Una idea.* Bogotá: n.p., February 26, 1868.

González, Saturnino. *Dos palabras en la cuestión Alianza.* Bogotá: n.p., June 13, 1868.

———. *Sociedad de la Alianza.* Bogotá: n.p., February 4, 1868.

González, Saturnino, José Antonio Cárdenas V., José L. Camacho, et al. *Representación al congreso nacional.* Bogotá: Impreso por Manuel de J. Barrera, 1868.

Heredia, Emeterio. *Contestación al cuaderno titulado "El desengaño o confidencias de Ambrosio López etc." por El Presidente que fue de la*

*Sociedad de Artesanos El 7 de Marzo de 1849.* Bogotá: Imprenta de Núcleo Liberal, 1851.

Heredia, Melitón Angulo. *Informe del secretario de la Sociedad de Socorros Mutuos.* Bogotá: Imprenta de Gaitán, February 6, 1873.

Jiménez, Ramón, et al. *La situación.* Bogotá: n.p., October 6, 1868.

León, Miguel. *¡Artesanos !desangaños!* Bogotá: n.p., August 6, 1853.

———. *Satisfacción, que da el que escribe, al Sr. M. Murillo Secretario de Hacienda.* Bogotá: n.p., January 19, 1852.

———. *Señor jefe político Doctor Eustaquio Alvárez.* Bogotá: Imprenta de Echeverría Hermanos, August 31, 1851.

Un liberal honrado. *A los artesanos sensatos.* Bogotá: Imprenta Constitucional, June 1, 1867.

Lleras, Lorenzo María. *República de la N. Granada.* Bogotá: Imp. por Juan N. Triana, October 30, 1838.

———. *San Bartolomé en 1855.* Bogotá: n.p., 1855.

———. *Señor Júez del crímen.* Bogotá: n.p., January 27, 1855.

Lombana, Tomás. *Manifestación.* Bogotá: Imprenta de la Nación, December 10, 1857.

López, Ambrosio. *El desengaño o confidencias de Ambrosio López, primer director de la Sociedad de Artesanos de Bogotá, denominada hoi "Sociedad Democrática" escrito para conocimiento de sus consocios.* Bogotá: Imprenta de Espinosa, por Isidoro García Ramírez, 1851.

———. *La guardia nacional de Bogotá.* Bogotá: n.p., n.d.

———. *El triunfo sobre la serpiente roja, cuyo asunto es del dominio de la nación.* Bogotá: Editorial Espinosa, 1851.

López, Blas, Miguel León, Anselmo Flórez, et al. *Protesta de los artesanos Blas López, Miguel León, Anselmo Flórez y otros.* Bogotá: Imprenta de Nicolás Gómez, June 17, 1853.

Madero, Isodoro. *El señor Cruz Sánchez i "La Alianza" ante el tribunal de la opinión pública.* Bogotá: n.p., September 30, 1868.

Manrique de Cárdenas, Gregoria e hijas. *A los miembros de la Sociedad Popular que pretenden renuciar.* Bogotá: Imprenta de El Día, por José Ayarza, May 17, 1850.

Mas de mil artesanos. *El 8 de junio.* Bogotá: n.p., June 9, 1853.

Mil ciudadanos. *El 8 de junio.* Bogotá: n.p., June 9, 1853.

Morales, Ignacio, Antonio Herrán, Felipe Bernal, et al. *Invitación que hace la Sociedad Católica de Bogotá a los fieles de la América.* Bogotá: Impreso por J. A. Cualla, May 10, 1838.

Muchos artesanos. *La reforma de la tarifa aduana i la cámera de representantes.* Bogotá: n.p., May 12, 1880.

Neira Acevedo, Pedro. *Carta abierta.* Bogotá: Imprenta del Neo-Granadino, July 21, 1856.

Plata, José María. *El gobernador de Bogotá a los habitantes de la capital.* Bogotá: Imprenta del Neo-Granadino, June 13, 1853.

Posada, Joaquín P. *Los revolucionarios de 1854 en las elecciones de 1856.* Bogotá. Imprenta de Nicolás Gómez, 1856.

*Primera banderilla: A los gólgotas en las Nieves.* Bogotá: n.p., June 1, 1853.

Quijano, Bonifacio, Ramón Torres, Gaspar Jiménez, et al. *HH. senadores i representantes.* Bogotá: Impreso por J. A. Cualla, April 16, 1839.

El redactor del Porvenir. *Al pueblo.* Bogotá: Imprenta de la Nación, November 10, 1857.

*Reglamento de la Sociedad de Artistas.* Bogotá: Zalamez Hermanos, 1891.

*Reglamento orgánico de la Sociedad Popular de instrucción mútua i fraternidad Cristiana.* Bogotá: Imprenta de El Día, por José Ayarza, 1849.

*Reseña histórica de los principales acontecimientos políticos de la ciudad de Cali, desde el año de 1848 hasta el de 1855 inclusive.* Bogotá: Imprenta de Echeverría Hermanos, 1856.

*La revolución: Orijen, fines, i estado actual de la revolución democrática que se prepara en esta ciudad.* 3d ed. Bogotá: Imprenta de F. T. Amaya, April 1858.

Rodríguez, Agustín. *Al director i miembros de la Sociedad Democrática.* Bogotá: n.p., 1849.

Rodríguez, Agustín, Vicente Vega, Juan Dederlé, et al. *HH. senadores.* Bogotá: Imprenta de Nicolás Gómez, May 5, 1846.

Rodríguez Leal, Juan. *Alianza católica.* Bogotá: n.p., June 29, 1863.

————. *Alianza católica (Esta es la bala).* Bogotá: n.p., n.d.

Seiscientos artesanos. *Muchos artesanos ante la sanción pública.* Bogotá: Impreso por F. Mantilla, July 30, 1869.

Silvestre, Francisco. *Descripción del Reyno de Sante Fé de Bogotá escrita en 1789 por D. Francisco Silvestre, secretario que fué de virreinato y antiguo governador de la provincia de Antioquia.* Bogotá: Universidad Nacional de Colombia, 1968.

Sociedad de Artesanos. *Reglamento para su réjimen interior i económico.* Bogotá: Imprenta de Nicolás Gómez, 1847.

*La Sociedad de Artesanos de Bogotá a la Nación.* Bogotá: Impr. de Sánchez y Compañía, March 8, 1849.

*Unión de artesanos.* Bogotá: Impreso por Foción Mantilla, June 19, 1867.

Uno que no vive de empleo sino de su trabajo. *Degollación de los artesanos.* Bogotá: Imprenta de la Nación, June 11, 1867.

Vega, Francisco, et al. *Cosas de artesanos.* Bogotá: Imprenta de Echeverría Hermanos, March 22, 1866.

Vega, José María, Santos Castro, José Antonio Saavedra, et al. *Los artesanos de Bogotá a la nación.* Bogotá: Imprenta de Echeverría Hermanos, November 15, 1857.

W. *Breves anotaciones para la historia sobre los sucesos del 19 de mayo ultimo.* Bogotá: Imprenta de Nicolás Gómez, May 27, 1853.

## Travel Accounts

Bennet, J. A. "My First Trip up the Magdalena, and Life in the Heart of the Andes." *Journal of the American Geographical Society of New York*, 9 (1879), 126–41.

Calderón, Clímaco, and Edward E. Britton. *Colombia, 1893.* New York: Robert Sneider, 1894.

Cané, Miguel. *En viaje, 1881–1882.* París: Garnier Hermanos, 1883.

Duane, William. *A Visit to Colombia, in the Years 1822 & 1823.* Philadelphia: Thomas H. Palmer, 1826.

*Guía oficial i descriptiva de Bogotá.* Bogotá: Imprenta de la Nación, 1858.

Hettner, Alfred. *La cordillera de Bogotá: resultados de viajes y estudios.* trans. by Ernesto Guhl. Bogotá: Banco de la República, 1956.

Holton, Issac F. *New Granada: Twenty Months in the Andes.* New York: Harper & Brothers, 1857.

Mollien, Gaspar Theodore. *Viaje por la República de Colombia en 1823.* Bogotá: Banco de la República, 1944.

Pérez, Felipe. *Geografía general física y política de los Estados Unidos de Colombia y geografía particular de la ciudad de Bogotá.* Bogotá: Imprenta de Echeverría Hermanos, 1883.

Reclus, Eliseo. *Colombia.* Bogotá: Papelería de Samper Matiz, 1893.

Röthlisberger, Ernst. *El Dorado: Estampas de viaje y cultura de la Colombia suramericana.* Bogotá: Banco de la República, 1963.

"Santa Fé de Bogotá." *Harper's New Monthly Magazine*, 71 (June–November 1885), 47–58.

Scruggs, William Lindsay. *The Colombian and Venezuelan Republics.* 2d ed. Boston: Little, Brown, 1910.

Steuart, John. *Bogotá in 1836–7. Being a Narrative of an Expedition to the Capital of New-Granada and a Residence there of Eleven Months.* New York: Harper & Brothers, 1838.

"Up and Down Among the Andes." *Harper's New Monthly Magazine* (1857), 739–51.

## Newspapers

Unless otherwise noted, all papers were published in Bogotá. Only those years cited in the text are listed. Two different papers with the same name are included in chronological order.

*Alcance a la Gaceta Oficial*, 1853.
*La Alianza*, 1866–68.
*La América*, 1848.
*La América*, 1872–74.
*El Amigo de los Artesanos*, 1849.
*El Amigo del Pueblo*, 1838.
*El Amigo del Pueblo*, 1890.
*El Ariete*, 1912.
*El Argos*, 1838.
*El Artesano*, 1854.
*El Artesano*, 1856.
*El Artesano*, 1867.
*El Artesano*, 1893.
*El Artista*, 1906, 1908.
*El Autonomista*, 1899.
*El Aviso*, 1848–49.
*El Baile*, 1850.
*La Bandera Nacional*, 1838.
*La Bandera Tricolor*, 1826.
*El Bien Público*, 1870–72.
*El Bogotáno*, 1866.
*El Bogotáno Libre*, 1855.
*Boletín del Crédito Nacional*, 1862–63.
*Boletín Eleccionario*, 1853.
*El Boletín Liberal*, 1849.
*Boletín Oficial*, 1862.
*El Cañón*, 1850.
*La Capital*, 1890.
*El Catolicismo*, 1853.
*El Cernícalo*, 1850.
*El Ciudadano*, 1856.
*La Civilización*. 1850–51.
*El Clamor de la Verdad*, 1847.
*Colombia*, 1911.
*Colombia Cristiana*, 1892–94.
*El Combate*, 1875.
*Comentarios*, 1911.
*El Comercio*, 1858.
*El Comercio*, 1881.
*El Comercio*, 1911.
*El Concurso Nacional*, 1908–9.

*El Conservador*, 1863.
*La Constitución*, 1902.
*El Constitucional*, 1846, 1853.
*Constitucional de Cundinamarca*, 1832.
*El Contemporáneo*, 1911.
*El Correo de Colombia*, 1875.
*El Correo Liberal*, 1919.
*El Correo Nacional*, 1890–94, 1904–5, 1908–9.
*La Correspondencia*, 1910.
*El Criterio*, 1883.
*La Crónica*, 1897–99.
*La Crónica Semanal*, 1832.
*El Deber*, 1879.
*El Demócrata*, 1850.
*El Día*, 1842–51.
*El Día Noticioso*, 1911.
*Diario de Cundinamarca*, 1870–81, 1889, 1893.
*Diario de Debates*, 1850.
*El Diario Nacional*, 1918.
*Diario Noticioso*, 1905.
*El Diario Oficial*, 1867, 1872, 1880.
*La Discusión*, 1852–53.
*La Doctrina*, 1878–79.
*El Domingo*, 1912, 1916.
*La Época*, 1875.
*La Época*, 1884.
*La Esperanza*, 1885.
*El Estandarte del Pueblo*, 1850.
*El Faro*, 1905.
*El Filotémico*, 1851.
*La Fusión*, 1910.
*La Gaceta Oficial*, 1849–55.
*La Gaceta Republicana*, 1909, 1911–19.
*Gil Blas*, 1912.
*El Grito del Pueblo*, 1897.
*El Guasca*, 1897
*Los Hechos*, 1904.
*El Heraldo*, 1890–92.

*La Ilustración*, 1870, 1873, 1875.
*La Ilustración*, 1881.
*El Impulso*, 1903.
*La Independencia*, 1868.
*El Instituto*, 1886–87.
*El Investigador Católico*, 1838.
*La Justicia*, 1880.
*La Juventud*, 1903.
*El Labrador i Artesano*, 1838–39.
*El Liberal*, 1853.
*El Liberal*, 1863.
*El Liberal*, 1869.
*El Liberal*, 1879.
*El Liberal*, 1911–17.
*La Libertad*, 1863.
*La Libertad*, 1867–68.
*La Libertad*, 1916.
*La Luz*, 1882–84.
*El Mensajero*, 1867.
*El Municipal*, 1863.
*La Nación*, 1886–88.
*El Nacional*, 1848.
*El Nacional*, 1856.
*El Nacional*, 1867.
*El Nacionalista*, 1898.
*El Neo-Granadino*, 1849–51, 1853–54, 1857.
*Las Noticias*, 1889.
*El Noticioso de Cundinamarca*, 1868.
*El Núcleo*, 1858–59.
*El Nuevo Mundo*, 1862.
*El Nuevo Tiempo*, 1909.
*La Opinión*, 1863–66.
*El Orden*, 1853.
*El Orden*, 1887–88, 1893.
*El Obrero*, 1865.
*Pan*, 1910.
*El Panameño* (Panama City), 1855.
*El Partido Obrero*, 1916.
*El Pasatiempo*, 1852–53.
*La Patria*, 1856.
*La Patria*, 1867.

*La Patria*, 1894.
*El Patriota*, 1853
*El Patriota*, 1883.
*El Patriota Imparcial*, 1850.
*La Paz*, 1868.
*El Porvenir*, 1849.
*El Porvenir*, 1856, 1859.
*El Precursos*, 1889.
*La Prensa*, 1867–68.
*La Prensa*, 1891.
*La Prensa*, 1907.
*Los Principios*, 1852–53.
*El Progreso*, 1848.
*El Progreso*, 1897.
*El Proteccionista*, 1910.
*El Público*, 1907.
*El Pueblo*, 1867.
*El Razón del Obrero*, 1910.
*La Reforma*, 1851.
*La Reforma*, 1879.
*Rejistro Municipal*, 1874.
*El Renacimiento*, 1886.
*El Repertorio*, 1853, 1855.
*La República*, 1867–68.
*El Republicano*, 1867.
*El Republicano*, 1896.
*El Republicano*, 1907.
*Salud Pública*, 1882.
*El Sentimiento Democrático* (Cali), 1849.
*El 7 de Marzo*, 1849–50.
*El 17 de Abril*, 1854.
*El Símbolo*, 1864.
*La Sociedad*, 1911–14.
*El Sufragio*, 1910.
*El Sur-Americano*, 1849–50.
*El Taller*, 1887–89, 1891–92.
*El Telegrama*, 1888–90, 1895.
*El Termómetro*, 1853.
*El 13 de Marzo*, 1910.
*3 y 2*, 1911.
*El Tiempo*, 1855–58.
*El Tiempo*, 1911–14, 1917.

El Tradicionista, 1872, 1874–75.    La Unión Obrera, 1913.
La Unidad, 1911.    XYZ, 1907, 1909.
La Unión, 1881.    El Yunque, 1905–6.
Unión Industrial, 1909.


## SECONDARY SOURCES

Abel, Christopher. *Conservative Politics in Twentieth-Century Antioquia (1910–1953)*. Oxford: Latin American Centre, St. Antony's College, Occasional Paper III, 1973.

Amato, Peter. "An Analysis of the Changing Patterns of Elite Residential Locations in Bogotá, Colombia." Ph.D. dissertation, Cornell University, 1968.

———. "Environmental Quality and Locational Behavior in a Latin American City." *Urban Affairs Quarterly*, 5:1 (September 1969), 83–101.

Anderson, Perry. "The Common and the Particular." *ILWCH*, No. 36 (Fall 1989), 31–36.

Anderson, Rodney. "Mexico," in *Latin American Labor Organizations*, ed. by Gerald Michael Greenfield and Seldon L. Maram. Westport, CT: Greenwood Press, 1987, 511–48.

———. "Race and Social Stratification: A Comparison of Working-Class Spaniards, Indians, and Castas in Guadalajara, Mexico in 1821." *HAHR*, 68:2 (May 1988), 209–43.

Andrews, George Reid. "Review Essay: Latin American Workers." *Journal of Social History*, 21:2 (Winter 1987), 311–26.

Arango Jaramillo, Mario. *Judás Tadeo Landínez y la primera bancarrota colombiana (1842)*. Medellín: Ediciones Hombre Nuevo, 1981.

Arboleda, Gustavo. *Historia contemporánea de Colombia desde la disolución de la antigua república de ese nombre hasta la época presente*. 6 vols. Bogotá: Casa Editorial de Arboleda y Valencia, 1918–35.

Archila, Mauricio. "La clase obrera colombiana (1886–1930)," in *Relaciones internacionales, movimientos sociales*, Vol. III, *Nueva historia de Colombia*. Bogotá: Planeta, 1989, 209–37.

———. "De la revolución social a la conciliación? Algunas hipótesis sobre la transformación de la clase obrera colombiana (1919–1935)." *Anuario Colombiano de Historia Social y de la Cultura*, No. 12 (1984), 51–102.

———. "La memoria de los trabajadores de Medellín y Bogotá, 1910–1945." Draft in author's possession.

———. "La otra opinión: La prensa obrera en Colombia, 1920–1934." *Anuario Colombiano de Historia Social y de la Cultura*, No. 13–14 (1985–86), 209–37.

Aristizabal, Luis H. "Las tres tazas: de Santafé a Bogotá a traves del cuadro de costumbres." *Boletín Cultural y Bibliográfico*, 25:16 (1988), 61–79.

Baena Paz, Guillermo, Rocío Guadarrama Olivera, Raúl Trejo Delarbre, and José Woldenberg. "Notas sobre la periodización del movimiento obrero (1860–1979)," in *El trabajo y los trabajadores en la historia de México*, ed. by Elsa Cecilia Frost, Michael C. Meyer, and Josefina Zoraida Vásquez. Mexico City: El Colegio de México, 1979, 2–33.

Baily, Samuel. "Las sociedades de ayuda mutua y el desarrollo de una comunidad italiana en Buenos Aires, 1858–1918." *Desarrollo Económico*, 21:84 (January–March 1982), 485–514.

Barman, Roderick J. *Brazil: The Forging of a Nation, 1798–1852*. Stanford, CA: Stanford University Press, 1988.

Basadre, Jorge. *Historia de la República del Perú, 1822–1933*. 17 vols., 6th ed. Lima: Editorial Universitaria, 1968.

Bensel, Richard. "Southern Leviathan: The Development of Central State Authority in the Confederate States of America," in *Studies in American Political Development: An Annual*. Vol. II. New Haven, CT: Yale University Press, 1987, 68–136.

Bergquist, Charles W. *Coffee and Conflict in Colombia, 1886–1910*. Durham, NC: Duke University Press, 1978.

———. *Labor in Latin America: Comparative Essays on Chile, Argentina, Venezuela, and Colombia*. Stanford, CA: Stanford University Press, 1986.

———. "Latin American Labour History in Comparative Perspective: Notes on the Insidiousness of Cultural Imperialism." *Labour/Le Travail*, 25 (Spring 1990), 189–98.

———. "On Paradigms and the Pursuit of the Practical." *LARR*, 13:2 (1978), 247–51.

———. "The Political Economy of the Colombian Presidential Election of 1897." *HAHR*, 56:1 (February 1976), 1–30.

———. "What Is Being Done? Some Recent Studies on the Urban Working Class and Organized Labor in Latin America." *LARR*, 16:1 (1981), 203–23.

Blanchard, Peter. *The Origins of the Peruvian Labor Movement, 1883–1919*. Pittsburgh: University of Pittsburgh Press, 1982.

Bogin, Ruth. "Petitioning and the New Moral Economy of Post-Revolutionary America." *William and Mary Quarterly*. 3rd series, 45:3 (July 1988), 391–425.

Borda, José Joaquín. *Historia de la Compañia de Jesús en la Nueva Granada*. 2 vols. Poissy: Imprenta de S. Lejay et Çe., 1872.

Boyer, Richard E., and Keith A. Davies. *Urbanization in 19th Century Latin America: Statistics and Sources*. Los Angeles. Latin American Center, 1973.

Braun, Herbert. *The Assassination of Gaitán: Public Life and Urban Violence in Colombia.* Madison: University of Wisconsin Press, 1985.

Briceño, Manuel. *La revolución de 1876–77. Recuerdos para la historia.* Bogotá: Imprenta Nueva, 1878.

Burns, E. Bradford. *The Poverty of Progress: Latin America in the Nineteenth Century.* Berkeley: University of California Press, 1980.

Bushnell, David. "Elecciones presidenciales colombianas, 1825–1856," in *Compendio de estadísticas históricas de Colombia,* ed. by Miguel Urrutia Montoya and Mario Arrubla. Bogotá: Universidad Nacional de Colombia, 1970, 219–314.

————. "The Last Dictatorship: Betrayal or Consummation?" *HAHR,* 63:1 (February 1983), 65–105.

————. *The Santander Regime in Gran Colombia.* Newark: University of Delaware Press, 1954.

————. "Two Stages of Colombian Tariff Policy: The Radical Era and the Return to Protection (1861–1885)." *Inter-American Economic Affairs,* 9:4 (Spring 1956), 3–23.

Bushnell, David, and Neil Macaulay. *The Emergence of Latin America in the Nineteeth Century.* New York: Oxford University Press, 1988.

Bustamante Roldán, Darío. "Efectos económicos del papel moneda durante la regeneración." *Cuadernos Colombianos,* 1:4 (1974), 561–660.

Butterworth, Douglas, and John K. Chance. *Latin American Urbanization.* New York: Cambridge University Press, 1981.

Caicedo, Edgar. *Historia de las luchas sindicales en Colombia.* Bogotá: Ediciones CEIS, 1982.

Calhoun, Craig. *The Question of Class Struggle.* Chicago: University of Illinois Press, 1982.

Camacho Roldán, Salvador. *Memorias.* 2 vols. Bogotá: Biblioteca Popular de Cultura Colombiana, 1946.

Cárdenas Acosta, Pablo E. *La restauración constitucional de 1867. Historia de un contragolpe de estado.* Tunja: Imprenta Departamental, 1966.

Cardoso, Fernando H., and José Luis Reyna. "Industrialization, Occupational Structure, and Social Stratification in Latin America," in *Constructive Change in Latin America,* ed. by Cole Blasier. Pittsburgh: University of Pittsburgh Press, 1968, 19–55.

Carrera Stampa, Miguel. *Los gremios en México. La organización gremial en Nueva España, 1521–1861.* Mexico City: EDIAPSA, 1954.

Castaño Castillo, Alvaro. *La policía, su origen y su destino.* Bogotá: Lit y Edit "Cahur," 1947, Vol. VIII.

Chaney, Elsa M., and Mary García Castro, eds. *Muchachas No More: Household Workers in Latin America and the Caribbean.* Philadelphia: Temple University Press, 1989.

Colmenares, Germán. "Formas de la conciencia de clase en la Nueva Granada." *Boletín Cultural y Bibliográfico*, 9:12 (1966), 2410–21.

———. *Partidos políticos y clases sociales en Colombia*. Bogotá: Universidad de Los Andes, 1968.

Cook, Scott, and Leigh Binford. *Obliging Need: Rural Petty Industry in Mexican Capitalism*. Austin: University of Texas Press, 1990.

Córdoba A., Marco A. *Elementos de sindicalismo*. Bogotá: Ediciones Tercer Mundo, 1977.

Cordovez Moure, José María. *Reminiscencias de Santa Fé de Bogotá*. 9 vols. Bogotá: Imprenta de La Cruz, 1910.

Cuervo, Angel, and Rufino José. *Vida de Rufino Cuervo y noticias de su época*. 2 vols. Bogotá: Biblioteca Popular de Cultura Colombiana, Prensas de la Biblioteca Nacional, 1946.

da Costa, Emilia Viotti. *The Brazilian Empire: Myths and Histories*. Chicago: University of Chicago Press, 1985.

———. "Experience versus Structure: New Tendencies in the History of Labor and the Working Class in Latin America—What Do We Gain? What Do We Lose?" *ILWCH*, No. 36 (Fall 1989), 3–24.

de Soto, Hernando. *The Other Path: The Invisible Revolution in the Third World*. New York: Harper & Row, 1989.

Deas, Malcolm. "Algunos interrogantes sobre la relación guerras civiles y violencia," in *Pasado y presente de la violencia en Colombia*, comp. by Gonzalo Sánchez and Ricardo Peñaranda. Bogotá: Fondo Editorial CEREC, 1986, 41–46.

———. "The Fiscal Problems of Nineteenth-Century Colombia." *JLAS*, 14:2 (November 1982), 287–328.

———. "Venezuela, Colombia and Ecuador: The First Half-Century of Independence," in *The Cambridge History of Latin America*, Volume III. *From Independence to c. 1870*, ed. by Leslie Bethell. New York: Cambridge University Press, 1985, 507–38.

Delpar, Helen. "Aspects of Liberal Factionalism in Colombia, 1875–1885." *HAHR*, 51:2 (May 1971), 250–74.

———. "Colombian Liberalism and the Roman Catholic Church, 1863–1886." *Journal of Church and State*, 22:2 (Spring 1980), 271–93.

———. "The Liberal Record and Colombian Historiography: An Indictment in Need of Revision." *Revista Interamericana de Bibliografía*, 31:4 (1981), 524–37.

———. *Red Against Blue: The Liberal Party in Colombian Politics, 1863–1899*. University: University of Alabama Press, 1981.

———. "Renegade or Regenerator? Rafael Núñez as Seen by Colombian Historians." *Revista Interamericana de Bibliografía*, 35:1 (1985), 25–39.

DeShazo, Peter. *Urban Workers and Labor Unions in Chile, 1902–1907.* Madison: University of Wisconsin Press, 1983.

———. "Workers, Labor Unions, and Industrial Relations in Latin America." *LARR,* 23:2 (1988), 145–56.

Di Tella, Torcuato S. "The Dangerous Classes in Early Nineteenth Century Mexico." *JLAS,* 5:1 (May 1974), 79–105.

Díaz Díaz, Fernando. "Estado, iglesia y desamortización," in *Manual de historia de Colombia.* 2d ed. 3 vols. Bogotá: Instituto Colombiano de Cultura, 1982, Vol. II, 413–66.

*Diccionario de la lengua Castellana.* Madrid: Imprenta Francisco del Hierro, 1726.

Duarte French, Jaime. *Florentino González: Razón y sinrazón de una lucha política.* Bogotá: Banco de la República, 1971.

Dulles, Foster Rhea, and Melvin Dubofsky. *Labor in America: A History.* 4th ed. Arlington Heights, IL: Harlan Davidson, 1986.

Dunlap, Vincent Baillie. "Tragedy of a Colombian Martyr: Rafael Uribe Uribe and the Liberal Party, 1896–1914." Ph.D. dissertation, University of North Carolina, 1979.

Erickson, Kenneth Paul, Patrick V. Peppe, and Hobart Spalding, Jr. "Research on the Urban Working Class and Organized Labor in Argentina, Brazil, and Chile: What Is Left to Be Done?" *LARR,* 9:2 (Summer 1974), 115–42.

Escobar Rodríguez, Carmen. *La revolución liberal y la protesta del artesanado.* Bogotá: Editorial Suraméricana, 1990.

Escorcia, José. "La sociedad caleña en la primera mitad del siglo XIX," in *Santiago de Cali—450 años de historia.* Cali: Alcaldía de Santiago de Cali, 1981, 101–25.

———. *Sociedad y economía en el Valle del Cauca, Tomo III. Desarrollo político, social y económico, 1800–1854.* Bogotá: Biblioteca Banco Popular, 1983.

Evans, Judith. "Results and Prospects: Some Observations on Latin American Labor Studies." *ILWCH,* No. 16 (Fall 1979), 28–39.

Faler, Paul G. *Mechanics and Manufacturers in the Early Industrial Revolution: Lynn, Massachusetts, 1780–1860.* Albany: State University of New York Press, 1981.

Fallas Monge, Carlos Luis. *El movimiento obrero de Costa Rica, 1830–1902.* San José: Editorial Universidad Estatal a Distancia, 1983.

Fals Borda, Orlando. *Historia doble de la costa,* Vol. II. *El Presidente Nieto.* Bogotá: Carlos Valencia Editores, 1981.

———. *Subversion and Social Change in Colombia,* trans. by Jacqueline D. Skiles. New York: Columbia University Press, 1969.

Franco V., Constacio. *Apuntamientos para la historia. La guerra de 1876 i 1877*. Bogotá: Imprenta de la Época, 1877.

Friedel, Juan, and Michael Jiménez. "Colombia," in *The Urban Development of Latin America, 1750–1920*, ed. by Richard M. Morse. Stanford, CA: Center for Latin American Studies, Stanford University, 1971, 61–76.

Frost, Elsa Cecilia, Michael C. Meyer, Josefina Zoraida Vásquez, eds. *El trabajo y los trabajadores en la historia de Mexico: Labor and Laborers Through Mexican History*. Mexico City: El Colegio de México and University of Arizona Press, 1979.

Galindo, Aníbal. *Historia económica i estadística de la hacienda nacional desde la colonia hasta nuestros días*. Bogotá: Imprenta de Nicolás Pontón i Compañía, 1874.

García Márquez, Gabriel. *One Hundred Years of Solitude*, trans. by Gregory Rabassa. New York: Avon Books, 1970.

Gaviria Liévano, Enrique. "Las Sociedades Democráticas o de Artesanos en Colombia." *Correo de los Andes*, No. 24 (January–February 1984), 67–76.

Gibson, William Marion. *The Constitutions of Colombia*. Durham, NC: Duke University Press, 1948.

Gilmore, Robert Louis. "Federalism in Colombia, 1810–1858." Ph.D. dissertation, University of California, 1949.

———. "Nueva Granada's Socialist Mirage." *HAHR*, 36:2 (May 1956), 190–210.

Gilmore, Robert Louis, and John P. Harrison. "Juan Bernardo Elbers and the Introduction of Steam Navigation on the Magdalena River." *HAHR*, 30:3 (August 1948), 335–59.

Godio, Julio. *El movimiento obrero de América Latina, 1850–1918*. Bogotá: Ediciones Tercer Mundo, 1978.

Gómez Picón, Alirio. *El golpe militar de 17 de abril de 1854: la dictadura de José María Melo, el enigma de Obando, los secretos de la historia*. Bogotá: Editorial Kelly, 1972.

González Quintana, Guillermo, and Jorge. *El Círculo de Obreros: La Obra y su espíritu, 1911–1940*. Bogotá: Editorial de la Litografía Colombiana, 1940.

Goodwin, Lawrence. *The Populist Moment: A Short History of the Agrarian Revolt in America*. New York: Oxford University Press, 1978.

Gootenberg, Paul. "Beleaguered Liberals: The Failed First Generation of Free Traders in Peru," in *Guiding the Invisible Hand: Economic Liberalism and the State in Latin American History*, ed. by Joseph L. Love and Nils Jacobsen. New York: Praeger Publishers, 1988, 63–97.

———. "The Social Origins of Protectionism and Free Trade in Nineteenth-Century Lima." *JLAS*, 14:2 (November 1982), 329–58.

Greenberg, Brian. *Worker and Community: Response to Industrialization in a Nineteenth Century American City, Albany, New York, 1850–1884.* Albany: State University of New York Press, 1985.

Greenfield, Gerald Michael, and Seldon L. Maram, eds. *Latin American Labor Organizations.* Westport, CT: Greenwood Press, 1987.

Grusin, Jay Robert. "The Colombian Revolution of 1848." Ph.D. dissertation, University of New Mexico, 1978.

Gudmundson, Lowell. *Costa Rica Before Coffee: Society and Economy on the Eve of the Export Boom.* Baton Rouge: Louisiana State University Press, 1986.

Gutiérrez Cely, Eugenio. "Nuevo movimiento popular contra el laissez-faire: Bogotá, 1875." *Universitas Humanística,* 11:17 (March 1982), 177–212.

Hale, Charles A. *Mexican Liberalism in the Age of Mora, 1821–1853.* New Haven, CT: Yale University Press, 1968.

———. "The Reconstruction of Nineteenth Century Politics in Spanish America: A Case for the History of Ideas." *LARR,* 8:2 (1973), 53–73.

Halperín-Donghi, Tulio. *Politics and Society in Argentina in the Revolutionary Period,* trans. by Richard Southern. New York: Cambridge University Press, 1975.

Hanagan, Michael P. "Artisan and Skilled Worker: The Problem of Definition." *ILWCH,* No. 12 (November 1977), 28–31.

———. *The Logic of Solidarity: Artisans and Industrial Workers in Three French Towns, 1871–1914.* Chicago: University of Chicago Press, 1980.

Hart, John M. *Anarchism and the Mexican Working Class, 1860–1931.* Austin: University of Texas Press, 1987.

———. "Los obreros mexicanos y el Estado, 1860–1931." *Nexos,* 4:37 (1981), 21–27.

Helguera, J. León. "Antecedentes sociales de la revolución de 1851 en el sur de Colombia, 1848–1849." *Anuario Colombiano de Historia Social y de la Cultura,* No. 5 (1970), 53–63.

———. "The First Mosquera Administration in New Granada." Ph.D. dissertation, University of North Carolina, 1958.

———. "Tomás Cipriano de Mosquera as President." *SELA,* 25:1 (June 1981), 1–14.

Helguera, J. León, and Robert H. Davis, eds. *Archivo epistolar del General Mosquera: Correspondencia con el General Ramón Espina, 1835–1866.* Bogotá: Editorial Kelly, 1966.

Hobsbawm, Eric. "Artisans or Labour Aristocrats?" *Economic History Review,* 2d Series, 37:3 (August 1984), 355–72.

———. *Workers: Worlds of Labor.* New York: Pantheon Books, 1984.

Hyland, Richard Preston. "The Secularization of Credit in the Cauca Valley, Colombia." Ph.D. dissertation, University of California, 1979.

James, Daniel. "Dependency and Organized Labor in Latin America." *Radical History Review*, 18 (Fall 1978), 155–60.

Jaramillo, Carlos Eduardo. "La guerra de los mil días: Aspectos estructurales de la organización guerrillera," in *Pasado y presente de la violencia en Colombia*, comp. by Gonzalo Sánchez and Ricardo Peñaranda. Bogotá: Fondo Editorial CEREC, 1986, 47–86.

———. "La guerra de los mil días, 1899–1902." in *Histórica política*, Vol. I. *Historia de Colombia*. Bogotá: Planeta, 1989, 89–112.

Jaramillo Uribe, Jaime. "La influencia de los románticos franceses y de la revolución de 1848 en el pensamiento político colombiano del siglo XIX," in *La personalidad histórica de Colombia y otros ensayos*. Bogotá: Editorial Andes, 1977, 181–201.

———. *El pensamiento colombiano en el siglo XIX*. Bogotá: Editorial Temis Librería, 1982.

———. "Las Sociedades Democráticas de Artesanos y la coyuntura política y social colombiana de 1848," in *La personalidad histórica de Colombia y otros ensayos*. Bogotá: Editorial Andes, 1977, 203–22.

Johnson, David Church. *Santander: Siglo XIX—Cambios socioeconómicos*. Bogotá: Carlos Valencia Editores, 1984.

Johnson, Lyman L. "Artisans," in *Cities and Society in Colonial Latin America*, ed. by Louisa Schell Hoberman and Susan Migden Socolow. Albuquerque: University of New Mexico Press, 1986, 227–50.

———. "The Racial Limits of Guild Solidarity: An Example from Colonial Buenos Aires." *Revista de Historia de América*, No. 99 (January–June 1985), 7–26.

———. "The Role of Apprenticeship in Colonial Buenos Aires." *Revista de Historia de América*, No. 103 (January–June 1987), 7–30.

———. "The Silversmiths of Buenos Aires: A Case Study in the Failure of Corporate Social Organization." *JLAS*, 8:2 (November 1976), 181–213.

Jones, Gareth Stedman. *Languages of Class: Studies in English Working Class History, 1832–1982*. New York: Cambridge University Press, 1983.

Kalmanovitz, Salomon. "Los orígenes de la industrialización en Colombia (1890–1929)." *Cuadernos de Economia*, 2d epoch, 5 (1983), 79–126.

Katz, Michael B. *The People of Hamilton, Canada West: Family and Class in a Mid-Nineteenth-Century City*. Cambridge, MA: Harvard University Press, 1975.

Keesing, Donald B. "Structural Change Early in Development: Mexico's Changing Industrial and Occupational Structure from 1895 to 1950." *Journal of Economic History*, 29:4 (December 1969), 726–30.

Klaiber, Jeffrey L. "The Catholic Lay Movement in Peru: 1867–1959." *The Americas*, 40:2 (October 1983), 149–70.

Klein, Herbert S. *Bolivia: The Evolution of a Multi-Ethnic Society.* New York: Oxford University Press, 1982.

Knight, Alan. *The Mexican Revolution*, Vol. 1. *Porfirians, Liberals, and Peasants.* New York: Cambridge University Press, 1986.

Latorre Cabal, Hugo. *Mi novela: Apuntes autobiográficos de Alfonso López.* Bogotá: Ediciones Mito, 1961.

Leal, Juan Felipe, and José Woldenberg. *La clase obrera en la historia de México. Del estado liberal a los inicios de la dictadura porfirista.* 3d ed. Mexico City: Siglo Veintiuno Editores, 1983.

––––––. "Orígenes y desarrollo del artesanado y del proletariado industrial en México: 1867–1914 (Bibliografía comentada)." *Revista Mexicana de Ciencia Política*, No. 81 (1975), 131–59.

Leal Buitrago, Francisco. *Estado y política en Colombia.* Bogotá: Siglo Veintiuno Editores, 1984.

Lemaitre, Eduardo. *Rafael Reyes: Biografía de un gran colombiano.* 4th ed. Bogotá: Banco de la República, 1981.

Levene, Ricardo. *Investigaciones acerca de la historia económica del virreinato del Plata.* 2 vols. Buenos Aires: Biblioteca Humanidades, 1928.

Liévano Aguirre, Indalecio. *El proceso de Mosquera ante el senado: Tres conferencias.* Bogotá: Editorial Revista Colombiana, 1966.

––––––. *Rafael Núñez.* Bogotá: Cromos, 1944.

Long, Gary. "Communists, Radical Artisans, and Workers in Colombia, 1925–1950." Draft in author's possession.

Lora, Guillermo. *A History of the Bolivian Labour Movement, 1848–1971*, ed. and abridged by Laurence Whitehead, trans. by Christine Whitehead. New York: Cambridge University Press, 1977.

Love, Joseph L. "The Origins of Dependency Analysis." *JLAS*, 22:1 (1990), 143–68.

Lynch, John. *Argentine Dictator: Juan Manuel de Rosas, 1829–1852.* New York: Oxford University Press, 1981.

McFarlane, Anthony. "The Transition from Colonialism in Colombia, 1819–1875," in *Latin America, Economic Imperialism and the State: The Political Economy of the External Connection from Independence to the Present*, ed. by Christopher Abel and Colin M. Lewis. London: Athlone Press, 1985, 101–24.

McGann, Thomas F. "The Assassination of Sucre and Its Significance in Colombian History, 1828–1848." *HAHR*, 30:3 (August 1950), 269–89.

McGreevey, William Paul. *An Economic History of Colombia, 1845–1930.* Cambridge: Cambridge University Press, 1971.

Madiedo, Manuel María. *Ideas fundamentales de los partidos políticos de la Nueva Granada.* 3d ed. Bogotá: Editorial Incunables, 1985.

Maingot, Anthony P. "Social Structure, Social Status, and Civil-Military Conflict in Urban Colombia, 1810–1858," in *Nineteenth-Century Cities: Essays in the New Urban History,* ed. by Stephen Thernstrom and Richard Sennett. New Haven, CT: Yale University Press, 1969, 297–355.

Martínez Carreño, Aída. *Mesa y cocina en el siglo XIX.* Bogotá: Fondo Cultural Cafetero, 1985.

Marx, Karl. *The Communist Manifesto of Karl Marx and Frederick Engels.* New York: Russell and Russell, 1963.

Mayor Mora, Alberto. *Etica, trabajo y productividad en Antioquia: Una interpretación sociológica sobre la influencia de la Escuela Nacional de Minas de la vida, costumbres e industrialización regionales.* 2d ed. Bogotá: Editorial Tercer Mundo, 1985.

Medhurst, Kenneth N. *The Church and Labour in Colombia.* Manchester, UK: Manchester University Press, 1984.

Medina, Mario Oliva. *Artesanos y obreros costaricenses, 1880–1914.* San José: Editorial Costa Rica, 1985.

Medina, Medófilo. *La protesta urbana en Colombia el siglo XX.* Bogotá: Ediciones Aurora, 1984.

Meisel R., Adolfo, and Alejandro López M. "Papel moneda, tasas de interés y revaluación durante la Regeneración," in *El Banco de la República: Antecedentes, evolución y estructura.* Bogotá: Banco de la República, 1990, 67–102.

Mejía Pavony, Germán R. "Las Sociedades Democráticas (1848–1854): Problemas historiográficos." *Universitas Humanística,* 11:17 (March 1982), 145–76.

Melo, Jorge Orlando. "De Carlos E. Restrepo a Marco Fidel Suárez. Republicanismo y gobiernos conservadores," in *Historia política,* Vol. I. *Historia de Colombia.* Bogotá: Planeta, 1989, 220–45.

Middleton, Alan. "Division and Cohesion in the Working Class: Artisans and Wage Labourers in Ecuador." *JLAS,* 14:1 (May 1982), 171–94.

Molina, Gerardo. *Las ideas liberales en Colombia, 1849–1914.* 6th ed. Bogotá: Ediciones Tercer Mundo, 1979.

Moncayo, Víctor, and Fernando Rojas. *Luchas obreras y política laboral en Colombia.* Bogotá: La Carreta, 1978.

Montgomery, David. *The Fall of the House of Labor: The Workplace, the State, and American Labor Activism, 1865–1925.* New York: Cambridge University Press, 1987.

———. *Workers' Control in America.* New York: Cambridge University Press, 1979.

Moreno Toscano, Alejandro. "Los trabajadores y el projecto de industrialización, 1810–1867," in *La clase obrera en la historia de México, Vol 1. De la colonia al imperio,* ed. by Enrique Florescano, Isabel González Sánchez, Jorge González Angulo, et al. 17 vols. 3d ed. Mexico City: Siglo Veintiuno Editores, 1983, 302–50.

Mosquera, Tomás Cipriano de. *Resumén histórico de los acontecimientos que han tenido lugar en la República, extracado de los diarios y noticias que ha podido obtener el General Jefe del Estado Mayor, T. C. de Mosquera.* Bogotá: Imprenta del Neo-Granadino, 1855.

Munck, Ronaldo. "Labor Studies Renewal." *Latin American Perspectives,* 13:2 (Spring 1986), 108–14.

Nash, June. "Gender Issues in Latin American Labor." *ILWCH,* No. 36 (Fall 1989), 44–50.

Neale, R. S. *Class and Ideology in the Nineteenth Century.* London: R.K.P., 1972.

Nieto Arteta, Luis Eduardo. *Economía y cultura en la historia de Colombia.* Bogotá: Editorial Viento del Pueblo, 1975.

Ocampo, José Antonio. "Comerciantes, artesanos y política económica en Colombia, 1830–1880." *Boletín Cultural y Bibliográfico,* 27:22 (1990), 21–45.

———. *Colombia y la economía mundial, 1830–1910.* Bogotá: Siglo Veintiuno Editores, 1984.

Orlando Melo, Jorge. "La economía neogranadino el la cuarta década del siglo XIX." *Universidad Nacional de Colombia. Medellín,* 2:3 (May–December 1976), 52–63.

Ortiz, Juan Francisco. *Reminiscencias de D. Juan Francisco Ortiz (1808–1861).* 2d ed. Bogotá: Librería Americana, 1914.

Ortiz, Venancio. *Historia de la revolución del 17 de abril de 1854.* Bogotá: Biblioteca Banco Popular, 1972.

Ospina Vásquez, Luis. *Industria y protección en Colombia, 1810 a 1930.* Bogotá: Editorial Santafé, 1955.

*The Oxford English Dictionary.* 13 vols. Oxford: Oxford at Clarendon Press, 1978.

Park, James William. *Rafael Núñez and the Politics of Colombian Regionalism, 1863–1886.* Baton Rouge: Louisiana State University Press, 1985.

Pécaut, Daniel. *Orden y violencia: Colombia, 1930–1954.* 2 vols. Bogotá: Siglo Veintiuno Editores, 1987.

———. *Política y sindicalismo en Colombia.* Bogotá: La Carreta, 1973.

Peralta de Ferreira, Victoria. "Historia del fracaso de la ferrería de Samacá." *Universitas Humanística,* No. 24 (July–December 1985), 127–58.

Pérez, Felipe. *Geografía general física y política de los Estados Unidos de Colombia y geografía particular de la ciudad de Bogotá.* Bogotá: Imprenta de Echeverría Hermanos, 1883.

Pérez Aguirre, Antonio. *25 años de historia colombiana: 1853 a 1878; del centralismo a la federación.* Bogotá: Editorial Sucre, 1959.

Pérez Vila, Manuel. *El artesanado: la formación de una clase media propiamente americana (1500–1800).* Caracas: Academia de la Historia, 1986.

Platt, D.C.M. "Dependency in Nineteenth Century Latin America: An Historian Objects," *LARR*, 15:1 (1980), 113–30.

———. "Reply." *LARR*, 15:1 (1980), 147–50.

Pombo, Antonio, and José Joaquín Guerra. *Constituciones de Colombia: Recopiladas y precedidas de una breve reseña histórica.* 4 vols. Bogotá: Prensas del Ministerio de Educación Nacional, 1951.

Portes, Alejandro, and John Walton. *Urban Latin America: The Political Condition from Above and Below.* Austin: University of Texas Press, 1976.

*Primer congreso eucarístico nacional de Colombia.* Bogotá: Escuela Tipografía Salesiana, 1914.

Quintero-Rivera, A. G. "Socialist and Cigarmaker: Artisans' Proletarianization in the Making of the Puerto Rican Working Class." *Latin American Perspectives*, 10:23, issues 37/38 (Spring–Summer, 1983), 19–38.

Ramírez Rojas, Manuel Alvaro, and Jesús Antonio Suárez Rosales. *El sector informal urbano en Colombia y las políticas de empleo, 1970–1980: Análisis de los planes de desarrollo y la informalidad económica.* 2d ed. Bogotá: Ediciones Tercer Mundo, 1987.

Rancière, Jacques. "The Myth of the Artisan: Critical Reflections on a Category of Social History." *ILWCH*, No. 24 (Fall 1983), 1–16.

*Recopilación de leyes y decretos del Estado Soberano de Cundinamarca, 1857–1868.* Bogotá: n.p., 1868.

Reina, Ruben E. *Paraná: Social Boundaries in an Argentine City.* Austin: University of Texas Press, 1973.

Restrepo, José Manuel. *Diario político y militar. Memorias sobre los sucesos importantes de la época para servir a la historia de la Revolución de Colombia y de la Nueva Granada, desde 1819 para adelante.* 4 vols. Bogotá: Imprenta Nacional, 1954.

———. *Historia de la Nueva Granada.* 2 vols. Bogotá: Editorial El Catolicismo, 1963.

Restrepo Posada, José. "La Sociedad Católica de Bogotá—1838." *Boletín de Historia y Antiqüedades*, 43:499–500 (May–June 1956), 310–21.

Reyna, María del Carmen. "Las condiciones del trabajo en las panaderías de la ciudad de México durante la segunda mitad del siglo XIX." *Historia Mexicana*, 31:3 (January–May 1982), 431–48.

Robinson, David J., ed. *Social Fabric and Spatial Structure in Colonial Latin America*. Syracuse, NY: Department of Geography, Syracuse University, 1979.

Rock, Howard B. *Artisans of the New Republic: The Tradesmen of New York City in the Age of Jefferson*. New York: New York University Press, 1979.

Rodríguez, Gustavo Humberto. *Santo Acosta: Caudillo del radicalismo*. Bogotá: Biblioteca de Cultura Colombiana, 1972.

Romero, L. A. *La Sociedad de la Igualidad: Los artesanos de Santiago de Chile y sus primeras experiencias políticas, 1820–1851*. Buenos Aires: Instituto Torcuato Di Tella, 1978.

Roxborough, Ian. "Issues in Labor Historiography." *LARR*, 21:2 (1986), 178–88.

Safford, Frank. "Acerca de las interpretaciones socioeconómicos de la política en la Colombia del siglo XIX: Variaciones sobre un tema." *Anuario Colombiano de Historia Social y de la Cultura*, No. 13–14 (1985–86), 91–151.

——. "Bases of Political Alignment in Early Republican Spanish America," in *New Approaches to Latin American History*, ed. by Richard Graham and Peter Smith. Austin: University of Texas Press, 1974, 71–109.

——. "Commerce and Enterprise in Central Colombia, 1821–1870." Ph.D. dissertation, Columbia University, 1965.

——. "The Emergence of Economic Liberalism in Colombia," in *Guiding the Invisible Hand: Economic Liberalism and the State in Latin American History*, ed. by Joseph L. Love and Nils Jacobsen. New York: Praeger, 1988, 35–61.

——. *The Ideal of the Practical: Colombia's Struggle to Form a Technical Elite*. Austin: University of Texas Press, 1976.

——. "On Paradigms and the Pursuit of the Practical: A Response." *LARR*, 13:2 (1978), 252–60.

——. "Politics, Ideology and Society in Post-Independence Spanish America," in *The Cambridge History of Latin America*, Vol. III. *Independence to c. 1870*, ed. by Leslie Bethell. New York: Cambridge University Press, 1985, 347–321.

——. "Social Aspects of Politics in Nineteenth-Century Spanish America: New Granada, 1825–1850." *Journal of Social History*, 5:2 (Spring 1972), 344–70.

Saldarriaga Vélez, Oscar de J. "Bogotá, la Regeneración y la policía 1880–1900." *Revista Universidad de Antioquia*, 37:211 (January–March 1988), 37–55.

Salgado, Cupertino. *Directorio general de Bogotá. Año IV, 1893*. Bogotá. n.p., 1893.

Samper, José María. *Ensayo sobre las revoluciones políticas y la condición social de las repúblicas colombianas (Hispano-Americanos)*. Bogotá: Biblioteca Popular de Cultura Colombiana, n.d.

————. *Historia de una alma, 1834 a 1881*. 2 vols. Bogotá: Biblioteca de Cultura Colombiana, 1948.

Samper, Miguel. *La miseria en Bogotá y otros escritos*. Bogotá: Biblioteca Universitaria de Cultura Colombiana, 1969.

Sánchez, Gonzalo. "La Violencia in Colombia: New Research, New Questions." *HAHR*, 65:4 (November 1985), 789–807.

Santa, Eduardo. *Sociología política de Colombia*. Bogotá: Ediciones Tercer Mundo, 1964.

Scobie, James R. *Secondary Cities of Argentina: The Social History of Corrientes, Salta, and Mendoza, 1850–1910*, completed and edited by Samuel L. Baily. Stanford, CA: Stanford University Press, 1988.

Scott, Joan Wallach. *The Glassworkers of Carmaux: French Craftsmen and Political Action in a Nineteenth-Century City*. Cambridge, MA: Harvard University Press, 1974.

Sewell, William H., Jr. "Uneven Development, the Autonomy of Politics, and the Dockworkers of Nineteenth-Century Marseille." *American Historical Review*, 93:3 (June 1988), 604–37.

————. *Work & Revolution in France: The Language of Labor from the Old Regime to 1848*. Cambridge, MA: Harvard University Press, 1980.

Shaw, Frederick J. "The Artisan in Mexico City (1824–1853)," in *El trabajo y los trabajadores en la historia de México*, ed. by Elsa Cecilia Frost, Michael C. Meyer, and Josefina Zoraida Vásquez. Mexico City: El Colegio de México, 1979, 399–418.

Shulgovski, Antaloli. "La 'Comuna de Bogotá' y el socialismo utópico." *América Latina*, 8:85 (August 1985), 45–56.

Socolow, Susan Migden. *The Merchants of Buenos Aires, 1778–1810: Family and Commerce*. New York: Cambridge University Press, 1978.

Sordo Cedeño, Reynaldo. "Las sociedades de socorros mutuos, 1867–1880." *Historia Mexicana*, Vol. 129, 33:1 (1983), 72–96.

Soriano Lleras, Andres. *Lorenzo María Lleras*. Bogotá: Editorial Sucre, 1958.

Sowell, David. "Agentes diplomáticas de los Estados Unidos y el golpe de Melo." *Anuario Colombiano de Historia Social y de la Cultura*, No. 12 (1984), 5–13.

————. "*La Caja de Ahorros de Bogotá*, 1845–63: Credit, Development, and Savings in Early National Colombia." Unpublished paper.

————. "The 1893 *bogotazo*: Artisans and Public Violence in Late Nineteenth-Century Bogotá." *JLAS*, 21:2 (May 1989), 267–82.

————. "José Leocadio Camacho: Artisan, Editor, and Political Activist," in *The Human Tradition in Latin America: The Nineteenth Century*, ed. by Judith Ewell and William H. Beezley. Wilmington, DE: Scholarly Resources, 1989, 269–79.

———. "'La teoría i la realidad': The Democratic Society of Artisans of Bogotá, 1847–1854." *HAHR*, 67:4 (November 1987), 611–30.

Spalding, Hobart, Jr. *Organized Labor in Latin America: Historical Case Studies of Workers in Dependent Societies.* New York: Harper & Row, 1977.

———. "Somethings Old and Somethings New." *ILWCH*, No. 36 (Fall 1989), 37–44.

Stein, Stanley J., and Barbara H. Stein. *The Colonial Heritage of Latin America.* New York: Oxford University Press, 1970.

———. "Comment." *LARR*, 15:1 (1980), 131–46.

Storch, Robert D. "The Plague of Blue Locusts: Police Reform and Popular Resistance in Northern England, 1840–57." *International Review of Social History* (1975), 61–90.

Szuchman, Mark D. *Mobility and Integration in Urban Argentina: Córdoba in the Liberal Era.* Austin: University of Texas Press, 1980.

Szuchman, Mark D., and Eugene F. Sofer. "The State of Occupational Stratification Studies in Argentina: A Classificatory Scheme." *LARR*, 11:1 (1976), 159–71.

Tanck de Estrada, Dorothy. "La abolición de los greminos," in *El trabajo y los trabajadores en la historia de México/Labor and Laborers Through Mexican History.* Mexico City: El Colegio de México and University of Arizona Press, 1979, 311–31.

Temoche Benites, Ricardo. *Cofradías, gremios, mutuales y sindicatos en el Perú.* Lima: Editorial Escuela Nueva, S.A., 1985.

Thompson, E. P. *The Making of the English Working Class.* New York: Vintage Books, 1963.

———. "The Moral Economy of the English Crowd in the Eighteenth Century." *Past and Present*, No. 50 (1971), 76–136.

Tirado Mejía, Alvaro. *El estado y la política en el siglo XIX.* Bogotá: El Ancora Editores, 1983.

Triana y Antorveza, Humberto. "El aprendizaje en los gremios neogranadinos." *Boletín Cultural y Bibliográfico*, 8:5 (1965), 735–42.

———. "El aspecto religioso en los gremios neogranadinos." *Boletín Cultural y Bibliográfico*, 9:2 (February 1966), 269–81.

———. "Examenes, licencias, fianzas y elecciones artesanales." *Boletín Cultural y Bibliográfico*, 9:2 (1966), 65–73.

———. "Extranjeros y grupos etnicos en los gremios neogranadinos." *Boletín Cultural y Bibliográfico*, 8:1 (1965), 24–32.

———. "La libertad laboral y la supresion de los gremios neogranadinos." *Boletín Cultural y Bibliográfico*, 8:7 (1965), 1015–24.

Urrutia, Miguel. *The Development of the Colombian Labor Movement.* New Haven, CT: Yale University Press, 1969.

Valencia Llano, Alonso. *Estado soberano del Cauca: Federalismo y regeneración.* Bogotá: Banco de la República, 1988.

Valenzuela, J. Samuel. "Movimientos obreros y sistemas políticos: Un análisis conceptual y tipológico." *Desarrollo Económico*, 23:91 (October–December 1983), 339–68.

Vargas Martínez, Gustavo. *Colombia 1854: Melo, los artesanos y el socialismo (La dictadura artesanal de 1854, expresión del socialismo utópico en Colombia).* Bogotá: Editorial la Oveja Negra, 1973.

Villegas, Jorge. *Colombia: Enfrentamiento iglesia-estado, 1819–1887.* Bogotá: La Carreta, 1981.

Wagley, Charles, and Marvin Harris. "A Typology of Latin American Subcultures," in *The Latin American Tradition: Essays on Unity and Diversity of Latin American Culture.* New York: Columbia University Press, 1968, 81–117.

Weinstein, Barbara. "The New Latin American Labor History: What We Gain." *ILWCH*, No. 36 (Fall 1989), 25–30.

Whiteford, Andrew Hunter. *An Andean City at Mid-Century: A Traditional Urban Society.* East Lansing: Michigan State University, 1977.

Wilentz, Sean. *Chants Democratic: New York City and the Rise of the American Working Class, 1788–1850.* New York: Oxford University Press, 1984.

Willems, Emilio. "Social Differentiation in Colonial Brazil." *Comparative Studies in Society and History*, 12:1 (January 1970), 31–49.

Winn, Peter. *Weavers of Revolution: The Yarur Workers and Chile's Road to Socialism.* New York: Oxford University Press, 1986.

Woldenberg K., José. "Asociaciones artesanas del siglo XIX (Sociedad Socorros Mutuos de Impresores, 1874–1875)." *Revista Mexicana de Ciencias Políticas y Sociales*, 83 (1976), 71–112.

Young, John L. "University Reform in New Granada, 1820–1850." Ph.D. dissertation, Columbia University, 1970.

Zdatny, Steven M. *The Politics of Survival: Artisans in Twentieth-Century France.* New York: Oxford University Press, 1990.

Zea, Leopoldo. *The Latin American Mind*, trans. by James H. Abbot and Lowell Dunham. Norman: University of Oklahoma Press, 1963.

Zeitlin, Maurice. *The Civil Wars in Chile (or The Bourgeois Revolutions That Never Were).* Princeton, NJ: Princeton University Press, 1984.

# INDEX

Political recruitment, 10, 30–31,
34–37, 52–53, 139, 142, 155,
162–65, 168
Pombo, Lino de, 40, 42, 50
Pombo, Miguel, 87
Pontón, Nicolás, 88, 91, 92
Popayán, 34, 72, 76, 126, 130, 131,
138, 203n.89
Pope Leo XIII, 140
Popular Society. *See* Sociedad Popular (1868)
Popular Society of Mutual Instruction and Fraternal Christianity.
*See* Sociedad Popular de Instrucción Mutua i Fraternidad Cristiana, La
Posada, Joaquín, 74
Posse, Florentino V., 49
Pradilla, Urbano, 49
Progresistas (progressives), 34, 35–37
Public Safety Society. *See* Sociedad de Salud Pública

Quinquenio, 29, 132
Quintero Calderón, Guillermo,
125, 136, 138
Quirós, Ramón, 70
Quito, 170

Radical Liberals, 58, 77, 87, 92,
103–5, 110, 114, 115, 116, 119
Radical Olympus, 77, 101
Ramírez, Fruto, 102
Rancière, Jacques, 225n.15
Ranjel, Bernadino, 113, 150
*Razón del Obrero, La*, 138
Regeneration, 22–23, 29, 98, 101–2, 103, 117–22, 125, 127, 158
Regionalism, 26–27, 115
Rengifo, Tomás, 117

Repression, 49, 51, 52, 125, 133–34; and Law of the Horses, 113,
124, 218n.103
Republicanism, 27, 161. *See also*
Artisan republicanism
Republican School. *See* Escuela Republicana
Republican Union. *See* Unión Republicana
*Rerum Novarum*, 140
Restrepo, Carlos E., 136, 137, 138
Restrepo, José Manuel, 17
Reyes, Rafael, 22, 26, 29, 104, 121,
131, 132–34, 135–36, 137, 158,
159, 163
Reyes Daza, Rafael, 139
Rio de Janeiro, 170
Rivera, Luciano, 95
Roa Ramírez, Felipe, 86, 96, 102,
115
Robayo, Eusebio, 68–69
Rock, Howard B., 9
Rodríguez, Agustín, 40, 41, 44, 59,
75, 89
Rodríguez, Bruno, 67, 69
Rodríguez, Camilo, 51
Rodríguez, Ignacio, 51
Rodríguez, Juan Nepomuceno, 122
Rojas, Ezequiel, 35, 36, 43, 87
Rosales, Ramón, 148
Röthlisberger, Ernst, 7
Ruiz, Tiburcio, 114

Saavedra, José Antonio, 73, 87–88,
91, 92, 110, 113, 115, 168,
208nn.33, 34, 209n.53
Safford, Frank, 27, 184n.56
St. Monday (hacer lunes, el lunes
de los zapateros), 13, 210n.57
Salesian Institute, 123
Salgar, Eustorgio, 102, 103, 104,
114, 115